ESSAYS
IN THE
ROMANTIC POETS

ESSAYS
IN THE
ROMANTIC POETS

By

Solomon Francis Gingerich

1969

OCTAGON BOOKS
New York

Reprinted 1969

by special arrangement with The Macmillan Company

OCTAGON BOOKS

A Division of Farrar, Straus & Giroux, Inc.

19 Union Square West

New York, N. Y. 10003

Library of Congress Catalog Card Number: 70-75994

Printed in U.S.A. by
NOBLE OFFSET PRINTERS, INC.
NEW YORK 3, N. Y.

PREFATORY NOTE

The essays on Shelley (1918) and Coleridge (1920) appeared in the *Publications of the Modern Language Association of America.* Both have been thoroughly revised and somewhat enlarged and are here reprinted by the kind permission of the Editor of the *Publications.*

S. F. G.

CONTENTS

INTRODUCTION

I

The growth of the 'deeper mind' of a true poet is continuous and, except in tragic or cataclysmic events in his personal life, steady. This is the case because he is always a seeker of truth and always in pursuit of giving that truth not merely good but supreme expression, satisfying and pleasurable, making us indeed 'heirs'

> Of truth and pure delight by heavenly lays.

However, the truth the poet is seeking is not primarily historic, or scientific, or philosophic, or religious truth, though he seeks all these, but it is the truth of experience —experiential—truth in that part of our being that is most alive and vital, that is actively engaged in adjusting the strictly personal with the totality of things; he is also seeking to render these adjustments, as he comes to them, in the phrase and literary form of finality, not to be changed or improved. He is therefore not a mere phenomenalist or dabbler, as so many seem to imply, nor is he a formalistic thinker with a closed system of thought. There is thus no standstill in him and no formal consistency; only there is the deeper consistency of constant growth, due to his unceasing efforts in adjusting the immediate personal experience with the universal, the ultimate truth 'general and operative'.

The true poet is largely subjective. Though he uses many devices to create the illusion of objectivity he really

1

never renounces or denies the personal element; consciously or unconsciously he writes himself into his works. Take for example, one of the most objective writers in appearing—Walter Scott. Any one reading a large quantity of Scott's writings is impressed by the fact that nothing is more certain than that he is moving in Scott's world and not in some one else's. The objective characterizations and the medievalism are impressed upon us by the mind of Walter Scott—they are his medieval world. Thus the sources of his art lie within his own mind, and are in so far truly subjective. This is true of all poets because the poet's personality, integrating properly the materials of his craft, is the life-giving force of his art.

The genuine poet is also truly psychological; he observes the workings of the minds of his characters, and often subtly divines the impulses and motives that lie just beyond the scope of common observation, thereby giving us a new insight into the hidden world of men's mental life. He also observes the inner processes of his own mind, and with fidelity renders them in his poems; or, if he belongs to the type not strictly introspective he still, by his native endowment as poet and by his sincerity in his art, gives us unconsciously the finer workings of his own mind. The authentic poet is a great informal psychologist.

He is likewise informally philosophical; he looks before and after, has an outlook upon life; not relinquishing the personal he yet comprehends the impersonal; he deals with concrete things, yet by imaginative implication he includes the abstract; he uses simple images but freights them with profound and revealing truth; he penetrates through the particular to the universal; he sees unity in diversity and diversity in unity; he is the creator of harmony and of spiritual satisfactions; he is not merely a bringer of joy but he indicates the causes and reveals the sources of joy. But he does not adhere to any set or fixed philosophical ideas, nor does he select indiscriminately now from this philosophy and now from another. Rather he brings all his conceptions gleaned from science, philosophy, religion, art, and from life, to bear upon the immediate experience that is to result in a poem. This immediate experience is a continuancy of his past in the same sense that a tree is the result of growth. His philosophy thus is flexible, adjustible, growing, and also informally coherent, by virtue of its being momentarily and forever tested by his personal experience.

The truth the poet seeks and renders is therefore the most composite kind of truth there is. It is the synthetic product of all the faculties of his mind, as perception, memory, emotion, intellect, will, imagination, with usually a slight dominance of emotion and imagination. Coleridge's emphasis on essentially this same fact about the nature of poetry is a memorable passage in modern literary criticism. The poet's truth is less specialized than the historian's, or the philosopher's, or the scientist's, because the poet aims at harmonizing the totality of life with personal experience. This is why he is more human, more essentially alive to us than others; this is why though he has lived a hundred or three hundred or a thousand years ago he is so real and vital to us—as one of ourselves. But he can earn this place in our affections and memories only because he learns by never-ceasing efforts and by a constant growing wisdom the inner and permanent meaning of our human existence, only because he is a truly growing, experimenting, human being like ourselves, but with the added gift of genius.

This composite nature of poetry lies at the root of its being essentially spiritual, or mystical, in character. Being "the breath and finer spirit of all knowledge," its truth cannot be apprehended by any one faculty of the mind acting separately, such as the intellect, but requires the interplay of all the faculties, requires that the whole personality bend, so to speak, toward its apprehension, which is essentially a spiritual act of the mind apprehending a spiritual reality.

The guiding light in a poet's life is conviction, a kind of sincerity with himself, an eagerness to find and experience the truth, from whatever source it may be derived. Though the facts are all against one's finding an ordered system of philosophy in any great poet, yet no poet can hold a profound conviction any length of time without revealing it in his writings. Opinions he may have without showing traces of them. He may hold the opinion, for instance, that democracy is a good thing, yet reveal purely aristocratic tendencies in his conduct and art. But should that opinion at any time become a passion, hints of it would at once be revealed in his work. It is at that point where opinion tends to pass into passion that it may be named conviction. From deep conviction spring the life and spirit of a poet's best work. Could criticism avoid taking mere opinion too seriously and refrain from formulating systems from poets' works it would save itself much trouble; could it always lay bare the conviction that inspired a poet to utterance it would be profoundly informing.

This does not mean that a poet cannot successfully simulate emotion. In drama especially, opposite passions are often presented with equal success in the same play. It is idle to suppose that either passion represents literally the conviction of the dramatist. Yet even as great authorities as Dowden and Raleigh and Brandes hold that Shakespeare, the greatest of all simulators, reveals his convictions in the total output of his work. "It was himself that he related to paper, his own mind that he revealed. . . . No man can walk abroad save on his own shadow," says Raleigh. Certainly non-dramatic poets reveal their convictions, for it is by convictions that they live.

Though in their nature steadfast, convictions are subject to subtle changes, being modified by a man's daily experiences. Or rather, they have the power of growth; each new day deepens them, or lessens them by calling new ones into being. Frequently the changes are unconscious, and a man may travel a long way before he is fully aware of what has taken place. Growth of conviction is particularly noticeable in the free, creative mind of the poet, open to new truth and subtly responsive to new influences. Such changes are especially to be expected where spiritual and religious truth are concerned, for here standards are indefinite and the truth itself unlimited and infinite. It is fascinating to put one's self at the central point of view of a poet and observe the growth and the gradual shifting of the ground of his convictions—it is really tracing the romance of his inner life. The following pages are dedicated largely to the task of tracing the inner spiritual growth of four English poets of the Romantic Age.

Of course the experiences and convictions of a poet are conditioned by the age in which he lives. Having as poet a sensitive, receptive and retentive mind, he has from his birth absorbed, from influences, environments, and currents of ideas of his own times and those just preceding, far more than he is conscious of and far more than can be measured. The poets of the Romantic Age are known to have made a sharp break with the poetry of the age preceding them, beginning particularly with the publication of the *Lyrical Ballads* by Coleridge and Wordsworth in 1798. Criticism concerns itself largely with the differences between poetry after this date and poetry before it. However, the spirit of the eighteenth century ran deeply in the youthful lives of Coleridge and Wordsworth, and in the whole careers of Shelley and Byron. The following pages aim to show indirectly to what extent this is true in philosophical and religious matters, which have been very greatly neglected in literary criticism.

The spiritual growth of these authors, as revealed not only in their poems but in their letters, prose writings, etc.—all taken in as strict chronological order as possible, shows in each case a remarkable self-consistency. The only way to illustrate this at all effectively has been to use selections somewhat copiously, in which there always lurks a certain amount of danger. The parts must never be taken for the whole, and passages must be read in their context. Nevertheless the selections have been made from what seems essential, and not incidental, in the poet's writings. The ideas that are repeated oftenest in a given period of an author's life are usually typical and representative of him, and undoubtedly lie close to his deeper consciousness. These indicate the main trend of his spiritual growth. And we must be satisfied to be able to find the main trend.

II

It may be worth while to suggest that the philosophic and religious terms it is necessary to use are used in a flexible rather than in a hard and fast manner. It is no aid to criticism, for instance, to name categorically Wordsworth, or Shelley, a Pantheist. What one finds are tendencies in poets in certain directions, and if a given tendency persists for a length of time it is significant, and yet is is not the whole truth concerning the author in question. Philosophic terms are used generally to indicate the direction in which the poet is moving.

It may be desirable that certain terms should be defined, not in any absolute sense, but merely in the form of working definitions for the specific use of this study. This, however, is done with the greatest diffidence, and any one may have the right to differ with these ideas of abstract things.

Pantheism, starting with the doctrine that the Universe considered as a whole is God, tends naturally to accentuate the senses and the laws of the material world as the embodiment of God. In its lowest and crudest form it identifies God with the tangible and physical elements of Nature; in its highest form it identifies God with the laws or the being of Nature. But the theory of *Immanence* asserts that, though God's Being is in no wise limited to the workings of Nature, God is present, is immanent, in every extant object of the Universe. According to this view one cannot touch the body of a child, or a growing tree, or a flower, but that one is made aware that God is in the object and behind it, and very close to us. Immanence is undoubtedly one of the great opera-

tive principles in the poetry of Wordsworth and in much
of the serious poetry since his time.

Necessity, Determinism, Predestination are antitheti-
cal to *Free-Will.* These terms may seem to have merely
a metaphysical interest, but in truth they have a very practical one. Whether the mind of man be as a cog in a
wheel, or a link in a chain, or as a harp to be played upon
by forces outside itself, or whether, on the other hand,
it possesses some unique self-determining and creative
power, by which in a measure it shapes its own destiny, is
of vital importance. Since it is obvious to common sense
that there are events and incidents and things—the pass-
ing of day and night, the coming and going of the sea-
sons, the stars in their course, the processes of all the
elemental forces of Nature, etc.—over which man, no
matter what he thinks and does, has no appreciable
control, it is easy enough to conceive the whole universe,
including man, so bound up and closed in by law and sequence that there is no room in it for the exercise of man's
free moral agency. Yet man has not been willing to
surrender his freedom, for with it he must needs surrender his sense of personal identity and of personal
responsibility. The antinomy of law and freedom is not
wholly explicable. One of the most serious occupations
of philosophers is to resolve it, as, for example, to show
that if man wills to live by fixed law he attains to freedom, or to distinguish between *must* as obtaining in one
realm and *ought* in another. Here we need not be dis-
turbed by the subtleties of the arguments. We shall hold
to the antithesis: if a poet be found to accept and express
the deterministic outlook on life he may be set down as
having a weak hold on will and personality, and if he be
an ardent exponent of free-will he will be a weak deter-

minist. It shall be seen that these attitudes are extremely important.

Indeed, literature of the nineteenth century is decidedly less deterministic than in the eighteenth. It appeals not only more strongly to the emotions but relatively more powerfully to the will, its characteristic distinction being that it renders imaginatively experiences compact of deep feeling and energetic will. It is that which separates it from the literature of the eighteenth century and links it in spirit to the literature of the latter part of the sixteenth and the early part of the seventeenth centuries. Though important exceptions must be made, it in general substitutes, for the determinism and necessitarianism regnant in the eighteenth century, the postulate of moral freedom; accordingly it appeals more profoundly to the human will.

The principle of *Transcendentalism* is closely allied to the principle of Free-will. Strictly speaking transcendentalism is a theory, not of intuition, but of knowledge. It lays bare the method, or mode, by which the intellect grows. It reverses the conception that all knowledge is derived from the senses, and asserts that the sense impressions that stream into the mind from the outer world were meaningless, a mere blotch on the canvas, had not the mind an original, active, organizing principle within itself by which it turns them into knowledge. Says Kant: "I call all knowledge *transcendental* which is concerned, not with objects, but with our mode of knowing objects so far as this is possible *a priori.*" This constituent force of the mind, which did not come by experience but which renders experience possible, makes the mind an active agent and not merely a passive recipient, implies that the mind is self-determining and the will free. This is

the so-called immortal discovery of Kant—the kernel of
what philosophers speak of when they say that Kant's
thinking revolutionized modern thought. The current of
philosophical thought in the eighteenth century in England as represented by Locke and Hume and others
started with the assumption that all knowledge is derived
from sensation, that the mind is 'compounded' out of the
senses, that it is an empty form until an impingement has
been made upon it by sense impressions. The mind thus
being a passive instrument, a product of sensation, it was
strictly necessitated, and not free, in its action. Here the
skeptical philosophers were at one with the believing
theologians, Calvin and Jonathan Edwards and their followers. For the doctrine of Necessity in philosophy is
the same as the doctrine of Predestination in religion.
The remorseless logic of the philosophers (granting their
major premise), supported by the remorseless logic of the
theologians, made it well-nigh impossible for a thinking
man, born in the tradition of the creed of Necessity, to
break through its iron chains. But the new trascenden-
talism offered a profound challenge to its central contention and in due course of time won a victory of vast significance to the thought of the nineteenth century.

The transendental principle did not get into the world
merely by the arguments of German philosophers and
such men as Coleridge and Emerson. Some speak of it
as though it were a thing invented by Kant, talked about
by Coleridge in his metaphysical moments, and elabor-
ated into a system by Emerson, and that it has no other
connection with the thought of the nineteenth century.
Nothing of course can be farther from the truth. It
entered the world as a presence, a force, an atmosphere,
pervasive and unescapable even by those who by tempera-

ment and express purpose were least inclined to countenance it. Like the theory of Evolution of a later generation, which influenced thousands of men who never read
Darwin, the principle of Transcendentalism influenced
thousands of persons who never read Kant. After Coleridge it had become common property among English
speaking peoples.

Transcendentalism   entered   Wordsworth's   mature
poetry unobtrusively and by slow gradations, making his
poetry prophetic for the thought of the century to follow;
it was the shaping influence in all of Coleridge's later
writings; it entered as an essential into the poetry and
prose of Emerson, the prose of Carlyle, and the poetry of
Tennyson; and it became an axiomatic truth in the poetry
of Browning. Tennyson thinks of it chiefly as a miracle:

> But this main-miracle, that thou art thou,
> With power on thine own act and on the world.

The transcendental principle, however, did not enter
poetry in its pure form. As a theory of knowledge it asserted that man is capable of a unitary experience only on
the basis that the mind itself, independent of sensations,
is possessed inherently of an active power by which it can
synthesize and transmute sensations into wider experiences of self-consciousness. In the following passage
from *The Prelude* Wordsworth expresses the doctrine
in its pure form:

> The mind is lord and master—outward sense
> The obedient servant of her will.

But generally the poets, who do not usually exercise as
rigid an intellectual logic as philosophers, conceived this
new principle of self-consciousness, with its power of initiative and development from within, not only as an abid-

ing and therefore immortal energy of the soul but as an intuition implanted in man by which he perceives Deity—which converts it into a spiritual and a poetic principle. Under its influence they exalted man's inner life of intuitions, passions, and volitions, not in any egotistical sense, but as divine powers sacredly entrusted to man, which are the insignia of his worth of soul.

Living under a rigid regime of Necessity men find it inherently difficult to maintain a profound respect for human individuality, since man is a mere puppet to the predestinating or deterministic powers; this regime produces, according to their respective natures, gloomy religionists, or skeptical philosophers, or light-hearted cynics and satirists, or sentimental moralists, with which different kinds among the leaders of English thought in the eighteenth century the roll of names is replete. The transcendental principle restores man's faith in his deeper self, because it gives assurance that he himself has a positive share in the shaping of his own destiny and the destiny of the race. This high faith lies at the root of the literature of the nineteenth century, taking vigorous growth in the mature poetry of Wordsworth and culminating perhaps in the poetry of Browning.

Of course so profound and freeing a principle as the transcendental brings with it the possibilities of grave abuse. Not taken in the right spirit it may unduly exaggerate the intuitions, or develop the merely egotistic, or make a man anti-social, or cause him to indulge in mere vagaries of soul development or soul affinities. But these risks must be taken for the essential worth of the principle, for it carries within itself the corrective of its own dangers, namely, the power of self-discipline and of self-sacrifice. In its fundamentals it is really nothing new—

it is as old as Plato and the Bible. Only modern thinking has given new and convincing grounds of its reason-
ableness and truth.

From the transcendental it is but a step to the *mystical.*
The mystic experience occurs when the total personality,
with volitional intensity, reaches forward to commune
with the powers, or Power, outside itself, identifies itself
with such Power. If it conceives Power as impersonal
and just Nature it is naturalistic mysticism; if it conceives
Power as Deity and as Personal it is theistic or pietistic
mysticism. This mystic principle lies at the root of all
poetry of high seriousness and deep spirituality.

In setting forth an abstruse matter Wordsworth some-
where complains of "the sad incompetence of human
speech," which may well be applied to the foregoing definitions. The terms, for instance, immanence, transcendence, and mysticism, vastly overlap in meaning and up
to a certain point are interchangeable. Immanence gives
the sense of the deepest power in the universe, or Deity,
as within Nature and within the individual; transcendence
asserts that the human individuality possesses something
that is not derived from sensation and that makes it
independent of the sense world in which we move; mysticism implies the communion of this individuality with the
universal power, or Deity, giving a sense of blending, or
becoming one with that Power. Beyond this perhaps
words are mere words and sadly incompetent. Vital
conviction, however, concerning any of these matters at
any time is of the greatest importance to the individual.

COLERIDGE

COLERIDGE

Coleridge and Wordsworth were more responsible than any two other men in changing the current of thought in English poetry from characteristic eighteenth to characteristic nineteenth century ways. Their early writings were deeply tinged with the eighteenth century tradition, from which both emancipated themselves as they grew to maturity. Their emancipation is not concerned merely or even primarily with matters of poetic diction, but with ideas, particularly ethical and religious. They did not gain the distinction of being prophets and seers without travail of spirit; this implied a change of attitude on certain important issues, for which they have been either praised or soundly berated by critics, according to the lights of the individual critic. But the fact of their spiritual struggle and its great significance to the thought of the world together with its special influence on nineteenth century literature cannot be gainsaid. Though Wordsworth left us a much larger body of creative literature, and is a more lasting influence, Coleridge, extraordinarily responsive to new ideas, eclectic from the beginning, and always something of a propagandist, registered swiftly in his writings the changing spirit of the age.

But Coleridge's outlook on life was always essentially religious. From his college days onward he considered himself, and was considered by his intimate friends, the champion of religion, and particularly of the Christian religion. In his spiritual history as reflected in his writings there are two broadly marked stages, divided at about the year 1798-9—the period of his visit to Germany. In the first stage he was a Necessitarian, and almost simultaneously a Unitarian, while in the second he became a Transcendentalist. The changes in his mind, though rather radical, can be accounted for both historically and psychologically. All his writings that touch on religion, including *The Rime of the Ancient Mariner,* fall chronologically into their place, showing a natural sequence in his spiritual development. In the first period (1794-8) the spiritual thought of the poet is governed chiefly by the conception that God, at the center of everything, predetermines (that is, necessitates) and regulates all physical and mental life into a sort of universal harmony, or unity. Expressed as opinion in the earlier poems, this conception is sublimated into a pervasive spiritual atmosphere in *The Rime of the Ancient Mariner.*

I

Religious Musings, by far the most ambitious poem of Coleridge's youth, was partially written in 1794, when the poet was twenty-two, and was completed and published in 1796. The poem indeed represents a very serious effort; but it is important for what it intends to perform rather than for what it performs. Its style is turgid and grandiose; it has nothing of the simple, terse, idiomatic English which Coleridge achieved in his later poems. Though it has no great intrinsic literary value, it was often considered in Coleridge's day as his most important deliverance,[1] and is significant as indicating the trend of his most serious thinking at that period when his mind was in a formative state. Its thought, complicated and not wholly self-consistent, is dominated by the principles of Necessity and of Unity.

"I am a complete necessitarian," Coleridge wrote to Southey at the time he was composing *Religious Musings,* "and believe the corporeality of *thought,* namely, that it is motion." In another letter of about the same time he speaks of himself as "a Unitarian Christian, and an advocate for the automatism of man." He thus conceived of mind not as a free agent but merely as an automatic and passive instrument through which the cosmic order, the omnipresent Love, finds an avenue of expression. In a letter to John Thelwall in 1796 in which he incidentally affirmed that even from the point of view of poetic sublimity Isaiah and St. Paul and St. John easily surpass Homer and Virgil, Coleridge wrote: "Now the religion which Christ taught is simply, first, that there is an omnipresent Father of infinite power, wisdom, and goodness, in whom we all of us move and have our being; and secondly, that when we appear to man to die we do not utterly perish, but after this life shall continue to enjoy or suffer the consequences and natural effects of the habits we have formed here, whether good or evil. This is the Christian *religion,* and all of the Christian *religion.*" It is striking that in this passage, which makes the bold claim to express the whole of Christian-

---

[1] "I have read all your *Religious Musings* with uninterrupted feelings of profound admiration. You may safely rest your fame on it."— Charles Lamb, in a letter to Coleridge, 1796.

"I was reading your *Religious Musings* the other day, and sincerely I think it the noblest poem in the language next after the *Paradise Lost.*"—Charles Lamb, in a letter to Coleridge, January 5, 1797.

ity, there is not even so much as a hint of the orthodox idea that man is sinful and is saved by grace, and that whatever harshness lurks in the Calvinistic conception of Necessitarianism is immediately removed by the Unitarian conception that since God is love, all are elect and no human being can be given over to eternal punishment. With Necessity at one pole of his thought and Unity at the other, the young poet felt he had solved the riddle of the universe and that he had a living message for the world.   This message, he proudly remarked in one of his letters, was to be found in his literary works; it is indeed completely summed up in *Religious Musings*.

The principles of Unity and Necessity fairly jostle each other in rivalry for the first place in the reader's attention.   As to Unity, the poet repeatedly suggests that "one Omnipresent Mind," whose "most holy name is Love," is diffused through all things; that in the "meek Saviour," "whose life was Love," is the only perfect revelation of the Godhead; and that when men are filled with this love they come to know themselves as "parts and portions of one wondrous whole."   As to Necessity, he likewise repeatedly speaks of "the elect of Heaven," who with steadfast gaze adore the Deity.   "Thus from the Elect, regenerate through faith, pass the dark passions," he reasserts, and declares that the Predestined are "by supernal grace enrobed with Light, and naturalized in Heaven," becoming one with the Father, which is "the Messiah's destined victory."   So the poet constantly passes from Unity to Necessity and back again, thus closely interweaving the two ideas in the poem.

Though the poem is speculative throughout, the poet aims to bring its philosophy to bear directly upon the evils of the day; he attempts to "cope with the tempest's swell" of "these tumultuous times"; and he strikes with all the energy of undisciplined genius. He vigorously attacks the "Fiends of Superstition, that film the eye of Faith, hiding the present God," "diffused through all, that doth make all one whole." He does not hesitate to mention specific offences against this religion, as, for example, the refusal, in January, 1794, of the House of Lords to accept a proffered peace from the French Republic. His wrath was kindled against those who held that the sole purpose of the war upon the French was the preservation of the Christian Religion. To defend the "meek Galilean," with his "mild laws of Love unutterable," by the scourge of war and the prayer of hate seemed to him nothing short of blasphemy. He roused himself even to greater indignation against social evils— "the innumerable multitude of wrongs by man on man inflicted." He expressed sympathy for poverty-stricken children, aged women, and men driven by want to deeds of blood—the wretched many "whom foul Oppression's ruffian gluttony drives from life's plenteous feast."

But in spite of this severe arraignment of all the wrongs committed by man, the poet is convinced that there will soon be a rapid regeneration of mankind, and that in fact all evil is but temporary in character and really the immediate source of greater good. Thus from avarice, luxury, and war, he asserts, sprang heavenly Science, and from Science, Freedom. Even the oppressors of mankind are beneficent instruments of Truth—

> These, even these, in mercy didst thou form,
> Teachers of Good through Evil, by brief wrong
> Making Truth lovely.

Coleridge's evil thus turns out to be no evil at all, but only a dream. His sense of the world's wrong, entirely vague and theoretical, quickly gives way to the conception, so common in the last decades of the eighteenth century, that very shortly the human race shall be changed into a blessed brotherhood of man. Coleridge thus optimistically peoples the earth with "the vast family of Love," each heart self-governed yet each belonging to the kingdom of Christ, and all parts of the one Omnipresent Mind. "A Necessitarian, I cannot possibly disesteem a man for his religious or anti-religious opinions —and as an *Optimist*, I feel diminish'd concern," —so wrote Coleridge to Thelwall in 1796 in reference to *Religious Musings*. A true Necessitarian cannot blame a man for holding any given opinion any more than he can blame a stone for lying where it lies—both positions being inevitable, and the one as remote from individual responsibility as the other. On the other hand, Coleridge's principle that God is all and is Love left no room in his scheme for the existence of evil, and he logically became an unqualified optimist. So the poet concludes as he began, breathing "the empyreal air of Love, omnific, omnipresent Love":

> Believe thou, O my soul,
> Life is a vision shadowy of Truth!
> And vice, and anguish, and the wormy grave,
> Shapes of a dream! [2]   The veiling clouds retire,
> And lo! the Throne of the redeeming God
> Forth flashing unimaginable day
> Wraps in one blaze earth, heaven, and deepest hell.

We may here ask from whence did the young Coleridge get the principles of Unity and Necessity? The

[2] "I thank you for these lines in the name of a Necessitarian and for what follows in the next paragraph, in the name of a child of fancy."—Charles Lamb, in a letter to Coleridge, June 10, 1796.

answer in its main outlines can be given briefly. As to necessity, aside from what of Calvinistic theories of Predestination came to him through the ordinary channels, he got his ideas directly from eighteenth century philosophers, among whom may be named: Hartley, naturalist and associational philosopher, who emphasized the theory that thought is corporeal and is motion, and who treated the mind as an automaton; Priestley, scientist and theologian, who in theology taught the doctrine of philosophical necessity; and Godwin, whose *Political Justice,* published in 1793, claimed to base all its reasoning on the principle of Necessity. Godwin's influence is especially noticeable in those parts of the poem that discuss the social and revolutionary problems of the day.

Besides, it must always be remembered in the eighteenth century poets and philosophers and divines thought much more commonly in terms of Necessity than in the nineteenth; whereas in the nineteenth they thought much more commonly in terms of Free-will. Pope's "Whatever is, is right," was a popular expression of an oft-repeated conception of eighteenth-century philosophy; while perhaps the profoundest expression of determinism was Jonathan Edward's book attacking the Freedom of the Will (1754), which Godwin quotes approvingly so far as it bears on philosophical necessity. It is to be expected that when Coleridge was disciplining his "young noviciate thought in ministeries of heart-stirring song," as he says in the poem, he would show that he had drunk deep from the prevailing philosophy of the preceding generation.

As to Unity, aside from what he gathered from such idealists as Plato, Plotinus, and Berkeley, he got his Unitarian ideas directly from the Bible, particularly from the writings of St. John. In the poem, such phrases as "his most holy name is Love," "Him whose life· was Love," "In whose sight all things are pure," "We and our Father one," and still others, are direct echoes of the Fourth Gospel.[3] In the notes, both those discarded from some of the earlier editions and those that were permanently retained, he also shows a close affinity in thought to the Book of Revelations.

In short, the poet attempted to harmonize his own interpretations of the Scriptures with the teachings of his favorite authors—philosophers and theologians. It was a magnificent effort, but unsuccessful—because of the inconceivability of any one's combining in a single scheme the philosophy of Plato and of St. John with that of eighteenth-century Materialists and Necessitarians. Yet the poet did achieve a certain harmony—satisfactory, it seems, to the people of his time—as, for example, to Charles Lamb—by blending the principles of Necessity and Unity.[4]   Temperamentally, Coleridge was easily

---

[3] The early Unitarians were literalists in interpreting the Scriptures and naturally held the Gospel of St. John in high esteem. But later this Gospel grew in disfavor with them because it emphasizes the Divinity of Christ. Coleridge, however, never followed the Unitarians very closely, either in their early literalism, or in their rejection of the Divinity of Christ. He always retained a profound reverence for the Gospel of St. John. See the quotation near the end of this essay from Notes on the Book of Common Prayer, also *Table Talk,* June 6, 1830: "It is delightful to think, that the beloved apostle was born a Plato," etc.

[4] Priestley made an almost identical combination of Necessity and Unity in his philosophy. A recent commentator, C. C. Everett, in *Immortality and Other Essays,* says of him: "His belief in necessity was simply an intense form of faith in God. Since everything was determined by God, what place is there for grief or anxiety? It was a marvel to his childlike mind that Calvinism, starting as it does from the thought of the sovereignty of God, could reach results so terrible. The sovereignty of God meant to him the sovereignty of a wise goodness. He believed that

inclined to try to reduce all things to one principle, to a Unity—that is, to see the One in the Many. And while in emphasizing the principle of Necessity he was harking back to eighteenth-century ideas, in drawing upon the more ancient sources of the Bible and Plato for the mystiçal principle of Unity, and attempting to express it in terms of the emotions and the imagination, he anticipated the spirit of the nineteenth century, and so far became a prophet of what was to be.

In the brief poem *To a Friend,* written also in 1794, Coleridge asserts that nothing can be gained by prayer— an extreme form of Necessitarianism, since it presupposes that God has literally predetermined every detail of life:

> He knows (the Spirit that in secret sees,
> Of whose omniscient and all-spreading Love
> Aught to implore were impotence of mind)—

Likewise in *The Eolian Harp* (1795) he conceives universal life as automatous:

> And what if all of animated nature
> Be but organic harps diversely framed,
> That tremble into thought, as o'er them sweeps
> Plastic and vast, one intellectual breeze,
> At once the Soul of each, and God of all?

The fragmentary poem, *The Destiny of Nations,* written in 1796, narrating the story of Joan of Arc, lengthily explains that "the infinite myriads of self-conscious minds are one all-conscious Spirit," and that all things in the

---

Calvinism thus carried at its heart a principle that would one day transform it into a system of beauty." It may be suspected but cannot be proved that Coleridge got his ideas ready-made from Priestley. First, there seems to be no direct evidence in the case. Secondly, it is well-nigh impossible to track Coleridge specifically in his borrowings, because of his subtly intermixing materials from various sources and of his interpenetrating them with something of his own. It appears he was only in general indebted to Priestley.

universe, including superstition, and evil itself, help, in a necessitarian spirit, to "evolve the process of eternal good." In the story Joan did not act upon her own initiative, "for a mighty hand was upon her." She went forth alone,

> Urged by the indwelling angel-guide, that oft,
> With dim inexplicable sympathies
> Disquieting the heart, shapes out Man's course
> To the pre-doomed adventure.

At the close the poet also pre-dooms, not only all Enthusiasts, however wild-eyed, but all Prophets, each to their respective fates, and hymns the praise of God:

> All-conscious Presence of the Universe!
> Nature's vast ever-acting Energy!
> In will, in deed, Impulse of All to All!
> Glory to Thee, Father of Earth and Heaven!

In the preface to the *Ode on the Departed Year* (1796) the poet asserts that "the Ode commences with an address to the Divine Providence, that regulates into one vast harmony all the events of time, however calamitous some of them appear to mortals."

Thus the principles of harmony, unity, and optimism, governed by the law of Necessity, furnish the chief intellectual matter of these poems (1794-1796). They are all somewhat abstractly conceived, and their religion may be said to be a religion of opinion rather than of experience. If justification were needed for dwelling so long on these poems of opinion which have no great intrinsic merit it would be that they show clearly that the strongest tendency of Coleridge's mind from the beginning was toward abstraction. In *Biographia Literaria* he says that "at a very premature age, even before my fifteenth year, I had bewildered myself in metaphysics,

and in theological controversy. Nothing else pleased
me. History, and particular facts, lost all interest in my
mind. . . . Poetry itself, yea, novels and romances,
became insipid to me." How different this is from the
early experiences of Keats, for instance. Keats, too, had
his bewildering workings of the mind—luxuriating in the
senses—a true sign that he would be poet for life.
Though Coleridge showed a vein of pure fancy in *The
Songs of the Prixies* (1793) and in *Lines Written at
Shurton Bars* (1795), yet the main powers of his mind
were directed toward discussion of abstract religious
opinions:

> To me hath Heaven with bounteous hand assigned
> Energetic Reason and a shaping mind.
> —*Lines on a Friend* (1794).

But in later poems (1797-8) we see the abstract ideas
gradually becoming humanized. This was the period
of the poet's finding himself, of change and growth, and
especially of the deepening of his spirit. The breaking
down of the scheme of Pantisocracy, upon which Coleridge had for a time staked his future, a serious rupture
with his most intimate friend, Southey, his marriage to
Sarah Fricker—all of which events occurred in the latter
part of 1795—his becoming father of children in 1796
and 1797, his ensuing struggles against serious financial
difficulties, brought him rather suddenly face to face
with actualities. His sense of responsibility for those
dependent on him, which was strong during these years,
wrought deeply on his naturally affectionate nature. It
not only humanized, but simplified his religious outlook.
Moreover, his acquaintance and ripening friendship with
Wordsworth in 1796 and 1797, immensely quickened his
intellectual powers, gave a profounder resonance to his

emotional life, and deepened his sympathy for individual and concrete things in life and nature. As a result, the religious poems of 1797 and 1798 were born of personal experience rather than of abstract speculation. The same principles, as formerly, govern the poet's thought, but they are now rendered by suggestion, and are approached by some simple, deep-felt, personal emotion. The poems are just as religious in spirit, but not so obtrusively religious as the earlier ones. They show a more intimate touch with nature and a far finer sympathy with the concrete objects of nature. The abstract "God diffused through all" of the *Religious Musings* becomes in *Fears in Solitude* (1798) "All sweet sensations, all ennobling thoughts, all adoration of the God in Nature," that keep "the heart awake to Love and Beauty;" or, as expressed in *This Lime-Tree Bower My Prison* (1797):

                                          So my friend
          Struck with deep joy may stand, as I have stood,
          Silent with swimming sense; yea, gazing round
          On the wide landscape, gaze till all doth seem
          Less gross than bodily; and of such hues
          As veil the Almighty Spirit, when yet he makes
          Spirits perceive his presence.

It is to be noted especially in *Frost at Midnight* (1798) how from a very simple situation—himself and his cradled infant at the hearth-fire of his cottage—he rises without seeming effort through personal experience to a grand climax which expresses profoundly and religiously his conception of Unity:

                    For I was reared
          In the great city, pent 'mid cloisters dim,
          And saw nought lovely but the sky and stars.
          But *thou*, my babe! shalt wander like a breeze
          By lakes and sandy shores, beneath the crags

Of ancient mountain, and beneath the clouds,
Which image in their bulk both lakes and shores
And mountain crags: so shalt thou see and hear
The lovely shapes and sounds intelligible
Of that eternal language, which thy God
Utters, who from eternity doth teach
Himself in all, and all things in himself.
Great universal Teacher! he shall mould
Thy spirit, and by giving make it ask.

But the highest and final expression of the spirit of
Unity and Necessity by Coleridge is to be found in the
greatest poem of his life—*The Rime of the Ancient
Mariner* (1797-8). This poem contains no reasoned
religion, no obtrusive theological arguments, but merely
the aroma, the fine flavor, the "breath and finer spirit"
of the poet's religious meditations. And this almost
against his will; for, as suggested in a note, he was consciously attempting to write a work of almost "pure
imagination." His imagination, however, did not escape
the shadow of all his previous religious musings, and the
religious atmosphere of the poem is connected with the
thought of all his earlier religious poems—is indeed its
logical outcome.

Though dealing with other things besides religion, the
poem is full of religious suggestiveness, whose source is
not so much the supernatural machinery the poet uses,
as that which is represented as taking place in the heart
of the mariner. With all its charm, subtlety, unearthly
music, and wild adventure, the poem indicates distin-
guishable stages in the mariner's moral and religious
experience by means of relating so wild a tale of strange
adventure. Or, to put it otherwise, the wonder is that
he has, without doing violence to either, fused such a tale
and such an experience into an harmonious whole. If the
poem ought to have had no more moral than an Arabian

Night's tale, as Coleridge himself once suggested, it
would have had to be completely rewritten and one of
its most unique qualities destroyed.

The thing which makes this blending of religious experience and marvelous adventure possible, and successful, is chiefly the character of the mariner—one of the
most distinctive creations in modern literature. Perhaps
the most striking characteristic of the mariner is that in
the story he does not act but is constantly acted upon—
a fact which Wordsworth considered a great defect, but
which for the purpose of the poem is no defect at all.
After the mariner had killed the albatross—an impulsive
rather than a deliberate act—spirits and powers, plastic
and vast, conjured up by the poet from the ends of the
earth, played upon his mind and conscience as on a harp.
Though in telling his own story the mariner has power
over the will of the wedding-guest and over any who may
be "pre-doomed" to listen to him, yet this power comes
to him as a visitation and is not in his keeping. He has
no will of his own: he is passive to the powers outside
himself and the new law of life revealed to him; that is,
he is a true Necessitarian:

> Forthwith this frame of mine was wrenched
> With a woful agony,
> Which forced me to begin my tale;
> And then it left me free.
>
> Since then, at an uncertain hour,
> That agony returns:
> And till my ghastly tale is told,
> This heart within me burns.
>
> I pass, like night, from land to land;
> I have strange powers of speech;
> That moment that his face I see,
> I know the man that must hear me:
> To him my tale I teach.

In any other hands but those of Coleridge so passive
a character would become insipid. But the mariner is
saved from insipidity chiefly by the poet's communicating
to him an unusual intensity of feeling. It is no doubt
fitting that the ancient man should be "venerable,
weather-beaten, and more or less oracular." It is also
well that he has a glittering eye endowed with the power
of fixing the attention of his listeners and of charming
them, for a time, into that suspension of unbelief concerning the external events of the poem which constitutes
poetic faith. But it is what goes on behind the glittering
eye that really gives the eye its peculiar significance and
power. It is what happens within the heart of the mariner that fixes him unforgettably in our imagination and
makes him appeal to us humanly. Of the poem Charles
Lamb wrote to Wordsworth: "I dislike all the miraculous parts of it, but the feeling of the man under the
operation of such scenery, dragged me along like Tom
Pope's whistle. . . . The Ancient Mariner undergoes
such trials as overwhelm and bury all individuality or
memory of what he was—like the state of a man in a
bad dream, one terrible peculiarity of which is, that all
consciousness of personality is gone." The audacity
of Coleridge's art in portraying the character, we may
say, was to offset his passivity with such an intensity of
feeling that he was on the verge of losing the sense of
his own identity. This inward intensity, derived from
Coleridge's own inwardness of mind, is the chief source
of that exalted and sustained lyricism that gives unusual
freshness and perpetual charm to the poem.

Simplicity and childlikeness of spirit further atone
for the mariner's passivity. Though the character is
old and weather-beaten, he throws himself with the abso-

lute faith and complete *abandon* of a child into the telling of his story.   This utter single-mindedness of the
mariner bewitches the wedding-guest, and also the reader.
Coleridge drank deep of the spirit of the folk ballad, and
at no point has he more completely caught the primitive
spirit of the ballads than in their childlikeness.   It was
a difficult feat for the poet to keep his own thought within
the circle of the mariner's mind and the mariner's thought
within the circle of a child's mind.   At places where the
mariner approaches generalizations and is in the greatest
danger of becoming sophisticated, his thought and
language becomes utterly simple and naïve.   Such, for
example, is the familiar passage near the end of the poem
which, though hackneyed by constant quotation, expresses, with artistic grace, the sum of the mariner's
religious wisdom.   The poem, in short, is the most superb
example of sustained naïveté in the language.

The failure to recognize this naïve spirit sufficiently
has caused some critics who have taken seriously the
moral of the poem to interpret certain important incidents erroneously.   The killing, for example, of an albatross that persisted in following a ship for nine days
would be considered, according to eighteenth-century
ethics, trivial; and according to the scientific ethics of the
twentieth century, natural, or necessary, or, at any event,
no great matter.   But the mariner's ethics is that of a
child.   He killed the bird impulsively and wantonly.   But
when his fellow-mariners attributed their fate and the
fate of their ship, whether for good or evil, but chiefly
for evil, to the killing of the albatross, and accounted the
act a crime, he accepted without question their verdict;
and straightway the crime became to him monstrous and
overwhelming. He had no scale of values, and he suffered

such intense agony as a child does when it is made to feel it has done an outrageously wicked thing, even though its compunction was of the slightest at the time of doing it. Perhaps no one has ever described more poignantly the prolonged agony that follows the inadvertent committal of a crime by an otherwise innocent person than has Coleridge:

> I looked to heaven, and tried to pray;
> But or ever a prayer had gusht,
> A wicked whisper came, and made
> My heart as dry as dust.
>
> I closed my lids, and kept them close,
> And the balls like pulses beat;
> For the sky and the sea, and the sea and the sky
> Lay like a load on my weary eye,
> And the dead were at my feet.

In truth, the sufferings and penances of the mariner are utterly out of proportion to the slightness of the crime. He is pursued by a dark and sinister fate. In his childlikeness he conceives the objects of nature as avenging personalities; the wind which drives the ship southward is the Storm Blast, tyrannous and strong, and the bloody and glorious Sun seems a living being, now appearing accusingly like a broad and burning face and now "like God's own head." The Moon and Stars and the Ocean are instinct with power and seem to conspire with the avenging Spirits against him. The only thing he can do is to lie passively under the terrifying strokes of fate and necessity. And because of the intensity of his feelings the mariner is the most effective, and because of his childlikeness he is the most attractive, Necessitarian in modern literature.

But the mariner is also a most engaging Unitarian.

He discourses sweetly and eloquently on the principle of universal love. To him, not evil, but love and loneliness are the two mighty contending forces in the Universe. In the story the mariner underwent an intense and suspended agony of spirit because of his separation, not merely from his comrades, but from the living world and from God:

> So lonely 'twas that God Himself
> Scarce seemed there to be.

To "abide alone" is more unendurable than flaming fire. But the mariner miraculously stood the test, although, as we have seen, he was all the while at the brink of losing consciousness of his own personality. At the same time he was intensely alive. The fate of his companions was a benediction as compared to the agony he endured in a living death:

> Seven days, seven nights, I saw that curse,
> And yet I could not die.

Those who hold that Coleridge violated poetic justice in the disposition he made of the crew either have a narrow conception of poetic justice or do not realize what it meant for the mariner to remain alive.

But love in the universe ultimately overcomes loneliness. The mariner had learned, not abstractly, but concretely, to love all things, both great and small. And this wisdom of love, though childlike, had in Coleridge's day, and still has in ours, momentous implications. The eighteenth century had placed much emphasis on man's duty to man; it had taught that the proper study of mankind is man; it had sung the short and simple annals of the poor. But its teachings were based either on the principle of selfishness, which insisted that when you show kindness to your fellow-men you are advancing your own interests, or on the principle of benevolence, which was often quite cold-hearted and full of mock pity. The new age, however, insisted on the Christian principle of becoming as little children in order to enter the kingdom of heaven. The note of it was struck in Blake's *Songs of Innocence,* its bearings worked out fully in the poems of Wordsworth, and its chief characteristics expressed in the person of the mariner by Coleridge. The new age also insisted that we have kinship, not merely with man, but with the whole animal creation. It may be urged that the instinctive affection a child shows for animals is based on an actual kinship with them, which is often ignored by adults, and was ignored especially by eighteenth century philosophers. But this sense of kinship was asserted in the poety of Cowper and of Burns; and in *The Ancient Mariner* Coleridge based it on the assumption that all creatures emanate from one Creator. This universal love gains its first victory in the poem when it is strong enough to make the mariner love the water-snakes. From that point it grows increasingly to the end, in larger and larger encircling reaches, till at last it embraces all living things in a sense of universal kinship, catching the mariner himself in its onward sweep, destining him in a necessitarian spirit to "pass, like night, from land to land" to tell the story of it, and causing him in particular to declare our universal human religious fellowship in one of the sweetest passages in our language:

> O sweeter than the marriage-feast,
> 'Tis sweeter far to me,
> To walk together to the kirk
> With a goodly company!—

> To walk together to the kirk,
> And all together pray,
> While each to his great Father bends,
> Old men, and babes, and loving friends
> And youths and maidens gay!

Thus the spirit of *The Rime of the Ancient Mariner* is closely allied to the spirit of Coleridge's earlier religious poems. In *The Ancient Mariner* the poet, in his own inimitable manner, has given, in a rarified, etherealized form, the exhalations and aroma of his personal experience of Necessity and Unity, "the blossom and the fragrancy of all" his earlier religious meditations.[5]

The Rime of the Ancient Mariner is also related to the earlier poems in the imagery it uses. In *The Destiny of Nations,* for example, the poet declares that since Fancy, by peopling the air with beings invisible, first unsensualizes the dark mind, he deems

> Those legends terrible, with which
> The poplar ancient thrills his uncouth throng:
> Whether of pitying Spirits that make their moan
> O'er slaughter'd infants, or that giant bird
> Vuokho, of whose rushing wings the noise
> Is tempest, when the unutterable Shape
> Speeds from the mother of Death, and utters once
> That shriek, which never murderer heard, and lived.

Again, he says that in the far distant polar region

> Dwells the fury Form, whose unheard name,
> With eager eye, pale cheek, suspended breath
> And lips half-opening with the dread of sound
> Unsleeping Silence guards. . . . Yet the wizard her,

[5] "Poetry is the blossom and the fragrancy of all human knowledge, human thought, human passions, emotions, language."—Coleridge, in *Biographia Literaria,* Chapter XV.

Armed with Torngarsuck's power, the Spirit of Good,
Forces to unchain the foodful progeny
Of the Ocean's stream.[6]

"Wild phantasies!" Coleridge ejaculates. Wild and crude they are for the making of poetry. Yet these ancients, wizards, pitying Spirits, unutterable Shapes, and fury Forms of the polar regions suggest the direct origin of much of the imagery in *The Ancient Mariner,* where they become things of beauty. In the earlier poems these spirits and powers have an educative influence on character, "teaching reliance, and medicinal hope," and leading toward faith and truth; to which purpose they are put, in a far finer spirit, in *The Ancient Mariner.*

Imagery similar to this is to be found in the prose fragment, *The Wanderings of Cain* (1798), as for instance: "There was no spring, no summer, no autumn; and the winter's snow, that would have been lovely, fell not on these hot rocks and scorching sands,"—which reminds one of the "hot and copper sky" of *The Ancient Mariner.*

The hero Cain, like the mariner, is a passive character, being pursued by mighty Powers: "The Mighty One that persecuteth me is on this side and on that; he pursueth my soul like the wind, like the sand-blast he passeth through me; he is around me even as the air! . . . The torrent that roareth far off hath a voice; and the clouds in heaven look terribly on me; the Mighty One who is against me speaketh in the wind of the cedar grove; and in silence am I dried up." There is never a

---

[6] The original sources of these passages are books of travel and history, such as Cranz's *History of Greenland.* The use Coleridge makes of them is all his own.

saint to take pity on Cain's soul in agony: "The spirit within me is withered, and burnt up with extreme agony."

In the first part of *Christabel,* written in 1797, Coleridge came nearer realizing his ideal of producing a poem of "pure imagination" than in *The Rime of the Ancient Mariner.* Yet the heroine, the lovely Christabel, like the mariner, inadvertently lays herself open to a sinister influence. Again like the mariner and like Cain, she is a passive character and is pursued and wrought upon by an evil spirit. This evil being—a witch in the form of a beautiful and oppressed maiden who apparently flings herself upon the mercy of Christabel—is more hideous and terrifying to the imagination than anything else conceived by Coleridge. By enacting spells the witch usurps power over the maiden's utterances and works indescribable confusion in her heart.

If the earlier poems were too obtrusively religious, as compared to the subtle implications of *The Ancient Mariner,* the first part of *Christabel* has almost fallen out of religion on the other side. It is extremely fragile and verges on the shadowy and impalpable. In this direction, then, the evolution of Coleridge's mind has gone as far as possible.[7] Later Coleridge added a second part, which, however, does not come up to the first in the qualities just mentioned. And because of the extreme fragility of the first part Coleridge afterwards was never able to write up to its level and therefore never able to complete the poem, though for a time he consciously willed to do so. Yet in atmosphere as well as in general structure it is very similar to *The Ancient Mariner,* its

[7] It may be said that *Kubla Khan* (1798) advances a step farther. But from it have vanished logical structure and discoverable sequence of ideas; what remains is a fragment of pure esthetic luxury.

first part closing with three lines that might have appeared in that poem:

> But this she knows, in joys and woes,
> That saints will aid if men will call:
> For the blue sky bends over all!

Had not Wordsworth suggested to Coleridge in *The Ancient Mariner* the incident of killing the albatross as a motive for punishing the mariner, it is doubtful whether Coleridge would have thought it necessary; for certainly in *Christabel,* a parallel case, the heroine has done nothing to merit the malignant persecution of the witch. In both cases Coleridge conceived that the sublime law of Necessitarian indifference would do its work effectively. For the verisimilitude to life in this principle he would have pointed to the manner in which his own footsteps had been dogged by an untoward fate.

Thus in this period Coleridge created none but passive, necessitarian-like characters, who are pursued by Shapes, Forms, Powers, Destinies, etc.; and wherever the story is completed the character is redeemed by universal love, and is reconciled to his world, the blue sky bending over all. What was asserted rather crudely as religious opinion of Necessity and Unity in the early poems was swiftly transmuted into spiritual implication and expressed with subtle suggestiveness in the poems written in those few short years that constituted the flowering period of Coleridge's poetic genius.

II

Late in his life Coleridge wrote concerning a poem of his youth, *The Destiny of Nations,* composed in 1796: "Within twelve months after the writing of this Poem, my bold Optimism, and Necessitarianism, together with the Infra, seu plusquam Socinianism, down to which, step by step, I had *un*believed, gave way to the day-break of a more genial and less shallow system. But I contemplate with pleasure these Phases of my Transition." Since Coleridge was often inaccurate concerning dates in his own life, it may be doubted whether this great change in his religious experience came as early as 1797 and as suddenly as he declares; for we have seen that the idea of Necessity continued to appear in his poems and writings after that time. The change seems to have come gradually and is not distinctly marked until around 1799, and later.

The first unmistakable sign of his change of heart is his attack upon the merely passive character of his former religious beliefs. In a letter to Thomas Poole, written early in 1801, he says: "Newton was a mere materialist. *Mind,* in his system, is always *passive,*—a lazy *Looker-on* on an external world. If the mind be not *passive,* if it be indeed made in God's Image, and that, too, in the sublimest sense, the *Image of the Creator,* there is ground for suspicion that any system built on the passiveness of the mind must be false as a system." Against the Necessitarian, materialistic, and associational philosopies of the eighteenth century this charge of passiveness is made again and again in Coleridge's later writings—*The Friend, Biographia Literaria, Aids to Reflection,* etc. It is striking that this charge should have been made so unequivocally thus early in his letter. He had remarkable prescience of truth which needed only the confirmation of other writers to bring it to fruition. One therefore can sympathize with his resentment against all attacks on him of plagarism. In another letter to Poole, written within a few days of the foregoing, he says: "If I do not greatly delude myself, I have not only *completely extricated the notion of time and space,* but have overthrown the doctrine of association, as taught by Hartley, and with it all the irreligious metaphysics of modern infidels—especially the doctrine of necessity." He thus repudiates not only an important phase of his earlier religious beliefs, but also his former teachers, on the basis of belief in the existence of a free, active energy in the mind of man; he is so far already committed to the transcendental principle.

As if to make his renunciation irrevocable Coleridge a few years later (1804) again wrote to Poole: "I love you, Poole, for many things; scarcely for anything more than that, trusting firmly in the rectitude and simplicity of your own heart, and listening with faith to its revealing voice, you never suffered either my subtlety, or my eloquence, to proselyte you to the pernicious doctrine of Necessity. All praise to the Great Being, who has graciously enabled me to find my way out of that labyrinth-den of sophistry, and I would fain believe, to bring with me a better clue than has hitherto been known to enable others to do the same." It might seem strange or absurd that a poet should feel an abasement of spirit for having held a certain metaphysical doctrine. But Coleridge was keenly aware that when he renounced this doctrine he was renouncing the whole trend and body of English thought from John Locke to William Godwin, and that a duty had been laid upon himself to find at least a working hypothesis to take its place.

Again, in 1803 he wrote concerning a certain necessitarian passage (written in 1794) as follows: "I utterly recant the sentiment contained in the lines—

> Of whose omniscient and all-spreading Love
> Aught to *implore* were impotence of mind,

it being written in Scripture, 'Ask, and it shall be given you,' and my human reason being moreover convinced of the propriety of offering *petitions* as well as thanksgiving to Deity." He thus accepted belief in Free-will; but only, it seems, after he had woven such strong threads of evil habits about his life that most of his career then seemed a sort of fatal necessity.

This new transcendental attitude of mind is indicated in a poem as early as 1799—*Lines Written in the Hartz Forest.* The theme of the poem is expressed in the lines—

> For I had found
> That outward forms, the loftiest, still receive
> Their finer influence from the Life within;—
> Fair cyphers else; fair, but of import vague
> Or unconcerning.

He illustrates this by saying that though standing on the height of the Brocken in Germany his eye shaped before him in the steady clouds the sands and high white cliffs of England (which he loved) so vividly that all the view

> From sovran Brocken, woods and woody hills,
> Floated away, like a departing dream,
> Feeble and dim!

Thus outward forms depend, for their beauty, upon what the perceiving mind contributes to them; mind is the active agency in determining the nature and quality of perception. The poet asserts that this matter must not be taken lightly, although he humbly admits that that man shows a sublimer spirit who can feel

That God is everywhere! the God who framed
Mankind to be one mighty family,
Himself our Father, and the World our Home.

Not a little interest may be attached to the fact that this poem, which for the first time in Coleridge's poetry expresses the transcendental conception of the might of the mind, should have been written in Germany, whither the poet had gone to study German philosophy. Yet it is practically certain that at this time he had but the slightest knowledge of Kant. Still, a meager knowledge only of that author together with the growth of his own many-sided interests would be sufficient to account for his having arrived at the sense of the shallowness of his former conceptions, especially as regards Necessity, or the passiveness of the mind.

And now, having outgrown the superficialities of his eighteenth-century teachers, Coleridge, at about the age of thirty, mature and unusually endowed and equipped, stood at the threshold of a period in which we should expect him to become the great transcendental and religious poet of his age. But in this we are almost completely disappointed. There are only a few straggling poems as a record of his achievement. His prose, upon which he spent his greatest efforts, is also fragmentary.

Various reasons have been assigned for Coleridge's failure in poetry. Some of them are obvious, others more subtle. Rheumatism and other physical ailments, and the use of opium, which became a confirmed habit with him about 1801, go far in explaining the failure. Subtler and even more potent causes were a congenital weakness of will and the lack of any sure anchorage in home affections.

Perhaps a more serious cause was a strong natural

tendency in Coleridge toward the abstract. Stopford
Brooke says that Coleridge had the power, in a far
greater degree than other poets, of "impassionating himself about intellectual conceptions." This is true of
Coleridge up to about 1799, but not thereafter. Indeed,
he later more than once expressed a yearning for just
this power, which had now left him. Two essential and
indispensable feelings had departed—joy and hope.
Without these he could not impassionate himself even
about intellectual conceptions. For

> Work without Hope draws nectar in a sieve,
> And Hope without an object cannot live.
>
> *(Work Without Hope, 1827)*

We have already seen that there was a tendency to
abstractions in Coleridge's earliest poetry, but that a
little later he succeeded in rendering these in his best
poetry in terms of concrete representation, imaginative
suggestion, and deep feeling. But now, bereft of some
essential feelings, he swung more strongly than ever
toward abstractions. It was not that at a certain time
in his life he began the study of German metaphysics
which destroyed the poet in him, as so many critics declare—his own new position, "we receive but what we
give," refutes the critics—it was simply that in the long
run his original natural impulse to abstractions was
stronger in him than the impulse to concrete poetical representation. Coleridge's prime interest in life was religion; but a man who would be the poet of a transcendental religion must look well to the simple, emotional, and
picturing side of his art. The great central antinomy
which lies at the root of Coleridge's prose—the superiority of Reason over mere Understanding—he was not

able to render successfully into story, incident, and poetic imaginings.

Moreover, as regards poetic method, Coleridge had perfected his art between the years 1794 and 1799. We saw how in that period his imagination made use of witches, wizards, polar spirits, etc., in a crude way in the earlier poems, but in a way nothing short of marvelous in *The Ancient Mariner* and *Christabel.* This imagery was perfectly adapted to that kind of poetry. Coleridge's use of it had become a habit, which was not easily to be shaken off. But this method of poetic representation was in no wise suited to a serious religious poetry that was to exalt the free powers of the mind and soul of man. It was almost literally necessary that he begin again at the beinning to develop an appropriate poetical method. No wonder that his "shaping spirit of Imagination" could not adapt itself to his new material and his new way of thinking![8]

Most of these failings are attested by Coleridge himself in the poem *Dejection: An Ode,* written in 1802. This poem also gives the fullest expression to be found in his poetry of the transcendental principle. Around the statement of this principle, set in the center of the poem, the poet weaves his personal experiences, which, in turn, are set against an external background of evening and night, gradually shifting from an ominous calm to a raging storm.

The poet is possessed with a feeling of dull pain; the

[8] Those who suppose that if his poetical powers had remained unimpaired Coleridge would have continued writing *Ancient Mariners* and *Christabels* imagine a vain thing. He never had an exalted opinion of *The Ancient Mariner* and did not publish *Christabel* until urged by Byron. In fact, these poems did not represent for him the highest truth of life after 1799.

western sky, clouds, stars, and the moon can make no impression on his failing spirit:

> I see them all so excellently fair,
> I see, not feel, how beautiful they are!

His capacity for thinking remains unimpaired; but the sources of his feelings are dried up,—he cannot get relief from external Nature:

> I may not hope from outward forms to win
> The passion and the life, whose fountains are within.

Therefore it naturally follows that

> O Lady! we receive but what we give,
> And in our life alone does Nature live; . . .
> Ah! from the soul itself must issue forth
> A light, a glory, a fair luminous cloud
>   Enveloping the Earth—
> And from the soul itself must there be sent
> A sweet and potent voice, of its own birth,
> Of all sweet sounds the life and element!

This generalization, which may be said to be the theme of the poem, is as radical transcendentalism as some of the poet's earlier conceptions were radical necessitarianism. The mind now is not an automaton, but an original creative force; nature becomes a mirror, a mere mechanical instrument, in which man's mind can reflect itself. All the color, warmth, beauty, life, and life's effluence, which we usually ascribe to outer Nature, are really derived from some inward energy of the soul.

Now this energizing force, this inward light, "this beautiful and beauty-making power" of the soul, the poet goes on to say, is Joy:

> Joy, Lady! is the spirit and the power,
> Which wedding Nature to us gives in dower
> A new Earth and new Heaven,

Undrempt of by the sensual and the proud—
Joy is the sweet voice, Joy the luminous cloud—
   We in ourselves rejoice!
And thence flows all that charms or ear or sight,
   All melodies the echoes of that voice,
All colours a suffusion from that light.

There was a time when the poet's joy dallied with distress, yet hope still remained with him. Now, however, both joy and hope have fled:

But now afflictions bow me down to earth:
Nor care I that they rob me of my mirth;
   But oh! each visitation
Suspends what nature gave me at my birth,
   My shaping spirit of Imagination.

Abstruse research, he says, became his· sole resource, his only plan,

Till that which suits a part infects the whole,
And now is almost grown the habit of my soul.[9]

The poet is aroused from his revery by the ravings of the nightwind, which symbolizes his own mental unrest, and peoples his mind with wild phantasies of a mad host in rout and of a little child lost in a storm. He concludes by pronouncing upon the Lady of the poem that benediction of joy which he himself does not possess. But here we must quote the poem as it originally appeared, which was addressed throughout, not to a Lady, but to the poet Wordsworth:

[9] A parallel passage in *Biographia Literaria* (1817) is: "And if in after time I have sought a refuge from bodily pain and mismanaged sensibility in abstruse researches, which exercised the strength and subtilty of the understanding without awakening the feelings of the heart; still there was a long and blessed interval, during which my natural faculties were allowed to expand, and my original tendencies to develope themselves;—my fancy, and the love of nature, and the sense of beauty in forms and sounds." Coleridge frequently refers to abstruse research as a solace when his feelings are benumbed.

O rais'd from anxious dread and busy care,
By the immenseness of the good and fair
Which thou see'st everywhere,
Joy lifts thy spirit, joy attunes thy voice,
To thee do all things live from pole to pole,
Their life the eddying of thy living soul!
O simple spirit, guided from above,
O lofty Poet, full of life and love,
Brother and friend of my devoutest choice,
Thus may'st thou ever, evermore rejoice!

The importance of this poem in Coleridge's spiritual history cannot easily be overestimated. The poet may be taken at his word, although literalness must not be carried too far. For instance, it is not to be concluded that Coleridge did not live many pleasant days after he had written this poem. Nevertheless it is strictly true that the kind of joy necessary for the working of his creative imagination never returned to him. Abstruse research, abstract reasonings, were the only substitutes possible. Had he had a profound conviction, such as Poe's, that sorrow and melancholy are the best themes for poetry, he undoubtedly could have written many marvellous poems in a doleful spirit. But like Wordsworth he held that truly creative art must be inspired by joy, that poetry is the spontaneous overflow of powerful emotions. The poet, Coleridge held, must be full of life and love, must have a sense of the immenseness of the good and fair; he must "bring the whole soul of man into activity, with the subordination of its faculties to each other according to their relative worth and dignity" [10]—imagination, will, intellect, emotion; not only must he have fine perceptions of spiritual truth, but his soul must be able, by an inward active energy, to create even the life and element

[10] *Biographia Literaria.* See the whole passage, close of chapter XIV.

of what it perceives. The contrast between this high transcendental and spiritual conception as an ideal of his art and the utterly depressing mood and waning power of the poet himself at the age of thirty, is as pathetic as anything in literary history. With a grace equal to its pathos he deferred to one who he deemed had the requisite qualifications—Wordsworth.

Seldom thereafter did he allow himself to sing in a strain similar to this—once in the poem *To William Wordsworth,* written in 1807, after he had read Wordsworth's *Prelude.* Here he asserts again the transcendental principle of the self-determining power of the mind, "the dread watch-tower of man's absolute self," as he describes Wordsworth's singing of

> Currents self-determined, as might seem,
> Or by some inner Power; of moments awful,
> Now in thy inner life, and now abroad,
> When power streamed from thee, and thy soul received
> The light reflected, as the light bestowed.

In sharp contrast to this conception is Coleridge's own mood of

> Fears self-willed, that shunned the eye of hope;
> And hope that scarce would know itself from fear;
> Sense of past youth, and manhood come in vain,
> And genius given, and knowledge won in vain.

These passages are strikingly similar to the corresponding passages in *Dejection: An Ode;* [11] only, the disparity between the poet's ideal and his prevailing mood is even greater here than in the earlier poem. He recognizes with bitterness the impossibility of ever realizing

---

[11] They begin respectively with, "O Lady! we receive but what we give," and, "But now afflictions bow me down to earth."

his ideal in poetry.   Yet he consoles himself with the
thought that

> Peace is nigh
> Where wisdom's voice has found a listening heart.

But in poetry the world demands a producer, not a lis-
tener.   However, if Coleridge could not produce the
poetry his heart could pronounce good, he would remain
silent; and silent he remained as a poet almost literally
the rest of his life.

Hymn Before Sunrise, in the Vale of Chamouni[12]
(1802), five years earlier than *To William Wordsworth*
and about the same time as *Dejection: An Ode,* aims to
be more specifically religious than the other two poems,
and shows a strong tendency toward the abstract:

> O dread and silent Mount! I gazed upon thee,
> Till thou, still present to the bodily sense,
> Didst vanish from my thought: entranced in prayer
> I worshipped the Invisible alone.

The poet's Thought, or Reason, comes into perfect union
with God,

> Till the dilating Soul, enrapt, transfused,
> Into the mighty vision passing—there
> As in her natural form, swelled vast to Heaven!

In *Dejection: An Ode* Coleridge conceives the finer
aspects of Nature as possessing what the mind of man
contributes to them; in *Hymn Before Sunrise* he asserts
a complimentary truth, namely, that Nature herself is
but a tool, a mouth-piece, of the Mind of the Divine.
The stupendous mountain, the wild torrents thundering

---

[12] For his conception Coleridge was indebted to the poem *Chamouni at
Sun-rise,* by Frederike Brun, a German poetess. But Coleridge, as
DeQuincey said, "created the dry bones of the German outlines into
fulness of life."

down the "precipitous, black, jagged rocks," the vale
beneath, all gorgeously described, are but so many voices
attesting the omnipotence of God:

> Thou kingly Spirit throned among the hills,
> Thou dread ambassador from Earth to Heaven,
> Great Hierarch! tell thou the silent sky,
> And tell the stars, and tell yon rising sun
> Earth, with her thousand voices, praises God.

The Mind of God and the Reason of Man are the two
sovereign entities of existence; the objects of Nature are
but the reflex of either:

> Whene'er the mist, that stands 'twixt God and thee,
> Defecates to a pure transparency,
> That intercepts no light and adds no stain—
> There Reason is, and then begins her reign! [13]

Hymn Before Sunrise is full of exclamatory sentences,
suggesting that the poet had difficulty in lifting his emotions and style to the height of his great argument. And
unless interfused by correspondingly deep emotions its
profound abstract conception yields more fruit for prose
than for poetry.

Both the expressed and suggested transcendental ideas
in the poems just considered are fully drawn out in *The
Friend,* a series of essays published as a weekly periodical
in 1809 and 1810, and revised and published in book form
in 1818. The display of immense learning and wide
reading, the unusually large number of latinized words
and complicated sentences, the extraordinary subtle and
abstract reasonings, show that Coleridge gave free rein
to that intellectual and abstracting power of the mind for
which he was famed among his contemporaries. The

---

[13] But he also quotes Dante to the effect that such Reason is unattainable.

treatise stands midway in his life and intellectual career, and represents his moral principles fully developed. It undoubtedly contains the essence of the matter he used in oral conversation, and is thus the foundation of the great influence he exerted over the thought of the generations following him. It therefore in no wise deserves the rather contemptuous treatment accorded it by most of his biographers and critics, who generally dismiss it with a short paragraph. Had Carlyle, for instance, studied it with the same thoroughness with which he usually studied historical documents he could have seen that Coleridge not only in a large measure anticipated his own thought but also the characteristic thought of the century, and could have saved his sneers at Coleridge. No apology is needed to set forth fully the leading ideas of this significant work.

By 1809 Coleridge was deeply immersed in the study of German metaphysics, which confirmed and helped to develop his own transcendental philosophy. Though for a time Schelling was in the ascendency, Kant in the long run was the most important influence. The works of Kant, Coleridge frankly asserts in *Biographia Literaria,* "took possession of me as with a giant's hand." Kant gave him the conviction of the essential difference between Reason and Understanding—a fundamental position in *The Friend.* But Coleridge was no mere imitator of Kant. For his great principle of method he was indebted to Plato and Bacon as well as to Kant. To Coleridge, whose reasonings, though subtle, were never rigidly logical, Plato's 'Ideas,' Bacon's 'Laws,' and Kant's 'Intuitive Reason' were all very much the same. For instance, in *Constitution of Church and State* Coleridge says: "That which, contemplated objectively (that is, as existing externally to the mind), we call a law; the same contemplated subjectively (that is, as existing in a subject or mind), is an idea. Hence Plato often names ideas laws; and Lord Bacon, the British Plato, describes the laws of the material universe as the ideas in nature" And with the ideas of these philosophers he interwove something distinctly his own.[14]

Though *The Friend* was too cumbrous to achieve with the reading public either an immediate or an ultimate success, its general drift is at once clear and positive. Its aim vigorously stated by the author in parts of two sentences, is "to support all old and venerable truths; and by them to support, to kindle, to protect the spirit; to make the reason spread light over our feelings, to make our feelings, with their vital warmth, actualize our reason;"—"to refer men's opinions to their absolute principles,[15] and thence their feelings to the appropriate objects and in their due degrees; and finally, to apply the principles thus ascertained to the formation of steadfast convictions concerning the most important questions of politics, morality, and religion."

"I am," he further says, "conscious that in upholding some principles of taste and philosophy, adopted by the

[14] In addition to the reason already given why it is almost impossible to track Coleridge in his borrowings from numberless authors, is his conception of the nature of truth. First: "I regard truth as a divine ventriloquist: I care not from whose mouth the sounds are supposed to proceed, if only the words are audible and intelligible." Secondly, he conceived truth as a process and a growth, and his own intellect as in a state of development, and therefore changing. Those who try to specify narrowly his indebtedness are inevitably driven to use such words as 'probably,' 'perhaps,' 'reasonable to suppose,' etc.

[15] The words 'refer,' 'ground,' 'bottom,' 'deduce,' used in the sense of grounding or bottoming opinions in principles, or of deducing them from principles, are great favorites with Coleridge.

great men of Europe, from the middle of the fifteenth till toward the close of the seventeenth century, I must run counter to many prejudices of many of my readers." Wordsworth is the only contemporary quoted approvingly, and in the 1818 edition he is quoted oftener than any other writer. It was the purpose of both Coleridge and Wordsworth to restore to English literature the freedom and the largeness that characterized it before Dryden, and in particular to bring back to it the transcendental spirit of the age of Shakespeare, and the puritan religious spirit of the age of Milton, shorn of its partisanship. In general, the venerable truths of the Bible, of the Ancient Classics, and of Elizabethan and Puritan poets and statesmen and divines are marshalled to do service in the cause of a transcendental religion.

The absolute principle in man, which gives him ultimate assurance of his higher spiritual and religious nature, in which his experiences must be grounded, and to which all his opinions must be referred, is Reason. Coleridge grows eloquent and poetic in describing this ultimate principle in man that assures man of his innate greatness of being:

"Reason! best and holiest gift of God and bond of union with the giver;—the high title by which the majesty of man claims precedence above all other living creatures; —mysterious faculty, the mother of conscience, of language, of tears, and of smiles;—calm and incorruptible legislator of the soul, without whom all its other powers would 'meet in oppugnancy';—sole principle of permanence amid endless change,—in a world of discordant appetites and imagined self-interests the only common measure. . . . Thou alone, more than even the sunshine, more than the common air, art given to all men, and to every man alike" (Section I, Essay II).

Reason is absolute, and therefore "is the same in all men, is not susceptible of degree;" it is impersonal, making men "feel within themselves a something ineffably greater than their own individual nature;" it is the organ of the supersensuous and of an inward sense, therefore it has "the power of acquainting itself with invisible realities or spiritual objects;" it implies free-will and conscience, giving "to every rational being the right of acting as a free agent, and of finally determining his conduct by his own will, according to his own conscience." "Man must be free; or to what purpose was he made a spirit of reason, and not a machine of instinct? Man must obey; or wherefore has he a conscience? The powers, which create this difficulty, contain its solution likewise: for their service is perfect freedom."

A faculty in man lower than reason and sharply distinguished from it is the understanding,—the instrument, so to speak, of reason. For "reason never acts by itself, but must clothe itself in the substance of individual understanding and specific inclination, in order to become a reality and an object of consciousness and experience." The understanding is not absolute but relative, "possessed in very different degrees by different persons," according to their enlightenment by past experience and immediate observation; it is not impersonal but personal, "the whole purport and functions of which consist in individualization, in outlines and differencings by quantity and relation;" it is not an organ of the supersensuous, but "a faculty of thinking and forming judgments on the notices furnished by sense," selecting, organizing, and generalizing; it does not imply free-will, but acts within the laws of cause and effect with reference to prudence and practical expediency.

Lower than the understanding in man are the organs of sense: "Under the term 'sense' I comprise," says Coleridge, "whatever is passive in our being, without any reference to the question of materialism or immaterialism; all that man is in common with animals, in kind at least—his sensations, and impressions" [16]   (Section I, Essay III).

From these principles as a working basis Coleridge attempts to interpret the ultimate realities of politics, morality, religion and art. As to politics, government is a science of relativity, which concerns itself with the ownership and distribution of property, and with the physical well-being and the security of the individuals who make up a nation. To gain these ends "we must rely upon our understandings, enlightened by past experiences and immediate observation, and determining our choice by comparisons of expediency," giving heed to "particular circumstances, which will vary in every different nation, and in the same nation at different times." That is, the understanding, rather than reason, must be the chief active faculty to determine the affairs of gov-

---

[16] "When I make a threefold distinction in human nature, I am fully aware, that it is a distinction, not a division, and that in every act of mind the man unites the properties of sense, understanding, and reason. Nevertheless it is of great practical importance, that these distinctions should be made and understood. . . . They are more than once expressed, and everywhere supposed, in the writings of St. Paul. I have no hesitation in undertaking to prove, that every heresy which has disquieted the Christian Church, from Tritheism to Socinianism, has originated in and supported itself by arguments rendered plausible only by the confusion of these faculties, and thus demanding for the objects of one, a sort of evidence appropriated to those of another faculty." (Section I, Essay III.)

ernment. It follows on the one hand, that man is not to
be governed by fear, or the power of the stronger, as
though he were a mere creature of the senses; and, on
the other, that man cannot, in the political aspect, be
governed by 'pure reason', which is absolute, impersonal,
and transcendental.

The system of Hobbes is an example of government by
the senses, which Coleridge dismisses with contempt as a
system that "applies only to beasts": "It denies all
truth and distinct meaning of the words, right and duty;
and affirming that the human mind consists of nothing but
the manifold modifications of passive sensations, considers men as the highest sort of animals indeed, but at
the same time the most wretched."—This is one of the
many severe strictures of Coleridge on all systems in
which "at all events the minds of men were to be sensual-
ized" and reduced to a passive state. An example, at
the other extreme, of government by reason is Rousseau's
Social Contract, which mistakenly exalts matters of the
understanding, relative, personal, prudential, into the
realm of pure reason, thus giving unlimited range to a
wild and dangerous individualism. Reason, grounded in
morality and conscience, is not possessed by men collec-
tively, but by individuals. Coleridge does ample justice
to Rousseau's disquisitions on pure reason and free-will as
inalienable qualities in man's being. But these high
powers must not be abased to the use of expediency and
worldly prudence which are primarily requisite in matters
of government. Therefore Rousseau's system, he argues,
"as an exclusive total, is under any form impracticable."

A wise government recognizes the inviolability of pure
reason in individuals and makes no regulations to inter-
fere with its freedom. It will content itself "to regulate

the outward actions of particular bodies of men, according to their particular circumstances," being guided largely by the enlightened intelligence of its public men. Thus reason acts as a constant corrective on the various phases of governmental changes and growth; so that

"The dignity of human nature will be secured, and at the same time a lesson of humility taught to each individual, when we are made to see that the universal necessary laws, and pure ideas of reason, were given us not for the purpose of flattering our pride, and enabling us to become national legislators; but that by an energy of continued self-conquest we might establish a free and yet absolute government in our own spirits" (Section I, Essay III).

Coleridge's political views had changed correspondingly with the changes in his religious development. In 1795 when he was in strong sympathy with the French Revolution, he recommended, in his Bristol address, "a practical faith in the doctrine of philosophical Necessity" as a panacea for the troubled times. In 1798, when he had lost faith in the leadership of France for liberty, he expressed the doubt in *France: An Ode* whether liberty could make its home anywhere but in the realm of nature —"nor ever didst breathe thy soul in forms of human power." But in 1809 he expressed the idea that true liberty is to be wrought out, not by means of political legislation, but in the souls of men in a transcendental spirit of self-conquest. Political government is thus the outcome, not the cause, of liberty.

It is, then, by the cultivation of individual morality and religion rather than by politics that the impersonal and absolute reason residing in the breast of every human being may incorporate itself in a thousand forms in all

the inclinations and activities of the personal and relative
understandings of men, and through their understandings
subdue and regulate the life of their senses, thus developing men to their highest capacities and making them free
indeed.

Morality and religion are essentially one. They "cannot be disjoined without the destruction of both." Whenever they are partially disjoined it invariably follows that
a short-sighted scheme of prudence, based on the mere
evidence of "sensible concretes," the rule of expediency,
"which properly belongs to one and the lower part of
morality," will be made the whole. To substitute this
worldly prudence "for the laws of reason and conscience,"
Coleridge says, "or even to confound them under one
name, is a prejudice, say rather a profanation, which I
became more and more reluctant to flatter by even an
appearance of assent." Reason, therefore, the organ of
the supersensuous and transcendental, with all that it
implies of conscience, free-will, and faith,[17] is the sole
arbiter of the inseparable forces of our moral and religious experience.

Philosophy, understood and pursued in the right spirit,
is an important aid to religion. The aim of philosophy is
to discover the absolute principles of existence, to find for
all that exists conditionally "a ground that is uncondi-
tional and absolute, and thereby to reduce the aggregate
of human knowledge to a system." But to reason at all
on principles of the absolute the mind must have some
kind of power to go out of its individual, personal self,

[17] "What is faith, but the personal realization of the reason by its
union with the will?" (Section II, Essay II.) "Faith is a total act of
the soul: it is the whole state of the mind, or it is not at all; and in this
consists its power, as well as its exclusive worth." (Section I, Essay
XV.)

and must think and act in accord with some discoverable method. By his emphasis on the science of method and on mental initiative, or an *apriori* activity of mind, as a prerequisite to all experiments and investigations Coleridge felt he had made his most distinctive contribution to religious philosophy.

These principles of mental initiative and of method are operative in our hourly and daily experiences, are the condition of our intellectual progress, and may "be said even to constitute the science of education, alike in the narrowest and most extensive sense of the word." The educated man is superior to the uneducated in this, that by a previous act and conception of the mind he selects with method the relative from the irrelative, the significant from the insignificant. Dame Quickly's want of method, old Polonius's form of method without its substance, and Hamlet's superb method when he is at his best, are examples of Shakespeare's mastery of the fundamental "principle of progressive transition." In short, all the failures in education may be ascribed to the "inattention to the method dictated by nature herself, to the simple truth, that as the forms in all organized existence, so much all true and living knowledge proceeds from within."

In scientific and speculative thought the prime materials of method are the relations of objects, and the contemplation of relations is the indispensable condition of thinking methodically. There are two kinds of relations—that of law and that of theory. The first is of "the absolute kind which, comprehending in itself the substance of every possible degree, precludes from its conception all degree, not by generalization, but by its own plentitude;" it is an attribute of the Supreme Being, inseparable from the idea of God, and from it must be derived all true insight into all other grounds and principles necessary to method. The second is a process of generalization based on facts and presupposes the ideas of cause and effect, being illustrated in the scientific arts of medicine, chemistry, physiology, etc. Thus it is implied that the first relation, partaking of the absolute, is of higher value than the second, our ideas, for instance, of the scientific arts being mere approximations of truth, changing in every generation.

In philosophy Plato most perfectly illustrated the principles of mental initiative and of method. The larger and more valuable of Plato's works have one common end—"to establish the sources, to evolve the principles, and exemplify the art of method. . . . The education of the intellect, by awakening the principle and method of self-development was his proposed object, not any specific information that can be conveyed into it from without." But this mental initiative, which is reason itself, has its ultimate source in a supersensual essence, the pre-establisher of the harmony between the laws of matter and the ideas of pure intellect. Thus for Plato philosophy ends in religion.

By showing that these same principles of method and of intellectual intuition—*lumen siccum*—were fundamental in Bacon's philosophic works Coleridge effected the so-called reconciliation of Plato and Bacon. Their very differences—that Plato sought the truth by applying the principle of method to the intellect, and that Bacon sought it by applying the principle of method to nature—tends only to accentuate the fact that their principles at bottom are one and the same.

Indeed the reconcilement of Plato and Bacon is but

one instance of the larger use Coleridge aims to make of the principle of method—he employs it as the means of reconciling all opposites. "Extremes meet" is to him a divine aphorism. "All method supposes a principle of unity with progression; in other words, progressive transition without breach of continuity." Even in the world of the senses an organism exists only by virtue of possessing "corresponding opposites" held in unity, and derives its character from an antecedent method of self-organizing purpose, the impulse of which comes from something above nature and is transcendental.[18] Likewise man's understanding grows by a similar process of reconciling "opposite yet interdependent forces," whose organizing impulse is derived from pure reason. The similarity of the processes in nature and in the understading makes it possible for the understanding to comprehend nature; thus by constant self-effort in experimenting and generalizing the understanding is led to comprehend gradually and progressively the relation of each to the other, of each to all—to perceive the world in unity and arrive at a general affirmation of the reality of a supreme being.

But here the understanding (the dialectic intellect) stops, and must give way to reason. Of the limitations of the understanding Coleridge says:

"It is utterly incapable of communicating insight or conviction concerning the existence or possibility of the world, as different from Deity. It finds itself constrained to identify, more truly to confound, the Creator with

[18] Man derives his sense of reality of the objects of nature from an experience which "compels him to contemplate as without and independent of himself what yet he could not contemplate at all, were it not a modification of his own being." (Section II, Essay XI.) This re-emphasizes that "in our life alone does nature live," as asserted in *Dejection: An Ode* (1802).

the aggregate of his creature. . . . The inevitable result of all consequent reasoning, in which the intellect refuses to acknowledge a higher or deeper ground than it can itself supply, and weens to possess within itself the centre of its own system is—and from Zeno the Eleatic to Spinosa, and from Spinosa to the Schellings, Okens and their adherents, of the present day, ever has been— pantheism under one or other of its modes, the least repulsive of which differs from the rest, not in its consequences, which are one and the same in all, and in all alike are practically atheistic, but only as it may express the striving of the philosopher himself to hide these consequences from his own mind. This, therefore, I repeat, is the final conclusion. All speculative disquisition must begin with postulates, which the conscience alone can at once authorize and substantiate; and from whichever point the reason may start, from the things which are seen to the one invisible, or from the idea of the absolute one to the things that are seen, it will find a chasm, which the moral being only, which the spirit and religion of man alone, can fill up.

"Thus I prefaced my inquiry into the science of method with a principle deeper than science, more certain than demonstration. . . . There is but one principle, which alone reconciles the man with himself, with others, and with the world; which regulates all relations, tempers all passions, gives power to overcome or support all suffering, and which is not to be shaken by aught earthly, for it belongs not to the earth: namely, the principle of religion, the living and substantial faith *which passeth all understanding,* as the cloud-piercing rock, which overhangs the stronghold of which it had been the quarry and remains the foundation; . . . this it is which affords the sole sure anchorage in the storm, and at the same time the substantiating principle of all true wisdom, the satisfactory solution of all the contradictions of human nature, of the whole riddle of the world" (Section II, Essay XI).

This remarkable passage and the following, which stresses the soul's freedom and immortality, reveal the heart of Coleridge's spiritual consciousness and the central springs of the philosophy of *The Friend:*

"God created man in his own image. To be the image of his own eternity created he man! Of eternity and self-existence what other likeness is possible, but immortality and moral self-determination? In addition to sensation, perception, and practical judgment—instinctive or acquirable—concerning the notices furnished by the organs of perception all which in kind at least, the dog possesses in common with his master; in addition to these, God gave us reason, and with reason he gave us reflective self-consciousness; gave us principles, distinguished from the maxims and generalizations of outward experience by their absolute and essential universality and necessity, and above all, by superadding to reason the mysterious faculty of free-will and consequent personal amenability, he gave us conscience—that law of conscience, which in the power, and as the indwelling word, of a holy and omnipotent legislator . . . unconditionally commands us to attribute reality, and actual existence, to those ideas and to those only, without which the conscience itself would be baseless and contradictory, to the ideas of soul, of free-will, of immortality, and of God. To God, as the reality of the conscience and the source of all obligation; to free-will, as the power of the human being to maintain the obedience which God through the

conscience has commanded, against all the might of
nature; and to the immortality of the soul, as a state
in which the weal and woe of man shall be proportioned
to his moral worth. With this faith all nature,

> —all the mighty world
> of eye and ear—

presents itself to us, now as the aggregated material of
duty, and now as a vision of the Most High revealing
to us the mode, and time, and particular instance of
applying and realizing that universal rule, pre-established
in the heart of our reason" (Introduction, Essay XV).

The Hebrew Scriptures alone give an adequate account
of these high matters. The Greeks made brilliant dis-
coveries in the region of pure intellect and are still
unrivalled in the arts of the imagination. The Romans
were given "to war, empire, law." "It was the Roman
instinct to appropriate by conquest and give fixure by
legislation." But

> The Hebrew may be regarded as the fixed mid point of the living
> line, toward which the Greeks as the ideal pole, and the Romans as the
> material, were ever approximating; till the coincidence and final syn-
> thesis took place in Christianity, of which the Bible is the law, and
> Christendom the *phenomenon* (Section II, Essay X).

Finally, the method in the fine arts—poetry, painting,
music, etc.—lies between law as absolute, or reason, and
theory as relative, or understanding. Outwardly art is
governed by the position of parts and mechanical relations, which require dexterity of manipulation, or understanding; inwardly it contains that which originates in
the artist himself and which partakes of the absolute—
his inner emotional and spiritual nature, his will and
reason. The depth and fulness, or "plentitude," of the
artist's real or true self contributed to the work of art

constitutes the degree of creative energy it possesses, and determines its worth. This is the root principle of Coleridge's esthetics, and the philosophical basis of his literary criticism.

The application of this transcendental principle, as developed in *The Friend,* to the art of poetry is the chief purpose of Coleridge's Notes on Shakespeare and his *Biographia Literaria* (1817), one of the great books in English literary criticism. Coleridge was undoubtedly gifted natively in literary appreciation, and from his youth onward was an excellent judge of poetry, independent of any school of art or of philosophy. Nevertheless almost the whole of his criticisms that have come down to us were produced after 1809, and grow out of his transcendental interpretation of life and art.

As in *The Friend* so in his literary criticism Coleridge's whole critical outlook springs from his deep sense of the principle of inwardness and of his grasp of the principle of organic unity. "One character," he says, "belongs to all true poets, that they write from a principle within, not originating in any thing without; and that the true poet's work in its form, its shapings, and its modifications, is distinguished from all other works that assume to belong to the class of poetry, as a natural from an artificial flower, or as the mimic garden from an enamelled meadow." Again, "The spirit of poetry, like all other living powers, must of necessity circumscribe itself by rules, were it only to unite power with beauty. It must embody in order to reveal itself; but a living body is of necessity an organized one; and what is organization but the connection of parts in and for a whole, so that each part is at once end and means? . . . The organic form shapes itself from within, and the fulness

of its development is one and the same with the perfection of its outward form" (Lectures on Shakespeare).
This transcendental method of perceiving the power of
the poet's mind from within and seeing it work itself
outward in the shapings of its art products makes of the
critic a true psychologist. And Coleridge's critical writings are replete with instances that reveal the insight of
one who in an extraordinary way understands the inner
workings of the human mind. We may wish that Coleridge had been less extreme in his transcendentalism, but
we must not forget that it was through his transcendental
method that he came into so intimate a knowledge of the
mind's deepest and most permanent traits.

Again, as in *The Friend,* so in his critical works Coleridge utilizes the principle of harmonization as expressed
in the aphorism, "Extremes meet." A poem is a true
work of art to the degree that it reveals "the balancing
and reconciling of opposite or discordant qualities, sameness with difference, a sense of novelty and freshness with
old or customary objects, a more than usual state of
emotion with more than usual order, self-possession and
judgment with enthusiasm and feeling" (*Biographia
Literaria*). One of the chief glories of Shakespeare
is his "signal adherence to the great law of nature, that
all opposites tend to attract and temper each other."
This of course satisfactorily explains Shakespeare's habit
of mingling comedy and tragedy in his plays. From the
fact that Shakespeare used not only this principle but
gave organic unity to his plays, working from within
outward, Coleridge proved that Shakespeare's intellectual
judgment was fully equal to his native genius, and
repudiated the prevailing eighteenth century critical
opinion that his genius was merely 'wild' and 'irregu-

lar.' In short, Coleridge was more responsible than any other single individual in changing current eighteenth century conceptions of Shakespeare to current nineteenth century conceptions of him.

Another fundamental trait of Coleridge's criticism is that it contemplates "reciprocal relations of poetry and philosophy to each other; and of both to religion, and the moral sense." In unmistakable language Coleridge declared: "It is my earnest desire—my passionate endeavor—to enforce at various times and by various arguments and instances the close and reciprocal connection of just taste with pure morality. Without that acquaintance with the heart of man, or that docility and childlike gladness to be made acquainted with it, which those only can have, who dare look at their own hearts—and that with a steadiness which religion only has the power of reconciling with sincere humility;—without this, and the modesty produced by it, I am deeply convinced that no man, however wide his erudition, however patient his antiquarian researches, can possibly understand, or be worthy of understanding, the writings of Shakespeare" (Lectures on Shakespeare). This means that a worthy critic, in Coleridge's estimation, must be not only a true psychologist but a religious philosopher. And whatever detailed comments Coleridge may be making on a play of Shakespeare, a drama of Aeschylus, or a poem of Milton, it is his psychological insight and his philosophical background that give to his comments their characteristic penetration and profundity. Milton's description of Death in Book II of *Paradise Lost,* to give one of numberless illustrations, elicits from the critic the following remark: "The grandest efforts of poetry are where the imagination is called forth, not to produce a distinct form, but a strong working of the mind, still offering what is still repelled, and again creating what is again rejected; the result being what the poet wishes to impress, namely, the substitution of a sublime feeling of the unimaginable for a mere image" (Lectures on Shakespeare and Milton).

It is therefore not surprising that in *Biographia Literaria* Coleridge should consider the growth of his philosophic and religious ideas germane to the development of his literary mind; indeed, what other critics would consider digressions were central to his purpose. It is likely that in writing *Biographia Literaria* he was influenced by Wordsworth in *The Prelude;* as Wordsworth told of the growth of his own poet's mind, based on his poetic and spiritual experiences, so Coleridge would tell of the growth of his critical mind, based on philosophical ideas.

As preliminary to literatary criticism proper he reviews and evaluates the different philosophical systems that have influenced him from his youth onward. Especially does he relate how he passed from Hartley and the eighteenth century associationists and materialists to Kant, with a vigorous onslaught on the sophistry of the Hartlean system of association that had beguiled him so long. From Hartley's system it follows "inevitably, that the will, the reason, the judgment, and the understanding, instead of being determining causes of association, must needs be represented as its creatures, and among its mechanical effects. . . . According to this hypothesis the disquisition, to which I am at present eliciting the reader's attention, may be as truly said to be written by Saint Paul's church, as by me: for it is the mere motion of my muscles and nerves; and these again are set in motion from external causes, equally passive, which external causes stand themselves in interdependent connection with every thing that exists or has existed. Thus the whole universe co-operates to produce the minutest stroke of every letter, save only that I myself, and I alone, have nothing to do with it, but merely the causeless and effectless beholding of it when it is done. . . . We only fancy, that we act from rational resolves, or prudent motives, or from impulses of anger, love, or generosity. In all these cases the real agent is a *something-nothing-everything,* which does all of which we know, and knows all that itself does. The existence of an infinite spirit, of an intelligent and holy will, must on this system be mere articulated motions of air" (Chapter VII).

During the interval between Hartley and Kant the Mystics, Jacob Behmen, George Fox, and others, he says, kept his mind from being imprisoned within the outlines of any single dogmatic system and aided him in keeping "the heart alive in the head." But it was Kant, as we have seen, who disciplined his understanding and gave him in "the categorical imperative of the conscience" and of the Reason a higher ground to postulate the freedom of the will and the 'dynamic ideas' and the inward reality which he worked out in *The Friend* and later applied to literary criticism. Here Coleridge enters a protest against the charge of plagarism both from Schelling in philosophy and Schlegel in criticism. This protest gains both point and force, especially with reference to Schlegel, when we consider, first, as has been shown here, that Coleridge's critical as well as his philosophical principles are clearly enunciated as early as 1809 in *The Friend,* and secondly, that he unstintingly admits the mighty influence of Kant upon him.

As in *The Friend* so in *Biographia Literaria* Coleridge finds the chief standards of literary and spiritual excellence in Shakespeare and Milton and in the current of thought of their age and in one great contemporary—Wordsworth. Though *Biographia Literaria* contains long dissertations on the difference between imagination and fancy and a detailed account of the author's differences with Wordsworth's *Preface to the Lyrical Ballads* and a summary of the defects of Wordsworth's poetry, the book mainly glories in the agreement of the two poets and in the excellency of Wordsworth's poetry, as triumphantly illustrating Coleridge's critical principles. "Lastly," he says, "and pre-eminently I challenge for this poet the gift of Imagination in the highest and strictest sense of the word. . . . In imaginative power, he stands nearest of all modern writers to Shakespeare and Milton; and yet in a kind perfectly unborrowed and his own" (Chapter XXII).

What a profound meaning Coleridge attached to the word Imagination is revealed in a passage at the close of Chapter XIV, which also is the heart of Coleridge's whole critical theory and one of the greatest single passages in modern literary criticism:

"The poet, described in ideal perfection, brings the whole soul of man into activity, with the subordination of its faculties to each other according to their relative worth and dignity. He diffuses a tone and spirit of unity, that blends, and (as it were) *fuses* each into each, by that synthetic and magical power, to which I would exclusively appropriate the name of Imagination. This power, first put in action by the will and understanding, and retained under their irremissive, though gentle and unnoticed, control, *laxis effertur habenis,* reveals itself in the balance or reconcilement of opposite or discordant qualities: of sameness, with difference; of the general with the concrete; the idea with the image; the individual with the representative; the sense of novelty and freshness with old and familiar objects; a more than usual state of emotion with more than usual order; judgment ever awake and steady self-possession with enthusiasm and feeling profound or vehement; and while it blends and harmonizes the natural and the artificial, still subordinates art to nature; the manner to the matter; and our admiration of the poet to our sympathy with the poetry. . . . Finally, Good Sense is the Body of poetic genius, Fancy its Drapery, Motion its Life, with Imagination the Soul that is everywhere, and in each and forms all into one graceful and intelligent whole."

Aside from balancing contrarieties and harmonizing all the faculties of the mind in creative work, perhaps the most original part of this passage is that which asserts that the activity of the imagination arises in the will and understanding and is unobtrusively controlled by them. The recognition of the volitional and dynamic quality in poetry harmonizes Coleridge's criticism with his philosophy, *Biographia Literaria* with *The Friend,* and also with his later writings.

The prose treatise *Aids to Reflection* (1825) has again the same general atmosphere and outlook as *The Friend;* it employs once more the principles of method and mental initiative and the distinction between reason and understanding as bases for interpreting morality and religion; and it asserts with equal emphasis that religion is the ultimate reality of life.

On the other hand, *Aids to Reflection* is much less subtle and abstruse, has a clearer outline and a more orderly arrangement of its matter, and is altogether a more readable book. Its frankly aphoristic style saves its author from the pitfalls of over-ingenuity which abound in *The Friend*. Not as arbitrary in its logic, it becomes a more profoundly human document. It admits of more latitude in argument and of greater flexibility in its distinctions. Reason, which in *The Friend* had been considered purely an absolute principle, is divided into speculative and practical reason, the former being relative and closely allied to understanding, the latter only remaining absolute. Prudence, thought of in *The Friend* as at best a very low form of morality that stands in opposition to higher spiritual life, is more reasonably admitted into the scheme of true morality. Though *The Friend* asserted that the reason recognizes the will and conscience as important agencies in man's spiritual development, *Aids to Reflection* exalts the will relatively to a more prominent position. Though the former work recognized Christianity as the true religion, the latter lifts it to a place of central interest in the reader's consciousness; what was implicit concerning Christianity in the former becomes explicit in the latter, in accordance with the natural evolution of Coleridge's mind.

In short, Coleridge's main purposes in *Aids to Reflection* is to harmonize the tenets and doctrines of orthodox Christianity with his own transcendental philosophy; to "translate the terms of theology into their moral equivalents;" as, for example, to render such words as "sanctifying influences of the Spirit" by "purity in life and action from a pure principle," or to contemplate the words "spirit, grace, gifts, operations, and the like" as ideas of "the reason, flowing naturally from the admission of an infinite omnipresent mind as the ground of the universe," with the aim of giving a fresh and deeper meaning to the old truths of religion. The inspiration and high hope of his work was that he might, in humility and modesty, "form the human mind anew after the Divine Image."

"The requisites," he says, "for the execution of this high intent may be comprised under three heads: the prudential, the moral, and the spiritual. . . . The prudential corresponds to the sense and the understanding; the moral to the heart and the conscience; the spiritual to the will and the reason, that is, to the finite will reduced to harmony with and in subordination to, the reason, as a ray from the true light which is both reason and will, universal reason, and will absolute." This threefold classification is logically adhered to in the three main divisions of the book, under the heads respectively of Prudential Aphorisms, Moral and Religious Aphorisms, and Aphorisms of Spiritual Religion Indeed.

Moral prudence is mainly prohibitive; *Thou shalt not* is its most characteristic formula. Its danger is to develop mere self-protection and self-love, and it must never be substituted for, or confused with, the higher morality. As a corrective on our sensual nature and a protector of virtue it is a necessity; it acts as a sort of doorway between the world of the senses and morality. "Though prudence in itself is neither virtue nor spiritual holiness, yet without prudence, or in opposition to it, neither virtue nor holiness can exist."

Higher than prudence is religious morality. Here are opened up at once questions concerning the relation of some of the essential doctrines of Christianity to the feelings, motives, the conscience, and the will, of man. Christianity, for instance, is superior to Stoicism in this, that while the latter attaches honor to the person who acts virtuously in spite of his feelings, the former "instructs us to place small reliance on a virtue that does not begin by bringing the feelings to a conformity with the commands of the conscience. Its especial aim, its characteristic operation, is to moralize the feelings."

Again, such phrases from the Scriptures as *the Spirit beareth witness with our spirit* cannot be explained except by postulating the freedom of the will in man: "The man makes the motive, and not the motive the man. What is a strong motive to one man, is no motive at all to another. If, then, the man determines the motive, what determines the man—to a good and worthy act, we will say, or a virtuous course of conduct? The intelligent will, or the self-determined power? True, in part it is: and therefore the will is pre-eminently, the spiritual constituent in our being." It is only with a free, spiritual being that we can imagine the Spirit to hold intercommunion.

Being spiritual, the will is not natural, that is, not in nature:

Whatever is comprised in the chain and mechanism of cause and effect, of course necessitated, and having its necessity in some other thing, antecedent or concurrent—this is said to be natural; and the aggregate and system of all such things is Nature. It is, therefore, a contradiction in terms to include in this free-will, of which the verbal definition is—that which originates an act or state of being. . . . It follows, therefore, that whatever originates its own acts, or in any sense contains in itself the cause of its own state, must be spiritual, and consequently supernatural; yet not on that account necessarily miraculous. And such must the responsible Will in us be, if it be at all. . . . These views of the Spirit, and of the Will as spiritual, form the ground-work of my scheme.[19] (*On Spiritual Religion Indeed,* Introduction to Aphorism X).

This conception of the will as above Nature and above the law of cause and effect is in flat contradiction to the philosophy of the Necessitarians, who assume "that motives act on the will, as bodies act on bodies; and that whether mind and matter are essentially the same, or essentially different, they are both alike under one and the same law of compulsory causation."

It is likewise utterly incompatible with Calvinism:

The doctrine of modern Calvinism, as laid down by Jonathan Edwards and the late Dr. Williams, which represents a will absolutely passive, clay in the hands of a potter, destroys all will, takes away its essence and definition, as effectually as in saying—This circle is square—I should deny the figure to be a circle at all. It was in strict consistency, therefore, that these writers supported the Necessitarian scheme, and made the relation of cause and effect the law of the universe, subjecting to its mechanism the moral world no less than the material or physical. It follows that all is nature. Thus, though few writers use the term Spirit more frequently, they in effect deny its existence, and evacuate the term of all its proper meaning. With such a system not the wit of man nor all the theodicies ever framed by human ingenuity, before the celebrated Leibnitz, can reconcile the sense of responsibility, nor the fact of the difference in kind between regret and remorse. (*On Spiritual Religion Indeed,* Aphorism I.)

Yet the reflecting man must admit that his own will is not the only and sufficient determinent of all he is, and

[19] "I have attempted, then, to fix the proper meaning of the words, Nature and Spirit, the one being the *antithesis* of the other: so that the most general and negative definition of nature is, whatever is not spirit; and *vice versa* of spirit, that which is not comprehended in nature; or in the language of our elder divines, that which transcends nature. But Nature is the term in which we comprehend all things that are representable in the forms of time and space, and subjected to the relations of cause and effect: and the cause of the existence of which, therefore, is to be sought for perpetually in something antecedent."

all he does. Something must be attributed to the "harmony of the system to which he belongs, and to the pre-established fitness of the objects and agents, known and unknown, that surround him." Moreover, in the world we see everywhere evidence of a unity, which the component parts are so far from explaining, that they necessarily pre-suppose it as the cause and condition of their existing as those parts; or even of their existing at all. This antecedent unity, or principle, or universal presence, or Spirit, acts "on the will by a predisposing influence from without, as it were, though in a spiritual manner, and without suspending or destroying its freedom." Thus *the Spirit beareth witness with our spirit*— man is a copartner with the Divine.

Furthermore, this intercommunion suggests the possibility of man's endless progress in the quest of the spirit. "Every state of religious morality, which is not progressive, is dead or retrograde." And "Christianity is not a theory, or a speculation; but a life;—not a philosophy of life, but a life and a living process." The law of method and of mental initiative with its principle of progressive transition, developed in *The Friend,* has its highest and ultimate application in the Christian's "ever-progressive, though never-ending" growth in spiritual truth. It is the culmination of what is a universal law of progress, from the lowest order of creation to the highest:

"The lowest class of animals or *protozoa,* the *polypi* for instance, have neither brain nor nerves. Their motive powers are all from without. The sun, light, the warmth, the air are their nerves and brain. As life ascends, nerves appear; but still only as the conductors of an external influence; next are seen the knots or ganglions, as so many *foci* of instinctive agency, which imperfectly imitate the yet wanting centre.   And now the promise and token of a true individuality are disclosed; . . . the spontaneous rises into the voluntary, and finally after various steps and long ascent, the material and animal means and conditions are prepared for the manifestations of a free will, having its law within itself, and its motive in the law—and thus bound to originate its own acts, not only without, but even against, alien stimulants.   That in our present state we have only the dawning of this inward sun (the perfect law of liberty) will sufficiently limit and qualify the preceding position, if only it have been allowed to produce its two-fold consequence—the excitement of hope and the repression of vanity" (*Moral and Religious Aphorisms, XV*). . . . "And who that hath watched their ways with an understanding heart, the filial and loyal bee; the home-building, wedded, and divorceless swallow; and above all the manifold intelligent ant tribes, with their commonwealths and confederacies, their warriors and miners, the husband-folk, that fold in their tiny flocks on the honeyed leaf, and the virgin sisters with the holy instincts of maternal love, detached and in selfless purity—and not say to himself, Behold the shadow of approaching humanity, the sun rising from behind, in the kindling morn of creation!   Thus all lower natures find their highest good in semblances and seekings of that which is higher and better.   All things strive to ascend, and ascend in their striving.   And shall man alone stoop?[20] . . . No! it

[20] These almost startlingly penetrative passages anticipate, so far as prophecy can anticipate, the evolutionary thought of a later generation, especially on its ethical side, as expressed, for instance, in the poetry of Browning.

must be a higher good to make you happy. While you labor for any thing below your proper humanity, you seek a happy life in the region of death. Well saith the moral poet—

> 'Unless above himself he can
> Erect himself, how mean a thing is man!' "
> *(Moral and Religious Aphorisms, XXXVI.)*

What is peculiar to man, however, and exclusively human is a struggle of jarring impulses within him; a mysterious diversity between the injunctions of the mind and the elections of the will; an inexplicable sense of moral evil in his nature. The means of redemption from this evil constitutes spiritual religion indeed—something higher than religious morality. This redemption cannot be effected merely by a progressive development toward moral perfection, but requires a special revealing and redeeming agency. "I regard," says Coleridge, "the very phrase, 'Revealed Religion,' as a pleonasm, inasmuch as a religion not revealed is, in my judgment, no religion at all." The historic Christ is the Revealer and Redeemer. "I believe Moses, I believe Paul; but I believe in Christ," succinctly expresses Coleridge's meaning. To show that the distinctive principles of Christianity as a redemptive religion are in full accord with right reason and highest conscience is the purpose of the third part of *Aids to Reflection*.

"The two great moments of the Christian Religion are, Original Sin and Redemption."[21] Without a distinct

---

[21] Coleridge considers many other articles of the Creed, such as Election, The Trinity, Baptism, etc., but since these are matters for the Speculative, not the Practical, Reason to consider, they admit of great varieties of opinion without affecting the character of the Christian.

comprehension of the meaning of the term original sin it is impossible to understand aright any one of the doctrines peculiar to Christianity. Original sin, then, is "sin originant, underived from without," that is, it is not a thing in nature, where all is Necessity, cause and effect, antecedent and consequent,—"in nature there can be no origin." Sin therefore is a spiritual, not a natural, evil, but the spiritual in man is the will; in and by the will sin must originate. It is a thing neither inflicted on man, nor implanted in him, nor inherited by him: "For if it be sin, it must be original; and a state or act, that has not its origin in the will, may be calamity, deformity, disease, or mischief; but a sin it can not be." The question, therefore, of the chronology of sin, or the chronicles of the first sinner, or of the supposed connecting links of an adamantine chain from the first sinner down to ourselves, has only a metaphysical and historical interest; and the question as to whether sin is of God or coequal with God becomes a barren controversy. What the individual must primarily concern himself with is, not what inherited tendencies or diseases he is afflicted with, but what moral evil he has originated in his own responsible will; for that alone is sin.

Nevertheless, original sin is confessedly a mystery, one which by the nature of the subject must ever remain such, which is felt to be such by every one who has previously convinced himself that he is a responsible being,—a mystery which admits of no further explanation than the statement of the fact. It is, however, not a fact and a mystery first introduced and imposed by Christianity, but of universal recognition. It is assumed or implied by every religion that retains the least glimmering of the patriarchal faith in God infinite, yet personal. A deep

sense of this fact is in the most ancient books of the
Brahmins; in the Atheism of the Buddhists; in the myths
of Prometheus, of Io, and of Cupid and Psyche,—"in the
assertion of Original Sin the Greek Mythology rose and
set." It is as great a perplexity for the philosophic Deist
as for the Christian; so that a man may not get rid of
the difficulty by ceasing to be a Christian.

It is in the Christian Scriptures alone, however, that
original sin is affirmed with the force and frequency proportioned to its consummate importance. And it is the
Christ alone of these Scriptures that supplies an adequate
redemption from its power. The Redemptive Act is complete and perfect in itself. Christ, sinless, voluntarily
took upon himself our humanity; and though his death
was violent, he accepted it with an inward willingness of
spirit, which was its real cause. The power of sin was
conquered by his Spirit. It is not merely by steadfastness
of will, or determination, but by *steadfastness in faith,*
faith in something higher than the will—the redemptive
power of Christ's love—that the will can be saved from
the consequences of original sin, that is, be regenerated,
and that the self can be emptied of evil and filled with
grace and truth.

Redemption is in no sense a credit-debit account
between two parties (God and man) into which a third
party (Christ) enters to pay the debt to satisfy the
creditor. But the Redeemer, by taking on human flesh
and conquering sin in the flesh, created a condition by
which man may be a co-agent with the Spirit of Christ;
and through repentance and faith, the two constantly in-
teracting, and through his will, working in conjunction
with both repentance and faith, man may attain to salvation. That is, redemption is a spiritual process and a

spiritual mystery.   And things spiritual must be apprehended spiritually.

The redemptive experience has a true inwardness and is transcendental.   A Christian cannot speak or think as if his redemption were a future contingent event, but must both feel and say, "I have been redeemed, I am justified."   Christ did not merely come to show us a way of life, to teach certain opinions and truths, and tell us of a resurrection; but he declared He is the Way, the Truth, the Resurrection, the Life.   God manifested in the flesh is eternity in the form of time.   The Absolute Reason in Christ became human reason.   And the method of redemption furnishes the means for the human reason to become one with the Absolute Reason, the human will with the Absolute Will.   Just as the understanding in man utilizes the material furnished by the senses to its own ends, just as the reason utilizes the understanding to its own and higher ends—just as, in other words, there is an antecedent and higher mental initiative in every act of mental and moral growth,—so the Redeemer furnishes the antecedent moral and spiritual initiative to the will that it might free itself, not only of its own original sin, but of ultimate corruption and carnal death, and become free indeed.   Thus the method of redemption offered in the Scriptures is in absolute harmony with right reason and highest conscience.

Since the redemptive experience is an inward process of purifying the heart and the will and must needs be had by every Christian, it follows that the question of miracles and the question of immortality are relatively of less importance as attesting the truth of religion.   As to miracles, it may freely be admitted and even contended that those worked by Christ were to the whole Jewish

nation true and appropriated evidences as to the nature
of him who worked them and proof of the truth of his
teachings. But what if, as Paley taught, these external
and historical data are substituted for the inward experience of religion itself as evidences of Christianity?
Coleridge retorts: "Evidences of Christianity! I am
weary of the word. Make a man feel the want of it;
rouse him, if you can, to the self-knowledge of his need
of it; and you may safely trust to its own evidence." Likewise an intellectual assent to belief in immortality, which
is a fundamental article of faith in all other religions as
well as Christianity, cannot be substituted for the possession of that inward grace and truth which came by Jesus
Christ.

In thus setting himself squarely against Jonathan
Edwards and Paley and all the Necessitarian and rational
theologians of the eighteenth century, and in transfusing
religion with imaginative and spiritual insight, Coleridge
became a prophet of the nineteenth century and an influential power in philosophy and literature as well as in
religion. He not only inveighed mightily against his own
early views and all theologies that conceive God as a law
of gravitation and that empty the words sin and holiness
of their real meaning, but against all schemes of conduct
based on calculations of self-interest. Of such schemes
he says:

They do not belong to moral science, to which, both in kind and
purpose, they are in all cases foreign, and, when substituted for it,
hostile. Ethics, or the science of Morality, does indeed in no wise
exclude the consideration of action; but it contemplates the same in
its originating spiritual source, without reference to space or time, or
sensible existence. Whatever springs out of *the perfect law of freedom,*
which exists only by its unity with the will of God, its inherence in the
Word of God, and its communion with the Spirit of God—that (ac-

cording to the principles of moral science) is good—it is light and righteousness and very truth. (*On Spiritual Religion Indeed,* XIII.)

This inward spiritual religion postulates a wider transcendence; namely, that in general of the spiritual over the material world, and militates against our habit of attaching all our conceptions and feelings to the objects of the senses: "I do not hesitate to assert, that it was one of the great purposes of Christianity, and included in the process of our redemption, to rouse and emancipate the soul from this debasing slavery of the outward senses, to awaken the mind to the true *criteria* of reality, namely, permanence, power, will manifested in act, and truth operating in life."   Indeed, thoughout *The Friend* and *Aids to Reflection* Coleridge insists that the visible objects of nature have reality only so far as there is in them a principle of permanence akin to the 'peculia' of humanity, "without which indeed they not only exist in vain, as pictures for moles, but actually do not exist at all:"— one long peroration on the text in *Dejection: An Ode* (1802): "We receive but what we give, and in our life alone does Nature live."

That the presupposition throughout *Aids to Reflection* of faith in God as personal, with moral attributes, and in Christ as more than human, meant something other to Coleridge than a matter of mere intellectual assent is attested by a letter to Stuart, in 1826, which expresses his personal acceptance of faith in God and in a Redeemer and belief in the efficacy of prayer.   In consequence he became more cheerful and more resigned than formerly. About this same time he freed himself measurably from the evil of opium; thenceforth he passed his days in the serenity of old age and in the spirit of a personal and transcendental religion.

But a revealed and transcendental religion, based on the Word of God, implies some special method or principle of interpreting the Bible. The question of interpretation Coleridge discusses in a little treatise *Confessions of an Inquiring Spirit,* posthumously published. The cautiousness with which he argues against Infallibility—the theory that the Bible throughout was literally dictated by Omniscience—indicates how universally the theory was held in Coleridge's day; the clearness and boldness with which he presents his own opposing view makes him one of the forerunners of the free and socalled 'higher' criticism' of later times.

Coleridge contends that the Bible should be approached in the same spirit that one approaches any other book of grave authority. One may, for instance, consider as un-Shakespearian passages in *Titus Andronicus* and other plays of Shakespeare, and yet speak with absolute certainty concerning the manifold beauties of Shakespeare, both in general and with detail. To deem every line in Shakespeare as authoritative and praiseworthy as every other line would be critical fanaticism. Likewise it is "superstitious and unscriptural" to consider that since the Bible was dictated by God Himself every word in it is as precious as every other word. In short, it is the spirit of the Bible, and not the detached words and sentences, that is infallible and absolute. And he who "takes it up as he would any other body of ancient writings, the livelier and steadier will be his impression of its superiority to all other books, till at length all other books and all other knowledge will be valuable in his eyes in proportion as they help him to a better understanding of his Bible."

Though Christianity has its historical evidences as

strong as is compatible with the nature of history, "the truth revealed through Christ has its evidence in itself, and the proof of its divine authority is its fitness to our nature and needs." For this transcendental or pragmatical test nothing can ever be substituted; the true inwardness of the Scriptures must find response in the true inwardness of man's soul. This Coleridge eloquently states in *Notes on the Book of Common Prayer,* where he speaks of preparations for taking the Sacrament of the Eucharist:

> Read over and over again the Gospel according to St. John, till your mind is familiarized to the contemplation of Christ, the Redeemer and Mediator of mankind, yes, of every creature, as the living and self-subsisting Word, the very truth of all true being, and the very being of all enduring truth; the reality, which is the substance and unity of all reality. . . . We are assured, and we believe, that Christ is God; God manifested in the flesh. As God, he must be present entire in every creature;—(for how can God, or indeed any spirit, exist in parts?)

This transcendent, monistic, and purely mystical Unity represents the final stage of Coleridge's spiritual development. Its strong religious intonation is accentuated in *My Baptismal Birth-day* (1833), which poem Coleridge recited to Emerson on the latter's visit to him, and which was one of the last of his compositions:

> Father! in Christ we live, and Christ in Thee—
> Eternal Thou, and everlasting we.
> The heir of heaven, henceforth I fear not death;
> In Christ I live! in Christ I draw the breath
> Of the true life!—

In *Religious Musings* of 1794, Coleridge began with the conception of Unity and with an effort to harmonize whatever light he possessed with the Scriptures; these two factors therefore are common to all the stages of his religious development. Thus Unity is both the most constant and the most important principle in his religious philosophy, while the Bible, in which St. John plays a special part, is the most important influence in shaping that philosophy. On the other hand, the widest divergence in his thought is this, that whereas in the first stage he represented Deity as impersonal and "not only as a necessary but a necessitated being," man as an automaton "pre-doomed" to a fixed course, and all things in the universe as regulated into a necessary universal harmony, in the second stage he gradually emancipated himself from this conception and became transcendental, conceiving God as personal[22] and self-determined and man as having conscience and free-will and other transcendental qualities, by means of which he is able to effect a higher Unity with the power and Will of God. Though this divergence involves a complete facing about on a fundamental issue, Coleridge's writings, when studied in chronological order, show a consistent growth, beginning with a thorough-going Necessitarianism and ending in a radical Transcendentalism. They were one of the most important influences in changing the current of English thought from characteristic eighteenth-century determinism and Necessitarianism to characteristic nineteenth-century Idealism.

[22] Of his transition period, Coleridge writes in *Biographia Literaria* (Chapter X): "For a very long time, indeed, I could not reconcile personality with infinity: and my head was with Spinoza, though my whole heart remained with Paul and John. Yet there had dawned upon me, even before I had met with the *Critique of Pure Reason,* a certain guiding light. . . . I became convinced, that religion, as both the corner-stone and the key-stone of morality, must have a moral origin; so far, at least, that the evidence of its doctrines could not, like the truths of abstract science, be wholly independent of the will."

WORDSWORTH

WORDSWORTH

Wordsworth was always primarily a poet and an artist. But he was also in a true sense a psychological and a philosophical poet, which fact or facts are necessary to grasp in order to understand the true import of his work. He not only "attended with care to the reports of the senses" and showed remarkable "ability to observe with accuracy things as they are in themselves," but also sedulously traced in his poems "the primary laws of our nature," attempting to show the action and reaction of mind upon its environment. Always strongly introspective, he revealed the workings of his own mind, or with rare insight transferred some of his own mental processes to those of his characters, giving them a verisimilitude to life. He was throughout his career profoundly interested in the growth of the mind, to which the long poem *The Prelude* is devoted.

Not only did he consider deeply the origin and nature of human knowledge, but it was almost habitual with him to contemplate a given object in its largest and ultimate relations. He viewed social problems, political issues, incidents of every-day life, and external nature, in the light of moral and spiritual principles. Even when dealing with an ordinary landscape or a simple story, his mind reached outward to a horizon that is infinite and penetrated inward to a world that is spiritual. By virtue of this interpenetrating energy of mind, which perceived the ideal in the real, the spiritual in the sensuous, and which reverently applied ultimate moral principles with transforming effect to many phases of life, Wordsworth's poetry may be said to embody a religious philosophy.

The spiritual growth of Wordsworth was steady and continuous. His outlook from any two points of his life more than a few years apart was not the same; he had undergone a change. He was constantly testing his past experiences by new truth or by new experiences, and thus he put into practice his deep belief in growth. The development in his philosophy of life was strikingly similar to that of Coleridge, although he was not so radically necessitarian in his youth nor so extremely transcendental in his mature years. The changes in him were also far more subtle than in Coleridge. Due, however, to a certain simplicity in his art and to his genuine sincerity, his poems accurately register the subtle changes; so that if one looks at the poems closely from a chronological point of view one can trace the story of the inner life of the poet.

I

The first chapter in this story is that of his childhood and youth. In the first two books of *The Prelude,* written between the age of twenty-eight and thirty, he gives an account of all that he could remember of significance that related to the building up of his soul in childhood. Although the Bible and the catechism were taught him, these did not take hold of him as did what we may call natural religion, derived at first hand from the influences of Nature. Though not able to define his experiences consciously, Nature from the beginning as of her own initiative wrought upon the sensitive mind of the child and held it as by fascination. Love, awe, and beauty were the prime elements in this devotion. Desire grew into love and rapture; a sense of danger into fear and awe. "I loved," he says, "whate'er I saw, nor lightly loved but most intensely." He loved the sun because he saw him lay his beauty on the morning hills. He "held unconscious intercourse with beauty, old as creation." He rejoiced to stand beneath some rock at night to watch a storm, to drink in the visionary power, and deemed the mood of shadowy exultation profitable because it gave his being a sense of sublimity and awe. Swayed now by love and now by awe, his feelings were alternately enkindled and restrained, intensified and disciplined.

Three special periods, or rather moments, of these early years, recorded in the Second and Fourth Books of *The Prelude*, are of great significance. The first tells of that momentous time when that which had been unconscious devotion in him became conscious. It was in his seventeenth year, he says, that he recognized that all the joy of his communion with Nature had a divine origin, that Deity (the Uncreated) was in and through and round all things and made them respire with meaning:

> I felt the sentiment of Being spread
> O'er all that moves and all that seemeth still;
> . . . Wonder not
> If high the transport, great the joy I felt
> Communing in this sort through earth and heaven
> With every form of creature, as it looked
> Towards the Uncreated with a countenance
> Of adoration, with an eye of love.
>   (*The Prelude*, Book II, lines 401-414.)

The second moment was more specific in point of time. He had returned for his summer vacation from his first year in college at Cambridge, and was in his eighteenth

year.   It was the first time he had for a long period been
absent from his native vales and mountains.   He tells
with great zest the overflowing joy of his return.   But in
the midst of his salutations of a thousand familiar objects
he suddenly became abstracted and saw himself apart
from his surroundings and became conscious of his own
soul, its free, creative, and immortal powers.   This great
revelation came to him almost instantaneously when first,
one evening, he made the circuit of Esthwaite Lake:

> Gently did my soul
> Put off her veil, and, self-transmuted, stood
> Naked, as in the presence of her God . . .
> —Of that external scene which round me lay,
> Little, in this abstraction, did I see;
> Remembered less; but I had inward hopes
> And swellings of the spirit, was rapt and soothed,
> Conversed with promises, had glimmering views
> How life pervades the undecaying mind;
> How the immortal soul with God-like power
> Informs, creates, and thaws the deepest sleep
> That time can lay upon her.
> *(The Prelude,* Book IV, lines 150-168.)

The third and climatic moment followed closely upon
the second, and was its natural sequel.   It was the hour
of his self-dedication—one of the supreme experiences
of his life.   In the moment of the baptism, as it were, of
the poet's soul, the spirit of poetry and the spirit of
religion met; and the fact, that in their so meeting neither
was belittled redounds to Wordsworth's everlasting
honor.   Reverently but unflinchingly he accepted the
dedication, which was not performed by him, but for him
by a power outside himself.   It was the moment when
the child put away childish things and became a man.   It
is psychologically natural that the dedication should have
come in a morning after a night of revelry, which be it

noted, for once and once only Wordsworth described
with as perfect a touch as the best in that kind:

> I had passed
> The night in dancing, gaiety, and mirth,
> With din of instruments and shuffling feet,
> And glancing forms, and tapers glittering,
> And unaimed prattle flying up and down;
> Spirits upon the stretch, and here and there
> Slight shocks of love-liking interspersed,
> Whose transient pleasure mounted to the head,
> And tingled through the veins.

The contrast between this night of gaiety and the con-
secration that followed as he walked home at the dawn
of morning immeasurably heightens the effect of the
latter:

> Magnificent
> The morning rose, in memorable pomp,
> Glorious as e'er I had beheld . . .
> Ah! need I say, dear Friend! that to the brim
> My heart was full; I made no vows, but vows
> Were then made for me; bond unknown to me
> Was given, that I should be, else sinning greatly,
> A dedicated Spirit.
>
> (*The Prelude,* Book IV, lines 311-337.)

These moments round out his boyhood experiences of
Nature, of his own soul, and of God, and are marked as
things from thenceforth to be hallowed in his memory.
He was keenly aware that he had not traveled the conventional road to spiritual light.   He avers, however, that
he still must raise his voice gratefully to the powers of
Nature, even

> If this be error, and another faith
> Find easier access to the pious mind.
>
> (*The Prelude,* Book II, lines 419-20.)

Along with his reverential attitude toward Nature and
God Wordsworth had an innate respect for humanity, or

rather human beings, which in due time took a central place in his thought. In *The Prelude* he traces as far back as he can the origin of this reverence for Man. Shepherds, he says, were the men that pleased him in his boyhood days. In a mountainous district he saw the shepherd against a background of Nature—sturdy, stalwart, independent, a freeman, "wedded to his life of hope and hazard"—

> A lord and master, or a power,
> Or genius, under Nature, under God,
> Presiding.
>
> (*The Prelude,* Book VIII, lines 258-60.)

Sometimes he beheld him through the mist a ghostly, giant-like appearance, or saw him glorified by the deep radiance of the setting sun:

> Thus was man
> Ennobled outwardly before my sight,
> And thus my heart was early introduced
> To an unconscious love and reverence
> Of human nature.
>
> (*The Prelude,* Book VIII, lines 275-279.)

But it was in his twenty-second year (1792), when he was in Revolutionary France, that his heart was for the first time all given to human beings and that his love was theirs. This was the opening of an epoch in his spiritual history, for from thenceforth Man was co-equal with Nature in his consciousness. Nature was ever an inspirer, a teacher, but his deepest thought and feeling were centered in humanity—"My theme no other than the very heart of man." (*The Prelude,* Book XIII, 1, 241.)

These experiences in his youth of Nature, Man, and God are undoubtedly colored by the language and philosophic thought of the poet at the time of composing

The Prelude (1799-1805). Nevertheless the feelings he had when a youth, such as the intensity of love, wonder, and awe, are rendered with absolute fidelity.

Early in 1793, in his twenty-third year, Wordsworth published in a separate volume the poem *Descriptive Sketches,* which marks the beginning properly of his public literary career. The material of this youthful poem is based upon a continental trip the poet made with his friend Robert Jones in 1790. Though his descriptions of the Grande Chartreuse, the Alps, and the Lake of Como bulk large and are loosely connected, there is evidence that the poet brought to his task "a mind aglow," struggling, but only now and then effectually, through the show of things to reality. Though the language is sometimes "knotty and contorted" he produced lines that indicate the Wordsworth of later years, such as, "black, drizzly crags," "deep that calls to deep across the hills," "—thy torrents shooting from the clear blue sky," Nature's "healing power," etc. "Seldom, if ever," says Coleridge, "was the emergence of an original poetic genius above the literary horizon more evidently announced."

The spirit of devoutness, fundamentally characteristic of Wordsworth, is manifested in this poem. In a letter to his sister in September, 1790, after he had visited the Alps, Wordsworth writes:—"Among the more awful scenes of the Alps, I had not a thought of man, or a single created being; my whole soul was turned to Him who produced the terrible majesty before me." This feeling of religious awe he attempted to put into the poem. Two passages may be quoted together as making clear his underlying feeling:

By floods, that, thundering from their dizzy height,
Swell more gigantic on the steadfast sight;
Black, drizzling crags, that beaten by the din,
Vibrate, as if a voice complain'd within;
Bare steeps, where Desolation stalks, afraid,
Unsteadfast, by a blasted yew upstay'd; . . .
—And sure there is a secret Power that reigns
Here, where no trace of man the spot profanes, . . .
How still! No irreligious sound or sight
Rouses the soul from her severe delight.

It is highly instructive to compare this passage with a later poem *The Simplon Pass* (1799, afterwards incorporated in *The Prelude*) on the same subject. The youth had been solemnly and religiously impressed by the magnificent view of the Simplon Pass. In *Descriptive Sketches* he did his best to interpret the scene. He was only partially successful, though he did convey something of its awfulness. It lingered in his mind and its majesty grew upon him. At last he was able to express his whole mind in one of the most magnificent religious passages in modern poetry. Here he exemplified the elements of great poetry—grace, vividness, harmony, concentration, the grand style, high seriousness, sublimity! Here the specific and the abstract, the sensuous and the spiritual, are fused together and held in perfect balance in a moving panorama. The poem was obviously the result of long meditation, inspired by the religious motive, basic in the poet's life and purposes. How far his art had advanced from 1793 to 1799!—

—Brook and road
Where fellow-travellers in this gloomy. Pass,
And with them did we journey several hours
At a slow step. The immeasurable height
Of woods decaying, never to be decayed,
The stationary blasts of waterfalls,
And in the narrow rent, at every turn,

Winds thwarting winds bewildered and forlorn,
The torrents shooting from the clear blue sky,
The rocks that muttered close upon our ears,
Black, drizzling crags that spake by the wayside
As if a voice were in them, the sick sight
And giddy prospect of the raving stream,
The unfettered clouds and region of the heavens,
Tumult and peace, the darkness and the light—
Were all like workings of one mind, the features
Of the same face, blossoms upon one tree,
Characters of the great Apocalypse,
The types and symbols of Eternity,
Of first, and last, and midst, and without end.

In *Descriptive Sketches* the poet also reveals his social and political enthusiasms, his recently awakened interest in Man. He describes sympathetically the Alpine shepherd who

Holds with God himself communion high
When the dread peal of swelling torrents fills
The sky-roof'd temple of the eternal hills.

He dilates on the spirit of Freedom that animates the Swiss people, recalling their heroic conflicts with their ancient enemies. He is stirred to a high pitch of enthusiasm by seeing in France Liberty actually in the making. He declares that in a country ruled despotically domestic joys everywhere tend to decay, while in a land of Freedom a new spirit of life spreads beyond the cottage hearth, making the air seem purer, skies brighter, fields richer. As the inhabitants of the Alps are a living illustration of the Rousseauistic Revolutionary creed, so the inhabitants of France, and perchance of all the world, are to achieve a similar freedom. He concludes his song with an appeal to the Almighty to give victory to the Revolutionary cause and with a sweeping denunciation of tyrant kings:

Oh give, great God, to Freedom's waves to ride
Sublime o'er Conquest, Avarice, and Pride,
To break, the vales where Death with Famine Scow'rs,
And dark Oppression builds her thick-ribb'd tow'rs:
And grant that every sceptred child of clay,
Who cries, presumptuous, "here their tides shall stay",
Swept in their anger from the affrighted shore,
With all his creatures sink—to rise no more.

In spite of the fact that *Descriptive Sketches* is a vigorous poem on Nature and radical revolutionary principles it clearly reveals the immaturity of the author. Its formal use of the heroic couplet with many cumbersome abstractions personified (as in last quoted passage), its adopting the current popular social views of liberty without giving them an individualistic character, are sufficient to prove the poem a promise rather than an achievement. The young author's attitude of devoutness toward Nature, Man, and God, is a hint of his future self, but his ideas here are of so general a character that we cannot say that the author has arrived at any distinct philosophy of life.

This lack of distinctness and the lack of a settled conviction followed the poet a good many years. Aside from his strongly naturalistic bent it is in general extremely difficult to determine by what central light Wordsworth's life was guided for half a decade after 1793. This is due partly to the fact that the period was a season of moral conflict within him, and of a political crisis, as well as a time of change and growth and of finding himself, and also to the fact of his extraordinary reticence, both in his letters and his poems, concerning the books he read, concerning certain phases of his personal experiences, and especially concerning his attitude toward Christianity.

When Wordsworth was sent to college under the guardianship of his uncles it was hoped by his relatives he would take orders in the church. He had been brought up as a member of the Anglican church, and his family was closely identified with the clergy; an uncle was a clergyman and his younger brother was preparing to be one. But as time passed he became less and less inclined to this profession. No doubt the distant example of Milton, who had been at Cambridge before him, with whose spirit he felt a conscious affinity in his second year at college, and who, as Wordsworth sings in *The Pre-lude* (Book III, lines 283-7),

> In his later day,
> Stood almost single; uttering odious truth—
> Darkness before, and danger's voice behind,
> Soul awful—if the earth has ever lodged
> An awful soul,

had its influence. Also Wordsworth's self-made religion of Nature and man from his youth unquestionably forced him to perceive the superficialities and absurdities that appeared in his day in the name of Christianity. Besides, he had felt that the mighty inspirations of a poet were already his, and had dedicated himself to them. Then in the year 1792 he was drawn powerfully into active sympathy with Revolutionary France, after which it was unlikely, if not impossible, that he should become a member of the English clergy.

Moreover, two radical teachers, Rousseau and Godwin, were influential in shaping Wordsworth's youthful mind. Rousseau's influence was more permanent than Godwin's; the poet experienced more quickly a sharp reaction against the teachings of the latter than he did against that of the former. The philosophies of Rousseau and Godwin are in no wise to be harmonized, but they are alike in their radical revolutionary tendencies and in their utterly ignoring the sense of historical continuity in human progress.

Rousseau emphasized the natural gifts of man, instinct, intuition, insight, with special stress on the inherent goodness of children. The Calvinistic and Puritan doctrine that a child is totally depraved by nature, purely of evil until some work of grace be wrought upon him, had very wide acceptance in the eighteenth century. Rousseau went completely to the other extreme by glorifying instincts as natively good in the child. This natural goodness, when developed according to the simple principles of primitive nature, makes the perfect man—the man of reason, naturalness, and individuality. Let it be universal that each individual, however humble, go back to primitive nature, follow her simple laws and his own instinct and reason, and develop a perfect individuality; then each one will be fitted to add his share to building up a perfect society—so runs the creed of Rousseau.

Godwin approached human perfectibility from an almost exactly opposite point of view. He indeed, like Rousseau, exalted human reason, but he attached a totally different meaning to the word. Rousseau identifies reason with a kind of insight; in Godwin reason is a purely intellectual and logical faculty and is governed solely by the abstract law of Necessity. Reason rigidly excludes instinct, insight, and sentiment, and Necessity excludes Free-will, from the world of human affairs. All knowledge, according to Godwin, is derived from sense experiences and there is nothing in morality or religion that reason cannot master. Since there is no freedom of the will or of choice there is no room in this system for the ideas of merits and demerits, guilt and accountability.

A man cannot be bound by promises and has no prefer-
ences or rights, but only duties. The exercise of reason
toward ascertaining and doing one's duty is the whole
purpose of life.

If Rousseau was an extreme Romanticist Godwin was
an extreme Rationalist; and as Rousseau's system tended
toward pure individualism so Godwin's tended toward
pure anarchy. The influence of Rousseau is noticeable in
Descriptive Sketches, the following passages, for instance, simply being Rousseau in meter:

> Once Man entirely free, alone and wild,
> Was bless'd as free—for he was Nature's child.
> He, all superiour but his God disdain'd,
> Walk'd none restraining, and by none restrain'd,
> Confess'd no law, but what his reason taught,
> Did all he wish'd, and wish'd but what he ought.

Godwin's influence is noticeable in *Guilt and Sorrow,*
completed in 1794, and both his influence and the poet's
reaction against it are obvious in *The Borderers* of 1795.
One teaching with the spirit of an evangelist and the
other with dogmatic authority, neither caring for the past
and each having his eyes wholly on the future, these masters led Wordsworth farther away from any distinct
Christian teachings that he may have cherished in his
affections, and tended to confirm him in his own peculiar
naturalistic religious experiences.

The strength of this native born devotion, this

> Subservience from the first
> To presences of God's mysterious power
> Made manifest in Nature's sovereignty,
> *(The Prelude,* Book IX., lines 233-5)

is eloquently attested by the manner in which he met the
greatest moral shock, on his own word, he had experienced throughout the first thirty years of his life—the

shock when in 1793 England declared war on the French Republic. Though his soul was "tossed about in whirl-wind," he did not resort for relief to distinct Christian love or mercy, but only fortified himself in his former revolutionary opinions, which clung to his mind "as if they were its life, nay more, the very being of the immortal soul." And when the worst came—France herself turning traitor to the cause of freedom—and he was "endlessly perplexed" to the point of despair, he sought consolation, not in the graces of Christian fortitude, but in speculative thought, and in the study of abstract science, without, however, any appreciable success. At last from this state of depression he was fortunately, the poet says providentially, rescued by the devotion of his sister, who maintained for him a saving intercourse with his true self; and by the ministry of Nature, whose powers gradually led him back through opening day "to those sweet counsels between head and heart," which are the cynosure of wisdom. Thus the grace of human love and the powers of Nature took on a deeper meaning than ever before. Both influences directed the whole power of his mind toward those early childhood experiences of life and Nature, the very root and foundation of his spiritual devotion, setting them apart doubly hallowed ever afterwards in his memory. No wonder that, with his new found joy which amounted to religious inspiration, he should rapidly grow into that maturity of power which we associate with the great Wordsworth of the *Lyrical Ballads*.

But in his farthest deviation from orthodoxy he cannot be said to have at any time been atheistical in his bent. "I did not walk with scoffers," he averred. In the midst of the Reign of Terror in France he even felt

possessed of something of the spirit of the ancient
Hebrew Prophet:

> So, with devout humility be it said,
> So, did a portion of that spirit fall
> On me uplifted from the vantage-ground
> Of pity and sorrow to a state of being
> That through the time's exceeding fierceness saw
> Glimpses of retribution, terrible,
> And in the order of sublime behests.
>
> (*The Prelude,* Book X, lines 447-453.)

The truth was then also received into his heart that if our
afflictions do not help us to grow into a higher faith and
sanctity the blame is ours, and that it was not the teaching
of this or that philosophy that caused the woe of France.

> But a terrific reservoir of guilt
> And ignorance filled up from age to age,
> That could no longer hold its loathsome charge,
> But burst and spread in deluge through the land:—
>
> (*The Prelude,* Book X, lines 477-480.)

which passage clearly indicates that even when he was
twenty-three he was no blind devotee of either Rousseau
or Godwin, because he saw the events of the Revolution,
as neither Rousseau nor Godwin could have seen them, in
their proper historical continuity with the past. And
when the report reached him that Robespierre, who
"wielded the sceptre of the Atheist crew", was dead, he
experienced a transport of religious ecstacy:

> Great was my transport, deep my gratitude
> To everlasting Justice, by this fiat
> Made manifest.
>
> (*The Prelude,* Book X, lines 576-8.)

On the other hand, there is the testimony of Coleridge,
in a letter to John Thelwall, dated May 13, 1796, in
which he speaks of "a very dear friend of mine, who is,
in my opinion, the best poet of the age," etc. . . . "And

this man is a republican, and, at least, a *semi*-atheist."
Since he does not mention Wordsworth's name Coleridge's editors have had difficulty in reconciling the statement with the fact that the two poets could hardly have been more than acquaintances at this date. However, Coleridge's soul had made its election, and the very fact that he does not name Wordsworth shows a delicate hesitancy to admit a third party to so new an acquisition; the person is unmistakably Wordsworth. Since Coleridge's description of him as a semi-atheist has been widely used by critics it seems strange that practically all should have ignored a far less dubious and a much weightier testimony by Coleridge after more than a year of most intimate companionship with him. In a letter of J. F. Estlin, written in May, 1798, Coleridge says of Wordsworth:

"I have now known him a year and six months, and my admiration, I might say my awe, of his intellectual powers has increased even to this hour, and (what is of more importance) he is a tried good man. On one subject we are habitually silent; we found our data dissimilar, and never renewed the subject. It is his practice and almost his nature to convey all the truth he knows without any attack on what he supposes falsehood, if that falsehood be interwoven with virtue and happiness. He loves and venerates Christ and Christianity. I wish he did more, but it were wrong indeed if an incoincidence in one of our wishes altered our respect and affection to a man whom we are, as it were, instructed by one great Master to say that not being against us he is for us."

Since on the testimony of his most intimate friend Wordsworth at this period included Christ and Christianity in his love and veneration, it is not only idle but false to speak of him as a semi-atheist, even though he was obviously (and this was perhaps the chief difference between them) not as ardent a propagandist of Christianity as Coleridge. How clearly Coleridge characterized his friend—his native reticence on complicated or deep subjects, his unwillingness to engage in destructive criticism, his dominant qualities of loving and venerating!

Had Wordsworth been a smaller man he would have connected atheism with his intense republicanism, as did John Thelwall and many another republican of that time. The extreme conservatives in England in the days of the French Revolution were exceedingly anxious to bring obloquy upon republican sympathizers; the easiest way to do it was to proffer the charge of 'infidel' or 'atheist' against them:

> "Whether ye make the Rights of Man your theme,
> Your country libel and your God blaspheme,"

says *The Anti-Jacobin,* a conservative journal, under the date of July 9, 1798. Some were infidels, but others named themselves such who in calmer times would not have been drawn so far from their natural orbit. Wordsworth remained silent, and nothing shows the largeness of his nature better than that while living under the opprobious name of republican he could not only refrain from partisan strife but could draw nurture from the fountain head of love, faith, and sanctity. It often happens that a sanely radical, a fearlessly progressive man of religion, in time of great public agitation, reaches the roots of Christian principle more nearly than either the conservative or the wildly radical. Though Wordsworth had met the greatest moral crisis of his early life with his own unaided strength of soul, yet the ministry of human love and of Nature which restored him to his normal habits of mind, was followed by a rapid development in him of a far wider range of sympathy and devotion than anything he had previously known, including reverence for Christianity itself. Though silent concerning the tenets of Christianity, Wordsworth, in those great years between 1797 and 1802, interpreted the life of lowly and humble people in such love and reverence that the world he created is extraordinarily similar to the world of original Christianity!

During the years of Coleridge's and Wordsworth's most intimate companionship (1797-99) Coleridge was an active advocate of Hartley and the associational school of philosophy from John Locke to William Godwin. Though we have but small evidence, it seems certain that Wordsworth learned a little directly, and much indirectly through Coleridge, of the principles of associationism—a philosophy perhaps most elaborately developed by David Hartley. Associationism asserts that all mental states are derived from sensations, that, to quote Hartley, "the ideas of sensation are the elements of which all the rest are compounded." It holds that through the power of association the internal feelings that arise from direct contact with the world around us are transmuted into thought, at first simple and then more complex, until we reach the most complicated thought possible to man; association furnishes a relationship, a 'next' to 'next,' of all the various ideas and faculties of the mind, and implies a unity of consciousness; association, in short, is the law of the mind as gravitation is the law of the physical world, and, it may be added, acts just as inflexibly and mechanically as that law. It thus claims to be wholly Necessitarian in its implications and philosophic outlook. It is a rather simple philosophy because it does not allow its adherents to go back of sensations and ask what causes them: it must take them for granted as the sole basis of all real knowledge. Nor does it do much more than give a descriptive word as to what takes place in the mind—the word association is all sufficient. It never asks as to how it is that the mind can 'associate' at all; or if it does, it answers, as Hartley answers, that association is caused by vibrations of ether which fill the universe and from whence comes the activity of the mind—a still more purely mechanical explanation. In fact, associationism is a psychology rather than a philosophy—a method of describing sensations and thought rather than an account of the ultimate constituent energies of the mind and the world. Fortunately one may accept its empyrical method, its psychology, without accepting its abstract metaphysical conclusions. As a psychology it had an important influence on Wordsworth. It aided him in classifying the emotions and gave him an increased range and variety in handling them; it confirmed his belief in the idea of growth, accentuating its importance; above all, it suggested to him "the manner in which we associate ideas in a state of excitement."

But Wordsworth's susceptibilities after all were greatest as poet, and his widest culture came from the study of poetry—which some critics seem to forget. He had studied his Chaucer, Spenser, Shakespeare, and Milton thoroughly, and hoped, not unreasonably, to create an ample but distinctive world not unworthy to be compared with theirs. He was well acquainted with Dryden and Pope, but felt they had narrowed the scope and spirit of English poetry. He was on very familiar

terms with the poetry of Thomson, Gray, Crabbe, Burns,
etc. It was Burns who showed his youth, he himself
says, for instance, how to build verse on humble truth.
Well grounded in his country's literary history and traditions, he in no wise attempted to controvert or destroy
its spirit, but aimed to widen its current, to add to "the
multiplicity and qualities of its moral relations," and
especially to bring back to it the breadth and amplitude
that characterized it before Dryden.

Thus far, then it has been noted that in his childhood
and youth Wordsworth had an experience of Nature,
his own soul, the soul of man, and God (it must always
be remembered that this to Wordsworth was an experience, not merely an opinion or an idea, remaining the
heart of him through life); that he passed through a
moral and political crisis in his later youth; that he
searched widely in abstract science, in speculative thought,
in the writings of Rousseau, of Godwin, of the Associationists, assimilating something from each to his own
central experience, but pursuing his own way to the truth
of things; that he became deeply versed in the poetry
of his own country, and aimed also to add something
unique to its glory; that through the companionship of
his sister and the ministry of his first love—Nature—he
grew rapidly into a wide-ranging experience of life, prepared to create a poetry of deep reality, inspired by love
and truth, in a kind "perfectly unborrowed and his own."

II

The first-fruits of this new psychological and spiritual
attitude toward life are the poems Wordsworth contributed to the *Lyrical Ballads* (published conjointly with
Coleridge, 1798), poems of naturalness and of a new

kind of inward reality, original and unique in every way. Though the advertisement prefacing this volume asserted that the poems were to be considered experiments as regards the use of conversational language, the poems contributed by Wordsworth were really more radical as experiments in the types of characters he chose to represent sympathetically and in the presentation of "natural piety."

There are five remarkable Nature poems by Words· worth in this volume—*Lines Written at a Small Distance from My House, Lines Written in Early Spring, Expostulation and Reply, the Tables Turned,* and *Lines Written a Few Miles Above Tintern Abbey.* The first four poems, which are brief, furnish a stepping stone to the last one, a longer production, which stands at the close of the volume and represents the high water mark of Wordsworth's Nature poetry. Not only that, but the five poems taken together, though they appear fairly early in Wordsworth's literary career, attain to so complete a mastery of both subject matter and style, that Wordsworth himself, in the realm of pure Nature poetry, never afterwards could surpass them. The explanation of this seems to be that all that he had felt in his childhood and all that he had most intimately experienced in his later communings with Nature seemed now to crystallize fully in his mind and become ripe for perfect expression. This was the golden period of his pure Nature poetry.

Wordsworth had an extraordinary memory for the experiences of his own past, particularly of his early childhood. He was far more deeply aware than most how much of the stock of knowledge we possess is due to the native activity of our senses from infancy onward.

Not only does Nature enkindle the senses to activity but she also restrains them from activity in dangerous directions: a child learns that fire burns and avoids it. Nature thus offers impulse that enkindles and law that restrains: and long before the individual receives moral precepts from sages Nature has furnished him with the solid foundation upon which his moral being may be reared. Therefore to be remanded to Nature for the method of growth is not a matter of a holiday mood merely, as some recent critics have insisted, but furnishes in all seriousness the solidest basis for real progress. The store of sense impressions which, with "aching joys" and "dizzy raptures," the poet had gathered in his childhood and youth, was but the foundation and beginning of the vaster stores that were now his. Yet sense impressions are but the raw material of experience. Here the poet was aided by the psychology of the associationists, who taught him that by the law of association "the primary sensations are transmuted, by a sort of chemical process into the 'purer' forms of thought, first into ideas of a simple sort, and then into more complex ones." There is, however, an element in Wordsworth's experience not represented in the "chemical process" theory of the associationists. In a famous passage in *Lines Above Tintern Abbey* Wordsworth speaks of

> All the mighty world
> Of eye, and ear,—both what they half create
> And what perceive;—

wherein he ascribes a creative act to the mind itself, which is a succinct statement of the modern psychological law of apperception. An artist and a lumberman look at the same tree from which they receive the same sense impressions, but with what different mental or spiritual results! The creative act of the mind and its previous experiences account for the difference. Moreover, there is still a further reach in Wordsworth's treatment of sense material. The creative mind uses the sense, sensation, and the language of the sense as portals of entrance into a world of spiritual reality. At the center of this world abide power, energy, joy, love, wisdom, to bless man, if he chooses to be blessed. This is the unique and original contribution of Wordsworth to the interpretation of Nature.

So in *Lines Written at a Small Distance From My House,* later named *To My Sister,* the poet's heart lies open to the temper of the day. Nature is pregnant with energies, stirring in the grass and mountains, and justifies her claim of being divine by disclosing "silent laws" for the heart's acceptance, and attuning man to the highest law of morals—the law of love. *Lines Written in Early Spring* chides the inhumanity of man and upholds the benignity of Nature, not in the strident voice of *Descriptive Sketches,* but with the persuasive wisdom of a seer. Nature offers to man joy and pain, with an over-balance of joy. Pleasure ranges from the smallest objects— twigs, flowers, birds,—to the widest spaces of Nature. Man is inseparably bound up with Nature's scheme of happiness and should be the highest expression of it. In *Expostulation and Reply* power comes to man from all the mighty sum of things forever speaking, while in *The Tables Turned,* a companion piece, Nature, blessing us with spontaneous truth, is the wisest teacher of mankind:

> One impulse from a vernal wood
> May teach you more of man;
> Of moral evil and of good,
> Than all the sages can.

Considerable ink has been spilled as to whether this passage is merely "a half-playful sally for the benefit of some too bookish friend," as Morley thinks, or whether "what Wordsworth here calls his faith is the corner-stone of his poetry, and no less," as Raleigh holds. Allowing for poetic license in the first line and making it read "impulses from Nature" we can be reasonably sure that catching in its own current the drift of the four poems, with their emphasis on love, pleasure, power, wisdom, this passage expressed a profound conviction of Wordsworth in the year 1798.

Should any doubt remain as to Wordsworth's serious intent one should read *Lines Above Tintern Abbey,* which, written about the same time, makes a more comprehensive claim for Nature, including the claim of the preceding passage. This poem is the most sublime expression of the general thought of the preceding four poems transformed into a larger and a more articulate religious conception. The doctrine of a "return to Nature," emphasized by Rousseau, was carried by the original and creative mind of Wordsworth into the realm of the religious. "To compare," says Myers, "small things with great—or rather, to compare great things with things vastly greater—the essential spirit of the *Lines Near Tintern Abbey* was for practical purposes as new to mankind as the essential spirit of the *Sermon on the Mount.*"

Yet the farthest deviation anywhere in Wordsworth from what is generally held to be orthodoxy is this poem, wherein he asserts that the nurture of his moral being is derived from the mystic influences of Nature, and wherein he conceives Deity, not as a personal entity, but as an impersonal Presence. This is Naturalism, and, when

pushed to extremes, Pantheism, though here, as everywhere in Wordsworth, it is relieved by a high mystic
spirituality.   The poem asserts that there is essential
unity in all existence, and that Nature and the mind of
man are but different emanations of one universal, impersonal Power.

But what made the spirit of this poem new and radical
in its day was not so much its abstract conceptions, which
were also commonly held by the Deists, but rather that
it rendered in terms of feeling and volition the mystical
union of man with the spiritual powers of Nature.
As a child Wordsworth had felt that there were in
Nature and distinctly outside himself powers that
impressed his mind.   Though his own being was an
entity separate from these powers, he felt a sense of
union with them, and through them a sense of union with
a spiritual Presence.   By means of a tenacious memory
and a voluntaristic power of soul he conserved and carried forward this experience into manhood.   As in his
youth he felt with bliss ineffable the "sentiment of Being
spread o'er all that moves," etc., so now he felt himself
one with a dynamic, energizing Power

> Whose dwelling is the light of setting suns,
> And the round ocean and the living air,
> And the blue sky, and in the mind of man;
> A motion and a spirit, that impels
> All thinking things, all objects of all thought,
> And rolls through all things.

"Perhaps the doctrine," says Hazlitt, "of what has
been called philosophic necessity was never more finely
expressed than in these lines."   Hazlitt also quotes
Wordsworth as saying to a young student of the Temple:
"Throw away your books of chemistry and read Godwin
on Necessity," and Coleridge declared in 1804 that

Wordsworth earlier had been a Necessitarian. It is almost too obvious for remark that in the universe there are forces and necessities over which man's mind has no real control—the elemental needs of our natures as food and light and air, the onward sweep of time, the "goings-on" of the universe, etc. To the Power that keeps the stars in their course Wordsworth paid his tribute later in the *Ode to Duty,* and by deliberate choice of his own will he surrendered himself to the will of the "Stern Lawgiver." But here the Power—an impersonal force—*impels* the thinking mind and all objects of all thought. Yet Wordsworth was not an extreme Necessitarian, for strict Necessity robs the mind of all choice and makes it an automaton. As if to qualify the assertion he speaks in the same passage—a few lines farther on—of the eye and the ear, instruments of the mind, as half-creating what they perceive—which, as has been said, implies a creative power in the mind itself. Besides, Wordsworth had such a naturally deep sense of personal identity and such energy of will that his Necessitarian theory, held for a short time, has but little more than a speculative interest in his works.

For the same reason that he was not a radical Necessitarian Wordsworth was not a mystic of the extreme type. The pure mystic feels his own being absorbed and lost in the eternal One. Nevertheless, the mystic truth of man's communing with the Divine through Nature, which may come to the pure in heart without the aid of "toiling reason," Wordsworth prizes most highly. He held that Nature has the power to build up our moral being, that her impulses have no slight or trivial influence in shaping the acts of men. Yet she bestows upon man a greater gift than this and of a more sublime aspect. From a divine source she illuminates the whole moral world of man with a spiritual light and lifts him, at intervals at least, to where he can "see into the life of things," where he feels a mighty "presence that disturbs him with the joy of elevated thoughts," where he obtains the beatific vision, which, once had, if only for an interval, is thenceforth recognized as a "great good" of the soul.

It is obvious that in this poem Wordsworth makes the highest demands of Nature that can ever be made of her and that he is convinced he obtains what he demands, even though his claims seem extravagant to other men. This does not mean that every one can have for the asking a supreme intuition of Nature, for it takes strength to be a seer. The ideal of an intimate communion with Nature that is to give spiritual illumination comes only as a rare experience and as the result of long training. The individual must meet Nature half way, and even more than half way. In single-hearted devotion to Nature, with power of penetration and depth of feeling, Wordsworth achieved the distinction of attaining to an experience in which Nature poured her riches into his "shut house of life."

There is an element of permanence in this attitude toward nature. For, whenever the outer world is perceived intensely and with feeling we are made aware that the physical order itself is illusive and is a reflection of a spiritual, that is, a mystical order, and that the common sense, that is, the natural science, aspect of truth is but one aspect of it. Since feeling and intensity of perception are permanent and universal powers of the mind it follows that the mystical experience is not a thing of time and place but belongs to all ages and races. To the primitive Indian, for example, as well as to the conscious philosopher the Great Spirit may be a Presence "Whose dwelling is the light of setting suns," etc.

But *Lines Above Tintern Abbey* does not lose itself in the clouds or run into what is popularly called the "vagaries of mysticism." A sensuous or naturalistic strain balances the mystical and keeps the poem close to earth. The many nature images, rendered with great clearness, make a continuous fabric of tactual objects for the eye and mind to rest upon, and indicate the wealth of physical sensations the poet could draw on at will. His Nature poetry will ever be "fresh with points of morning dew" because he rendered into it something of the primal impulses of Nature herself. We cannot out-grow it. For, however far we may advance in knowledge and experience we must still have to do with elemental forces, must still recline on Earth's bosom and be wrapped round by the visible creation of earth, air, sky and stars. The Nature forces in Wordsworth's poetry are thus of great and lasting artistic worth.

Yet this naturalistic strain does not make the poem less spiritual. It only serves to keep the mystical within proper bounds and give it articulation. The two strains are drawn into the closest affinity possible, counter-balancing each other perfectly. The use of the one aids the poet in giving expression to the other. Wordsworth dared to be so naturalistic because he was so great a mystic: he dared to travel so far into the region of the mystical because he held so firmly to sensuous elements. The one strain saves his poetry from vagueness: the other from earthiness; drawn together they furnish the basis of a unique creation—solid and beautiful, individual and whole. The strength of Wordsworth's genius is the strength by which he has created a world of his own out of the diverse elements of the mystical and the natural-istic—the dynamic of a new spiritual force.

Beautifully intertwined in the whole of this creation are also the human qualities of memory and of hope. The poem begins with a memory of an experience now five years old—a former visit to the Wye. With great subtilty the poet shows how the beauteous forms of the Wye valley had during his absence wrought consciously and unconsciously on his spiritual nature—a perfect example of "emotion recollected in tranquillity." Then he becomes reminiscent of the days of his boyhood when the sounding cataract haunted him like a passion. Here he sketches the different stages he has gone through in his experience with Nature—that of the coarser pleasures of his boyhood days and their glad animal movements, that of passionate enjoyment of the sensuous beauty of Nature as it appealed to his eye and ear, that of the rapt and solemn elevation of spirit as produced by the humanizing and chastening power of Nature, and that of his soul's mystic communion with the spiritual and volitional forces of Nature which enlarged his personality by bringing it in touch with the Divine. Again, he is looking backward when he reads his former pleasures in the voice and eyes of his sister.

But all memories—from childhood upward—are prized only as in the service of hope. The best of our past and our present is to be conserved and carried forward into the future. This is a sound psychology and a sound philosophy of life:

> While here I stand, not only with the sense
> Of present pleasure, but with pleasing thoughts
> That in this moment there is life and food
> For future years.

The thought of these lines is similar to the following from *To My Sister:*

> Some silent laws our hearts will make,
> Which they shall long obey;—

indicating again how closely this group of poems is related in spirit and purpose. And thus through the twin-born faculties of memory and hope the mind runs backward and forward, opening up vistas that look toward the 'Uncreated'—

> The blessed power that rolls
> About, below, above.

Underlying the whole of *Lines Above Tintern Abbey* is a profound spiritual joy, which has its springs deep in the poet's nature. There are the joys of his happy childhood memories, of a sacred and intimate companionship with his sister, of being a genuine lover of Nature who adheres tenaciously to the faith that all that we behold is full of blessings, of possessing both a perceiving and a creating mind, and the deep power of joy in being in harmony with the mighty and volitional energy of that Presence that forever works through Nature and forever sustains human life.

But natural piety concerns itself even more about Man than about Nature, for it is in the heart of man that Deity is most immanent. Of the nineteen poems Wordsworth contributed to the *Lyrical Ballads* thirteen (the proportion is significant) deal with human characters, and indicate the poet's spiritual attitude toward humanity. They are not as uniformly excellent in execution as the Nature poems. Though some are satisfactory in their kind, Wordsworth had not yet attained that sure touch in depicting character and that power of interpreting by

simple outward incident the deep things of the mind
which he was presently to achieve.   The poems present
a most remarkable list of personages—a neglected young
man of genius, a female vagrant, a poverty-stricken old
woman who gathered sticks from her neighbor's hedge,
an old huntsman, a boy who resorted to lying when too
closely questioned, a little girl who insisted her dead
brother and sister were as though alive, an outcast
woman suspected of child murder, a poor shepherd who
had lost all his flock, a mad mother, an idiot boy, a very
old man, a forsaken Indian woman, and a convict.

No one can doubt the sincerity and the courage of
Wordsworth in selecting such a group of characters. The
account of how he came to make so remarkable a selec-
tion is not fully given either in the advertisement to the
first *Lyrical Ballads* or in the prefaces to later editions,
but in Book Thirteen of *The Prelude,* which was written
only six years after the first publication of the poems,
and which should always be read with the prefaces:

> Long time in search of knowledge did I range
> The field of human life, in heart and mind
> Benighted; but, the dawn beginning now
> To re-appear, 'twas proved that not in vain
> I had been taught to reverence a Power
> That is the visible quality and shape
> And image of right reason.   (lines 16-22)

For this Power taught him

> To look with feelings of fraternal love
> Upon the unassuming things that hold
> A silent station in this beautous world.   (lines 45-47)

Thus he found in humble man "an object of delight, of
pure imagination, and of love." Then he began to inspect
the social structure of society to determine, if possible,

how much virtue and happiness those possess who labor by bodily toil, carrying on his observations

> Among the natural abodes of men,
> Fields with their rural works.   (lines 102-3)

Great happiness attended his search as he wandered on from day to day, where, he says,

> I could meditate in peace, and cull
> Knowledge that step by step might lead me on
> To wisdom. (lines 131-3)
>   . . . When I began to enquire,
> To watch and question those I met, and speak
> Without reserve to them, the lonely roads
> Were open schools in which I daily read
> With most delight the passions of mankind,
> Whether by words, looks, sighs, or tears, revealed;
> There saw into the depth of human souls,
> Souls that appear to have no depth at all
> To careless eyes. (lines 160-8)

He became convinced that the formalities which go under the name of Education have little to do with real feeling and just sense, and that such books as seek "their reward from judgments of the wealthy few" are misleading and debasing. This conviction was confirmed by the fact that he himself had heard

> From mouths of men obscure and lowly, truths
> Replete with honour; sounds in unison
> With loftiest promises of good and fair. (lines 183-5)

He perceived, however, that "where grace and culture hath been utterly unknown," where oppression, poverty and labor are daily in excess, love and truth cannot thrive. But if the humble, such as he had known in his youth in the familiar circuit of his home, have reasonable comforts and leisure they so reveal the inborn greatness of our human nature that the poet is constrained to bend in reverence to "the power of human minds, to men as they are men within themselves":

> How oft high services is performed within,
> When all the external man is rude in show . . .
> Of these, said I, shall be my song; of these,
> If future years mature me for the task,
> Will I record the praises, making verse
> Deal boldly with substantial things: in truth
> And sanctity of passion, speak of these,
> That justice may be done, obesiance paid
> Where it is due; thus haply shall I teach,
> Inspire; through unadulterated ears
> Pour rapture, tenderness, and hope,—my theme
> No other than the very heart of man,
> As found among the best of those who live—
> Not unexalted by religious faith,
> Nor uninformed by books, good books, though few—
> In Nature's presence: thence may I select
> Sorrow, that is not sorrow, but delight;
> And miserable love, that is not pain
> To hear of, for the glory that redounds
> Therefrom to human kind, and what we are,
> Be mine to follow with no timid step
> Where knowledge leads me: it shall be my pride
> That I have dared to tread this holy ground,
> Speaking no dream, but things oracular. (lines 227-8. 232-253)

This sublime and essentially spiritual purpose is the explanation of his choosing that remarkable group of characters in the *Lyrical Ballads*. In the simplest language and in a realistic manner he sympathetically portrays each character and asks our affection for each. It is not that we are to assent to an abstract principle of liberty and equality, which were easy enough, but are invited into the closest spiritual fellowship with the lowliest and most forsaken of the earth. In extreme cases, as in *Goody Blake and Harry Gill*, where the heroine might be subject to legal restrictions, or in *The Convict*, where the character is an outcast of society, the poet is wholly on the side of the offenders. A far-reaching charity, neither sentimental nor condescending, embraces them all.

In another extreme case—*The Idiot Boy*—Wordsworth showed the courage of his convictions, supported by prose comments which reveal the ultimate, or spiritual, foundation of his purpose. In a letter to John Wilson only four years after the poem was published the poet said:

"I have often applied to idiots, in my own mind, that sublime expression of scripture, that their 'life is hidden with God.' . . . I have, indeed, often looked upon the conduct of fathers and mothers of the lower classes of society towards idiots as the great triumph of the human heart. It is there that we see the strength, disinterestedness, and grandeur of love."

As Wordsworth had penetrated through the show of outward things to the primal impulses of Nature, so he cleaved through the accidental and secondary elements in man to those primary qualities essential and common to all human beings. The grand elemental principle of love works deeply in the heart of the mother and completely envelops, in self-abnegations, the poor idiot boy. So in *The Mad Mother* the betrayed woman in alternate moments of startling sanity and wanderings of the mind enfolds her child in a love of infinite amplitude. In *The Thorn,* Martha's wailings are like the ancient Rachel's weeping for her children and refusing to be comforted. Night by night her cries of misery for her dead child and her lost love ring through the tempest-swept hills and her vigils are known to every star and to every wind that blows. *The Complaint of the Forsaken Indian Woman* again illustrates the power of maternal "love and longings infinite." The heroine, left in sickness by her tribe in a solitary place to die, consoles herself with the grand spectacle of the heavens and fortifies her soul with the reflection that if she were to be reunited with her child she could die utterly happy. *Simon Lee* indicates dramatically and poignantly the extraordinary rarity of real kindness. In *Anecdote for Fathers* the poet bends his spirit in reverence to catch wisdom from the unsophisticated mind of a child. He does not merely wonder at the reply of the child when forced to answer a question on which it has no conviction, nor merely at the suggestion of the subtle origins of evil, but rather he seems to have gotten a glimpse of a deeper nature within the child, a hidden self-preservative spiritual instinct, which keeps its personality immune from possible vicious influences of environment. *We Are Seven* shows that it is natural for a child to believe in life as the real thing in existence and death as the exceptional—which unswerving intuition may prove to be the true light to life. *Anecdote for Fathers* and *We Are Seven* are important as the first of many poems that deal with child intuitions, that imply from the first an inviolable inner nature in man which gives him moral dignity and makes him a spiritual being.

The Old Cumberland Beggar belongs to the time of the *Lyrical Ballads* and is important as illustrating Wordsworth's broad humanitarianism. As the members of a family are benefitted by acts of love toward their own aged or helpless, so the members of the larger family —the community—are by acts of personal charity insensibly drawn "to virtue and true goodness." The aged mendicant is a benediction as he goes his rounds among the farms and thinly-scattered villages; the toll-gatherer generously lifts the latch to let him pass; the housewife,

pressed by her own wants, gives him of her store of meal
and "builds her hope in heaven." Bearing "the good
which the benignant law of Heaven has hung around
him" he is far from useless:

> 'Tis Nature's law
> That none, the meanest of created things,
> Of forms created the most vile and brute,
> The dullest or most noxious, should exist
> Divorced from good—a spirit and pulse of good,
> A life and soul, to every mode of being
> Inseparably linked.

It is a universal principle that 'man is dear to man,' that
even 'the poorest poor' longs for some moment in a
weary life to know and feel that he has been kind to such

> As needed kindness, for this single cause
> That we have all of us one human heart.

This is the deeper strain in Wordsworth, and it is
seldom that he deals with fierce, cruel, or vicious characters. One exception is the character in *Peter Bell,* a
poem also written in 1798 and intended as a rival to
Coleridge's *Ancient Mariner.* Its significance lies not
only in the fact that it deals with a religious conversion
but that it shows Wordsworth's belief that the soul of
the most hardened sinner has such susceptibilities to good
that it may be profoundly wrought upon by a series of
real and human incidents.

The poem was not published until 1819 and after it
had undergone various revisions. It is unfortunate that
we do not have it in its original form; yet in essentials it
is undoubtedly as it was written in 1798. In the second
edition of the *Lyrical Ballads* (1800) Wordsworth, in a
note to Coleridge's poem, pointed out as two cardinal
faults that the principle person has no distinctive profes-

sional or supernatural character, and that he does not act but is continually acted upon. Accordingly Wordsworth chose for his hero a distinctive character, active, rugged, and aggressive, but low-minded and full of evil deeds. He was a potter and a mighty rover, plying his trade in all parts of the country, and marrying many wives and breaking many hearts. He was not moved by human sympathy or human justice; nor was he consciously susceptible to influences of Nature.

Again, in Coleridge's poem the hero is wrought upon by supernatural spirits and powers which are conjured up by the imagination and are to be believed in only as poetic agencies. Wordsworth, on the contrary, felt that the imagination "may be called forth as imperiously and for kindred results of pleasure, by incidents, within the compass of poetic probability, in the humblest departments of daily life." Wordsworth's hero is accordingly arrested from his set hard-heartedness by a natural though unusual human incident. Having lost his way in a wild and rocky country he saw in the moonlight a stray ass by the river side. Administering a most cruel beating to the beast, which refused to stir from the spot, he suddenly beheld the apparition of the creature's dead master in the river and as a consequence fell into a momentary trance. Awakening, he was sufficiently softened to engage in the humane effort of recovering the corpse, and riding the animal wherever it would lead him.

From thenceforth a series of natural and human agencies, sufficient to turn any man from an evil course, touched the heart of Peter into a new spiritual consciousness. The wierd cry in the silent night of the little woodland boy seeking his dead father, a withered leaf sporting after Peter in the wind, the wild fantastic rocks, like

mosques and spires, seeming to gaze at him, a drop of
blood on a stone, fallen from the wounds he had
inflicted on the beast, a rumbling noise made by a troup
of miners under the earth without his knowing the cause,
sounds of drunkenness from an inn on the roadside, all
startled him and wrought in his soul 'conviction strange.'
Besides, from the inner recesses of his mind there was
released a new spirit, hitherto locked up, that produced
confusion in his thoughts and caused him to act strangely.
Then, by a brake of furze under shivering aspens he saw,
in hallucination, the Highland girl whom many years
before he had betrayed and who had died of a broken
heart. While the sweat was still pouring down his face
as the result of this miserable vision he heard in a wayside tabernacle the voice of a fervent Methodist, preach-
ing repentance and offering redemption. Peter was now
in such a state of mind that he heard the words of
salvation with joy; he felt through all his iron frame a
gentle, relaxing power; touched with hope and tenderness he became as meek as a child. And when he reached
the widow's home he was filled with an overwhelming pity
for her widowhood and the children's plight. He was at
last.

Taught to' feel
That man's heart is a holy thing.

As the Mariner learned to love the water-snakes, so a
spring of love gushed from Peter's heart for the poor
beast that carried him thither. Renouncing forever his
past folly he in time permanently "became a good and
honest man."

Poetically *Peter Bell* is not a serious rival to *The
Ancient Mariner*. Though Peter is a vigorous and
strongly drawn character, having back of him something

of the energy of Wordsworth's mind, the Mariner is so intensely, intimately, and humanly realized that from him as an entity there wells up such a strain of lyric loveliness as has made him a universal favorite. Though *Peter Bell* contains some of the finest touches of Wordsworth the poem as a whole lacks congruity and genuine simplicity. The poet's attempts at playful humor are not always successful, while in the serious parts he does not actually achieve high seriousness. The poem is great in intent rather than in achievement, and is important chiefly as indicating the strong bent of its author's mind. Wordsworth's greatest divergence from the author of *The Ancient Mariner* is that he wished to have done with all supernatural machinery as an aid in rendering the moral and spiritual experiences of his hero.

[1]But the issue is a far wider one than the difference between two poems or even two poets. Wordsworth was intent on ridding himself of all outer and ceremonious accessories dear to the heart of both poetry and religion in past generations—demons, witches, ghosts, gnomes, naiads, local deities, limbos, nether worlds, purgatories, etc. Daringly he cut through the accumulated superstitions, mythologies, and hide bound creeds of the past to the essential passion and power of man's deepest and inmost nature. If nineteenth century literature and life is freer from such literary and religious accessories than earlier centuries and is more inclined to treat man as man, perhaps more is due to the example of Wordsworth than that of any other single individual. It was no part of his purpose to set limits to the highest imaginative

---

[1] This paragraph and some other brief passages and sentences scattered through this essay appear in my book, *Selected Poems of Wordsworth* (Houghton, Mifflin Company).

power of poetry or to oppose religion. Rather, he found the center for both in the very heart of man. He demanded that good men feel the soul of Nature and realize the energy and mystery of their own inward being. He asserted unequivocally and illustrated with almost startling literalness the ancient doctrine that "the Kingdom of Heaven is within you." He is the most modern of moderns in his constant insistence on the principle of immanence: God is not an absentee Being in relation to His Universe—He is *in* Nature and *in* Man.

In the fragment of the *Recluse,* very probably composed in 1800, the poet asserted that

> Of Truth, of Grandeur, Beauty, Love, and Hope,
> And melancholy Fear subdued by Faith;
> Of bless'd consolations in distress;
> Of moral strength, and intellectual Power;
> Of joy in widest commonality spread;
> Of the individual Mind that keeps her own
> Inviolate retirement, subject there
> To Conscience only, and the law supreme
> Of that Intelligence which governs all—
> I sing.   . . . Not Chaos, not
> The darkest pit of lowest Erebus,
> Nor aught of blinder vacancy, scooped out
> By help of dreams—can breed such fear and awe
> As fall upon us often when we look
> Into our Minds, into the Mind of Man—
> My haunt; and the main region of my song.
>   (lines 767-794)

Surely here is enough imaginative, sublime, and spiritual matter to more than compensate for the supernatural world of *The Ancient Mariner,* or even for the spacious cosmography and the supernatural characters of *Paradise Lost.* Also here is plainest evidence that it was not Nature but the Mind of Man that occupied Wordsworth's chief and deepest thought. And though he de-

lighted to meditate on the general question as to how
the individual mind and the external world are fitted to
each other, yet he felt he must often turn from such
speculations to

> Travel near the tribes
> And fellowship of men, and see ill sights
> Of madding passions mutually inflamed;
> Must hear Humanity in fields and groves
> Pipe solitary anguish; or must hang
> Brooding above the fierce confederate storm
> Of sorrow, barricaded evermore
> Within the walls of cities. (lines 826-833)

If his purpose, he says, of giving an authentic account
of such things without becoming downcast or forlorn,
and of relating something of his personal experience,

> May sort with highest objects, then—dread Power;
> Whose gracious favour is the primal source
> Of all illumination,—may my life
> Express the image of a better time,
> More wise desires, and simpler manners;—nurse
> My Heart in genuine freedom:—all pure thoughts
> Be with me;—so shall thy unfailing love
> Guide, and support, and cheer me to the end!
>
> (Lines 853-860)

Obviously to achieve so high a purpose numerous
preparatory efforts, as the character studies in the
Lyrical Ballads and *The Old Cumberland Beggar,* half-
successes, as in *Peter Bell,* and the slow maturing of all
the poet's powers, are required. But the heights were
scaled numbers of times between 1799 and 1802, among
which instances is *Michael,* [2] written in 1800 and published in the same year in the second edition of the

[2] The story of *Margaret* (1797) was perhaps Wordsworth's first great
success in this kind. But the story lacks the dignity and grandeur
of *Michael. Ruth* (1799) and *The Brothers* (1800) are companion
pieces of *Michael,* though they, too, fall just a little short of its tower-
ing greatness.

Lyrical Ballads. This poem pipes solitary anguish in fields and groves, and gives such glimpses into the mind of man that breed more fear and awe than aught that may be scooped out by help of dreams.

It is a tragedy of an old man's broken hopes—the tale of a shepherd's loss of his only son, who, giving himself to evil courses, fell into ignominy and shame. It especially illustrates the distinction that Wordsworth claimed for all his poems—"the feeling therein developed gives importance to the action and situation and not the action and situation to the feeling." The deep-seated affections and, in the end, the incurable sorrow yet unconquerable heroism in the heart of the aged man are the moving force in the poem. The story advances slowly, almost leisurely. None but the simplest literary devices are used; no conventional contrasts are introduced to heighten the effect. The presentation, without exaggeration, of detail after detail, from the shepherd's daily family life, gradually lifts the hero in our admiration; thread after thread is so woven about our interest that when the crisis comes we feel a poignant sense of personal loss. Everything that occurs before the defection of the son reveals the immense depth and indomitable strength of the hero's affections; "stout of heart and strong of limb" he gradually looms before our imagination as a sublime personality.

Michael's attachment to the soil and to his inherited property and his mountain home was of such slow growth and so deeply rooted that he seemed an integral part of his natural surroundings. In his daily outdoor life he took his place in the 'goings-on' of Nature as inevitably as clouds and valleys and hills. The mountains, "which had impressed so many incidents upon his mind of hard-

ship, skill or courage, joy or fear," contributed something of their inviolate freshness and energy to his character. They were as much his second self as his own
breathing. A fragment intended for this poem recovered
from a Ms. book of Dorothy Wordsworth, says that in
Michael's thoughts concerning earth and sky were

> Wonder, and admiration, things that wrought
> No less than a religion of his heart.

But his devotion to the land and the hills, however deep
and strong, was transcended by his affection for the son
of his old age. It was unselfishly for the sake of Luke
that he wished the land to be free. If an old man's
attachments are not as numerous as a younger person's
they are likely to be far more intense; the energy of
Michael's devotion to the boy seemed as of iron. And
when he proposed that his son go away to the city to aid
in paying off the indemnity which had suddenly fallen on
their property he made as great and supreme a self-
renunciation as did Abraham in sacrificing his son in
devotion to the wishes of the Almighty:

> 'Heaven forgive me, Luke,
> If I judge ill for thee, but it seems good
> That thou should'st go.'

After the ceremony of laying the corner-stone of a proposed new sheepfold was performed, with the simplicity
and solemnity of an ancient Hebrew ritual, the father
declared they had been bound together only by the links
of love, concluding—

> 'Now, fare thee well—
> When thou return'st, thou in this place wilt see
> A work which is not here: a covenant
> 'Twill be between us: but, whatever fate
> Befall thee, I shall love thee to the last,
> And bear thy memory with me to the grave.'

The language here, in its simplicity and austerity, as in many places in the poem, is remarkably like the language of the Scriptures; besides, the character and conduct of Michael constantly remind one of many of the great, simple heroes of the Bible.

The record from this point onward is brief. It is an account of the world-old story of sons breaking their fathers' hearts. Wordsworth is nowhere greater than in handling this conclusion. The poem now moves with the utmost swiftness. Every line is pregnant with tragic energy. Michael attests his supreme greatness in this, that no cry escapes his lips as he goes about in solitary anguish to perform his duty. There is something more compelling in his quiet grief than if he had given way to torrents of passion at the ingratitude of children. He sought consolation only in the source from whence sprang his grief, that is, from a purely inward source:

> There is a comfort in the strength of love;
> 'Twill make a thing endurable, which else
> Would overset the brain, or break the heart.

The struggle through years of the broken-hearted old man, forlorn but unvanquished and unyielding, to build the sheepfold that was to stand as a covenant between himself and his son on his son's return, is as pathetic and sublime as anything recorded in literature. Looking into his mind strikes one with a sense of fear and awe. Yet nothing attests more eloquently man's innate greatness of being and his unconquerable spirit, even though death overtake him, than this:

> The length of full seven years, from time to time,
> He at the building of the Sheepfold wrought,
> And left the work unfinished when he died.

Since heroism can go no farther and since Michael breathed religion as natively as the air of his own fields and mountains, he is one of the sublime spiritual heroes of literature. Abstracted by art from the destructive influences of time he stands in the imagination, with pathos and sublimity, as enduring as the eternal hills.

A companion piece of *Michael* and a more pronounced assertion of the Divine in man is *Resolution and Independence,* written in 1802. The poem deals with a single incident—the casual meeting of the poet with his hero, the Leech Gatherer. It is the supreme example of Wordsworth's making the most of a slight, almost trivial, incident. The poet represents himself as being assailed by strange fancies and unnamable fears which cause him to sink into a state of utter dejection as he travels over a solitary moor on a morning after a rainstorm. Suddenly, almost startlingly, as though by "a leading from above, a something given," he in this lonely spot came face to face with a human being!—an old man "beside a pool bare to the eye of heaven."

The power of Wordsworth's imagination is at its highest in describing and interpreting this character. He compares him to natural objects—a huge stone, a seabeast reposing on the sand, a motionless cloud—so that the old man seems an elemental energy of the solitary moor, a power rising out of the earth as a monitor startling the poet from his wayward thoughts—like a still small voice of the desert charging the atmosphere with spiritual significance. Upon being questioned by the poet he said he had come to these waters to gather leeches.

> And he had many hardships to endure,
> From pond to pond he roamed, from moor to moor;
> Housing, with God's good help, by choice or chance,
> And in this way he gained an honest maintenance.

Yet the aged man smiled under his burden, looked kindly
from beneath "the sable orbs of his yet vivid eyes,"
uttered a stately speech in "choice word and measured
phrase, above the reach of ordinary men." In short, he
seemed possessed of the secret of happiness under the
most adverse circumstances, being completely sustained
by some inward power of being.

Then as by a touch from the divine within the man
the poet, longing to be freed from "the fear that kills,"
felt suddenly transformed into a new spirit of self possession. He had gotten a vision of "the hiding places of
man's power," a glimpse into that part of man's being
where God is revealed, and was subdued and awed.
Humbly he took to heart this new insight into the divine
mystery of man's spiritual nature:

> I could have laughed myself to scorn to find
> In that decrepit Man so firm a mind,
> "God," said I, "be my help and stay secure;
> I'll think of the Leech Gatherer on the lonely moor."

But nowhere is the Divine more concentratedly immanent than in the heart of a child. This conviction seems
gradually to have deepened in Wordsworth's mind. In
Anecdote for Fathers and *We Are Seven* (1798) he
expressed the bold surmise that a child's intuitions may
be a most important source of spiritual wisdom. In *Lucy
Gray* (1799) he spiritualized the little girl as a permanent mystic presence on the lonesome wild. In many
poems that followed, like *The Sparrow's Nest* and *To a
Butterfly,* his mind dwelt, wistfully and entranced, upon
those "sweet childish days that are as long as twenty days
are now." In *The Fountain* and *Two April Mornings*
(1799) he suggests that no substitution can be made of
one child's personality for another, that there remains

something intact and inviolable at the center of each. In *Michael* (1800) he struck a deeper note, where the boy's heart is the source, not of ideas 'compounded' out of the senses, but of mysterious spiritual influences that regenerate the father's mind. "Why should I relate," the poet asks,

> That from the boy there came
> Feelings and emanations—things which were
> Light to the sun and music to the wind;
> And that the old Man's heart seemed born again?

As in *Resolution and Independence* in 1802 the faith that the divinity in one man may have a vital transforming effect on another was first fully revealed, so in the Sonnet *It is a Beauteous Evening Calm and Free,* also in 1802, the principle of the indwelling of Deity in children and its regenerative influence became fully articulate. A child may be mischievous or even show violence of temper, but beneath such moodiness is always a deeper self, not tainted with original sin but made up of heavenly attributes. So that if one were to look for a visible resemblance of God and a close touch of Him in the world one could as readily see and feel it in the face and heart of a child as anywhere. Though the child in the Sonnet appears untouched by the solemn thought which fills the mind of the elder person it is nevertheless divine.

> Thou liest in Abraham's bosom all the year;
> And worship'st at the Temple's inner shrine,
> God being with thee when we know it not.

Thus up to 1802 or thereabouts the drift of Wordsworth's mind was towards a deeper and deeper inwardness—from naturalism to immanence, from the mystic in Nature to the mystic in man. At first he placed emphasis on Deity in Nature, but gradually he came to place greater emphasis on Deity in Man. One cannot touch the body of a child or a man without being made conscious that God is indwelling there. "What ye have done to the least of these ye have done unto me" was the mystic law that governed the poet. In the broadest sense, the earth is a sacred dwelling and all visible objects are somehow charged with revelations of spiritual truth. Or, to put it otherwise, the Presence at the heart of all things, working through natural objects, childhood intuitions, memory, and human character and human conduct, has a redemptive and re-creative influence on all who, with reverence, heed its power. For this reason Wordsworth's poetry is permeated with a spirit akin to the spirit of the deep and mystical truths of the New Testament. And for this reason it will be read and re-read in every generation and have many and different interpreters.

III

But after this doctrine of immanence had reached its full development it passed by slow and natural gradation into the doctrine of transcendence, or rather, without relinquishing immanence the poet added to it transcendence—which fact marks an important transition stage in Wordsworth's spiritual history. Immanence and transcendence are not used here as representing sharply fixed philosophical concepts, but as indicating tendencies in Wordsworth's spiritual growth. Wordsworth cannot be put into any one formula, and the truth about him has been beclouded by the efforts of critics to do so, to make him, for instance, a Pantheist (Elton), or an Associationist (Beatty), or a Philosophic Sensationalist (Garrod),—to cite but a few examples of recent critics. The growth of Wordsworth's mind, instead of being simple, as is usually supposed, is extraordinarily complex. One of the chief causes of this complexity is that Wordsworth was loath at any time to relinquish what he had once gained. When Coleridge became a transcendentalist he renounced in round terms his former belief in Necessity and in Associationism. Wordsworth, on the other hand, attempted to conserve and carry forward the best parts of his former conceptions, to adapt them by modification to the truth of his wider experience. Or, where such adaptations could not be made, he by a kind of grand inconsistency let them pass out of mind, which furnishes sufficient matter for small criticism. Perhaps the best that can be done is to trace the main tendencies as manifested in his works chronologically.

Again, immanence and transcendence are not mutually exclusive. One can conceive of Deity as operating in Nature and in man, and yet as above them; that is, Deity is at once immanent and transcendent. Likewise one can conceive of the mind of man as deeply immersed in Nature, and yet as possessing something alien to Nature, something derived from a higher source than Nature, which makes man transcendent. In general this view is something other than Naturalism or Pantheism.

As formerly, Wordsworth was filled with wonder at the ineffableness of Nature and at the Godlike in man; but he now also gradually began to conceive of Deity as personal and of both Deity and the mind of man as above Nature, and therefore transcendent. That is, Nature, as an entity, now ceased to be the ultimate source of all reality; and instead of considering the mind as being impelled by an impersonal Presence, the poet felt the need of an adequate theory of the will, as originative and free, and acting as a counterpoise to the feelings in poetry. The practical exercise of the will was present from the beginning in Wordsworth's sturdy nature, and it saved him from many romantic extravagancies. Its power is implicitly present in such characters as Michael and the Leech Gatherer; but it now becomes explicit as a theory and as a new force in his poetry. Besides, the subject of immortality, but slightly if at all treated before 1802, from this time on becomes a vital part of the poet's thought. In its wider aspects this whole attitude toward life may be termed religious idealism.

As early as 1800 in *Hart-leap Well* there are slight traces of the conception of a personal Deity, who is here spoken of as maintaining

> A deep and reverential care
> For the unoffending creatures whom he loves.

A strictly naturalistic religion does not permit one to speak of Deity as a Being who cares and loves, and in the earlier years Wordsworth maintained an attitude consistent with naturalism. But now it is different. As in *Hart-leap Well* so in *Fidelity* (1805) Wordsworth conceived of God not only as personal but as above Nature. In commemorating the faithfulness of a dog, who remained through three month's space in a wild spot by the side of his dead master, he concludes:

> How nourished here through such long time
> He knows, who gave that love sublime;
> And gave that strength of feeling, great
> Above all human estimate.

In the poems from about 1802 onward Wordsworth's God 'sees into the heart' (*The Prelude, Bk.* III), knows loves, and cares,—a Being, though manifest in Nature, is not contained in Nature. The difference between belief in Deity as impersonal and identified with Nature, and Diety as personal and above Nature, is sufficient to distinguish between an extremely radical and a moderately liberal faith. These are but the hints and beginnings of what became more pronounced in his later poetry.

Traces of the conception that the mind of man transcends Nature are found as early as 1802. In *Michael* and in earlier poems Wordsworth was content with accepting the Godlike in man on a par, so to speak, with Divinity in Nature; but he naturally grew to conceive the indwelling spirit to make the conscious being—man— superior to Nature. The change in Wordsworth was very gradual and subtle. One hears the prophecy of it in the closing lines of the Sonnet *Toussaint L'ouverture* (1802):

> Thy friends are exultations, agonies,
> And love, and man's unconquerable mind.

The 'firm' mind of the Leech Gatherer becomes 'unconquerable' in Toussaint—a love, a power, and a will, comparable to which there is nothing to be found in Nature.

A more positive expression of this principle is the Sonnet *Near Dover*. This and the *Toussaint* belong to a large group of Political Sonnets written in 1802, which interpret politics in terms of moral and idealistic principles. As his spiritual experiences were leading him from naturalism to transcendence, so his political conceptions were slowly changing from radicalism to idealism. The greatness of a nation depends not so much upon its natural and material resources as upon the possession of an inward transcendental power of soul. It is likely that very early Wordsworth felt that to regenerate nations required a driving power from a source higher than that which any philosophy of Nature could supply.

Though a mighty bulwark of safety for England in 1802, the winds and the waters of the English Channel were nothing in themselves; there was something idealistic in the soul of the nation which made it obedient to a spiritual human law higher than any law of Nature:

> Winds blow, and waters roll,
> Strength to the brave, and Power, and Deity;
> Yet in themselves are nothing! One decree
> Spake laws to *them,* and said that by the soul
> Only, the Nations shall be great and free.

We may take, then, the year 1802 as something of a landmark in Wordsworth's inner history. We may pause to note that it was the year of his marriage and the period when he was completely reconciled politically to his own country, to the type of liberty represented by her—a compromise between individualism and restraint, wrought out by slow degrees. The radicalism of his youth and whatever of extreme naturalism appeared in the poems of 1798 are toned down to balance with other values of life. The short Nature poems after 1802— *To the Small Celandine* (two poems, 1802), *To the Daisy* (three poems, 1802), *The Green Linnet* (1803), *Yew Trees* (1803), *I Wandered Lonely as a Cloud* (1804), *To the Cuckoo* (1804), and others—show as passionate a love for Nature as any of his poems, but do not at all contain the bold generalizations of the Nature poems of 1798. To be sure the daisy in at least one poem is apostolical and the daffodils flash upon the poet's inward eye and the voice of the cuckoo is transmuted into a spiritual presence. Yet whatever philosophy these poems contain is acceptable to all alike, and they have never caused the sharp dissention among critics as the earlier poems. In these later ones the voice of the poet is the voice of humanity at its best. And though in the parts of *The Prelude* written after 1802 the poet again and again relates the wonderful things Nature has done for him, yet he no where declares, as he once did in *Lines Above Tintern Abbey,* that Nature is the soul of all his moral being. Freqently considered by critics as the final wisdom of Wordsworth, this generalization and those in the Nature poems of the same period, none of which were ever repeated by Wordsworth in their extreme form, have been given an undue importance in critical history. In brief, Naturalism as a religious philosophy held Wordsworth but for a short time. This is as it should be, for any one bent, as Wordsworth was, on searching.

> Human nature and her subtle ways,
> As studied first in our own hearts, and then
> In life among the passions of mankind.
> (*The Prelude,* Book XIV, lines 323-5)

is bound to discover facts about the human mind that do not readily sort with the rather simple and somewhat attenuated philosophy of pure naturalism. And despite the splendor and beauty and dynamic energy of *Lines Above Tintern Abbey* there is still something slightly immature in its daring and unqualified generalizations. Wordsworth reached intellectual maturity a little later; by 1802 there is a better balance and a broader sanity in his work, a larger and more convincing synthesis of the essential facts of experience. The years approximately between thirty and thirty-seven represent him at full maturity.

It is not an accident that the *Intimations of Immortality* (1802-6), which by common consent reaches the high water mark of Wordsworth's genius, should fall

within the compass of these years. The first four stanzas
were written in 1802 or 1803; the remainder was written
some three years later.   There is a deeper humanity
and a larger scope of movement in this poem than in
Lines Above Tintern Abbey. Though it is less personal
in form of expression it penetrates deeper into the secrets
of human power and human faith and connects man with
a larger cosmic order of existence.   As in the earlier poem
so in this the human qualities of memory and hope, or
rather memory and faith, are interwoven in close affinity.
But here they are more intimately related to the main
theme.   Indeed, memory and hope bound together by
the power of the central will, furnish the whole foundation of the poem.   By means of these faculties the mind
travels backward through childhood and birth and forward through age and death into a transcendental world.
The philosophic significance of the poem is that in it the
two great currents of immanence and transcendence meet
and are held in perfect balance by the law of continuity.

The poem does not offer logical argument or formal
proof of immortality, for immortality is a thing which
cannot be demonstrated.   In this life we can only have
intimations of it, which almost always produce deep convictions in our hearts or do not touch us at all.   The
poet has recorded his deepest convictions on the subject,
which are that of immanence and of transcendence—that
in the center of man's being is a spiritual and creative
energy which makes him immortal, and that beyond
Nature there is an invisible and spiritual world, which
supports and gives meaning to our physical world and
which is the true home of man's higher nature.

Now both these convictions are supported by and
really arise from the poet's recollections of his early

childhood, as the subtitle of the poem indicates. There
are, no doubt, degrees of difference in the capaciousness
of men's memories, and there have been men who have
had more capacious memories than Wordsworth. But
there are also degrees of difference in men's capacities to
remember certain things, or kinds of things. And it is
to be doubted whether there was ever another man who
remembered the experiences of his early childhood as
tenaciously as did Wordsworth, of which the first two
books of *The Prelude* are an eloquent testimony. There
he expresses, in a little more naturalistic form, the seed
thoughts of the great *Ode*—a sense of a creative and
indestructible force within him that would not be subdued by the regular action of the world, and a sense of
a spiritual order of beauty and being, old as creation,
that gives to forms and images a breath and everlasting
motion.

Wordsworth also found confirmation of his remembered experiences by what he observed in children. There
seems to be a divine intelligence in the heart of a child
that brings it nearer to some truths than we can arrive
at by our reasoning powers. The fact that its mind has
not as yet been subjected to the falsities that certainly
do exist in the world of adult thought make it possible
that its wisdom at some points may be more trustworthy
than man's wisdom. A child may, for instance, easily
perceive the outer world as phantasmal and may transform it without effort into "an unsubstantial faery place,"
and thereby make the invisible seem the real,—which,
according to Wordsworth, is the deeper and truer meaning of things.

In a prose note to the poem Wordsworth asserts the
principle of immanence: "Nothing was more difficult

for me in childhood than to admit the notion of death as a state applicable to my own being. . . . It was not so much from feelings of animal vivacity that my difficulty came as from a sense of the indomitableness of the Spirit within me;" and also the principle of transcendence: "I was often unable to think of external things as having external existence, and I communed with all that I saw as something not apart from, but inherent in my own immaterial nature.   Many times while going to school have I grasped at a wall or tree to recall myself from this abyss of idealism to the reality."

Though expressed in an original way in the poem these ideas of immanence and transcendence are not altogether original—they belong to the traditions of Christianity. The faith of Christianity asserts as two cardinal principles that a man's soul is worth more than the whole world because it is immortal, and that the visible worlds were framed by a spiritual power, "so that," as St. Paul says, "the things which are seen are not made by the things that do appear."   The main lines in Wordsworth's thinking were slowly converging toward these central truths of Christianity; it is easy to make the identity.   In short, the poem is an exposition of the faith of liberal Christianity.

Then, too, it was Christianity that set a child in the midst of grown up persons and insisted that these persons must become like it as a first step of entrance into the kingdom.   The world in Wordsworth's day had lost the whole meaning of this phase of the Christian dogma. Wordsworth came upon it anew, though by very strange paths; and in so doing he discovered something deep in humanity and something deep in religion.

This something is the principle of continuity—an abiding sense that at the very center of our natures there has existed, from our earliest childhood, a quality, or force, which preserves our personal identity throughout life—

> So was it when my life began;
> So is it now I am a man;
> So be it when I shall grow old,
>   Or let me die!
> The Child is father of the Man;—

and which in itself has such spiritual dignity and greatness that it demands on our part a faith that it gives continuity to our existence throughout eternity. "Creative sensibility," "the primal sympathy," "the light that never was on sea or land," "man's unconquerable mind," "the immortal soul,"—these are a few of the different expressions Wordsworth uses to designate it. The central will, it may be called, since it carries with it especially a sense of the soul's immunity from decay and its essential freedom, and is just that part of our being which defies analysis. To have a steady faith in this power within us implies a steady faith in immortality. This power, which asserted itself so unmistakably in Wordsworth's consciousness in childhood, gave him, as he beautifully says in the poem, "the faith that looks through death." *My Heart Leaps up when I behold,* partly quoted above, and this poem make an advance in Wordsworth because they articulate for the first time the sense of an abiding reality in the inmost part of our natures. It is thus not so much the intuitions of childhood that Wordsworth prizes as it is the sense of a continuous personal identity. This law of continuity also harmonizes the principles of immanence and transcendence.

Wordsworth believed that the soul comes from God and is not merely of earthly or sensuous origin. But this faith rests upon the sense of the indomitableness of the spirit within him and not upon shadowy recollections of that origin. The Platonic recollections of a former existence are but an ornamental part of his faith; for one may have no such recollections and still as firmly hold the belief that the soul comes from God. In this connection the following phrases from stanzas nine and ten must be carefully considered: "obstinate questionings," "high instincts," "first affections," "shadowy recollections," "the primal sympathy," "faith that looks through death," "the philosophic mind;" all these phrases, in different ways, tell of the inviolate Reality within us that gives us conviction of immortality. Now it should be noted, first, that among these elements "shadowy recollections" is but one element in our instinct of immortality and that a subordinate one. But the majority of critics treat it as the main element and oftentimes as the only element, and thereby falsely interpret the poem. Secondly, the Platonic recollections must be sharply distinguished from "the thought of our past years" upon which the matter of the poem is essentially based. And third, the total entity these phrases aim to set forth is not derivable from sensation, is a deeper reality within us than sensation, deeper than "sense and outward things." Wordsworth rightly says in his note on pre-existence: "It is far too shadowy a notion to be recommended to faith as more than an element in our instinct of immortality. . . . . Having to wield some of the mind's elements when I was impelled to write this poem on the 'Immortality of the Soul,' I took hold of the notion of pre-existence as having sufficient foundation in humanity for authorizing me to make for my purpose the best use of it I could as a poet."

The use that he makes of the Platonic "shadowy recollections" *as a poet* is that they suggest a connection, a continuous existence of the soul, from the past to the present through that mysterious period that we call birth. The purpose of this poetical device is to give continuousness and largeness of movement, or something like epical dimensions, to the poem, to give the reader a sense of imaginative completeness.

Another device is the contrast between lamentations in the first part and exultations in the latter part of the poem. In the opening stanzas the poet laments the loss of celestial light he possessed in his childhood. In the closing stanzas he exults in the strength that remains behind, in the potency of his present recollections of the past which have power to reduce "noisy years" to "moments in the being of the eternal Silence." The purpose of this device is to heighten by contrast the victory of the soul against its temporary losses, the joy of its permanent possessions.

Still another device is that of contrasting spiritual life to physical life, the heavenly to the earthly, at the expense of the latter. The world is conceived as a prison-house which closes in upon the soul; mere earthly pleasures and habits of imitation deepen the prison gloom. But spiritual powers within the mind itself are set in resistance to this earthly encroachment:

> Obstinate questionings
> Of sense and outward things,
> Fallings from us, vanishings;—

These powers of the mind, alien to the mere knowledge derived from sensations and outward things, make man aware that he is a creature moving about in a world of larger compass than this earthly one. They are "high instincts" that successfully combat the tendencies of our mere mortal nature and can lead us in sight of "that immortal sea which brought us hither." This contrast deepens our sense of the transcendence of the spiritual order both in the mind and in God over the forces of Nature.

Now it is chiefly the use of these contrasts that has caused various admirers of Wordsworth to find something unsatisfactory in the *Ode*. One discovers that the lament in the four first stanzas verges on the sentimental and is neither characteristic nor worthy of Wordsworth. Another feels that the sixth and seventh stanzas, in which Wordsworth represents the earth as making man to forget the glories he has known, are not in keeping with the spirit of a true Nature poet. A third, as for instance, Matthew Arnold, finds that Wordsworth is really making declamatory efforts to lift himself to the height of his great argument.

In one sense all these objections are well grounded. In *Michael* and in many another simple and artless poem where literary devices all but vanish, Wordsworth created so high a standard of taste, which, if applied to the *Ode* make it seem lacking somewhat in simplicity, naturalness, and in a certain nameless grace. On the other hand, Wordsworth here used only such devices as are legitimate, and used them, in the main, with success; they are no more obtrusive or unsuccessful, for instance, than those Gray used in the *Elegy*, or Coleridge in *The Ancient Mariner*, or Tennyson in *In Memoriam*. To be sure, the *Ode* is more conventional than many other poems of Wordsworth; but partly because it is more conventional he has received a wider hearing through it than through any other poem, which fact must not be lost sight of.

Indeed, we may say that here Wordsworth has struck
the right balance between what is permanently conventional in poetry and what is original in his own mind.

There are, however, several minor defects in the poem
arising from the use of these contrasts. It is sometimes
difficult for the poet to make his transitions from one
part of the theme to another. The transition from the
seventh to the eighth stanza is slightly abrupt, while that
from the eighth to the ninth is distinctly abrupt. Another
defect is that the poet dwells too long on the pre-existent
idea, creating thereby a plausible center of thought for
the whole poem. So that instead of being a circle with
one center it is an ellipse with two centers—a plausible
one in the fifth and a real one in the ninth stanza. And
this defect in structure accounts for much of the complicated and oftentimes wrongheaded criticisms of the poem.

Yet the poet certainly has his recompenses for the use
of these contrasts. Besides the advantages already mentioned it so happens that the pre-existent idea furnishes
some superb poetry for its own sake in the fifth stanza.
Also, the shuttle-like, backward and forward movement
of the thought caused by their use aids further in giving
a sense of large outline and epic sweep to the poem; then,
too, after the poet is well under way with them and has
left some of them behind him he rises, which he could not
do without them, to a supreme height of moral grandeur.
From the beginning of the ninth stanza to the end of the
poem, through some seventy lines, he presents the best
sustained passage of religious sublimity that can be found
in English poetry since Milton.

These three last stanzas are the real heart of the poem
and contain the ripe fruition of all that has gone before.
For here the poet, as by a sudden divination, resolves

his contrasts into a continuity, by finding a deeper basis for them in human experience. And this law of continuity, looked at from the standpoint of the central will, reveals that the principles of immanence and transcendence are parts of the self-same thing. This sudden revelation comes with almost overwhelming effect upon the reader's mind. The heaven that lay about his infancy the poet still finds residing, fresh and blooming, in his own heart. The primal sympathy, having been, must ever be. Even the somewhat exaggerated assertions in the eighth stanza concerning the child that reads the "eternal deep" is illuminated by the startling power with which the poet expresses the potency of those early experiences that breed in us "perpetual benediction" and that "are the fountain light of all our day." Though certain elements of Nature, as represented earlier in the poem, lay a heavy weight upon the soul, now every hill and brook and cloud and flower give him intimations of immortality—"thoughts that lie too deep for tears." The shadowy idea of pre-existence itself is lost in the glory of man's present divinity. The past and the future, birth and death, and memory and hope, are drawn into the living present of the soul's mystic being; and earth and heaven, and Nature and God, the clouds that gather round the setting sun and the eye that keeps watch over man's mortality—all attest to the high instincts and mighty volitions within us that cannot die, and to the eternal tenderness and hope in that human heart by which we live.

A close parallel in thought to the last three stanzas of *Intimations of Immortality* and falling only a little short of their sublimity is the *Ode to Duty* (1805). It is likely that it was written before the last part of *Intimations of*

Immortality was completed; if so, it may be considered as a high preparation for that larger flight. It is more restricted in scope. It does not aim to look "through death" to an ultimate future; nor does it accentuate the law of continuity. But it even more intensely reveals the principles of immanence and transcendence. In a free paraphrase of Kant, it exalts the starry heavens above and the moral law within. Feeling too much the "weight of chance desires" and of "unchartered freedom" the poet supplements the promptings of the "high instincts" of childhood and youth by the guidance of the law of Duty. With a complete self-surrender, which requires the exercise of a unique imaginative energy, the poet draws the very Godhead that keeps the most ancient heavens fresh and strong to the humble function of living within himself and becoming to him a permanent guide. He realizes heaven, in the instant, here on earth.

Before completing the *Intimations of Immortality* Wordsworth was called upon to put his religious faith to a practical test. In 1805 his brother John, who was a little younger than the poet, and who had been his intimate companion, lost his life in a shipwreck. In a letter to Sir George Beaumont, to whom he lays open his feelings, the poet argues that he can only reconcile himself to the facts of pain and sorrow in this world "upon the supposition of another and a better world." In another letter to Sir George he speaks of John's unselfish devotion to the poet's interest and of a mystic bond between them: "He would work for me (that was his language)—for me and his sister; and I was to endeavour to do something for the world. . . . I shall never forget him, never lose sight of him. There is a bond between us yet, the same as if he were living,—nay far more sacred,—calling upon me to do my utmost, as he to the last did his utmost, to live in honour and worthiness."

The finest fruit of this bereavement is *Elegiac Stanzas Suggested by Peele Castle in a Storm* (1805):

> A power is gone, which nothing can restore;
> A deep distress hath humanised my Soul. . . .
>
> The feeling of my loss will ne'er be old;
> This, which I know, I speak with mind serene.

Greatly softening his energetic nature, this sorrow did not weaken, but rather strengthened and deepened his spirit. It released some hitherto hidden energies from a deeper level of his being, revealing that, as by the grace of God, he too was in possession of "man's unconquerable mind":

> But welcome fortitude, and patient cheer,
>   And frequent sights of what is to be borne!
> Such sights, or worse, as are before me here.—
> Not without hope we suffer and we mourn.

This is one of the best examples of Wordsworth's extraordinary power to elicit soothing thoughts out of human suffering, new hope and new strength of soul from the shocks of life.

In spirit the *Character of the Happy Warrior* (1806) is closely allied to the *Ode to Duty* and *Elegiac Stanzas*. The hero is confronted by the most adverse circumstances, particularly by the exigencies of war. The transcendental faculty that dwells in his breast is expressed in a number of striking phrases—his "high endeavours are an inward light;" in the presence of pain, fear and bloodshed he exercises "a power which is our highest human dower;" if he be called upon to face some awful moment to which

Heaven has joined great issues he is "attired with sudden brightness, like a man inspired;" he is "indued as with a sense and faculty for storm and turbulence," and

> Is yet a Soul whose master-bias leans
> To homefelt pleasures and to gentle scenes.

By these transcendent powers of mind he conforms his life to the best impulses of his early boyhood, builds up his moral being from within, gives continuity and harmony to the growth of his life, and achieves such self-mastery that in the most trying circumstances he does not swerve from his ideal of perfect conduct; so that at the last he

> Finds comfort in himself and in his cause;
> And, while the moral mist is gathering, draws
> His breath in confidence of Heaven's applause.

With majestic plainness of manner this poem gives in small compass the distilled essence of transcendental wisdom.

Thus by 1806 Wordsworth had become markedly transcendental. The record thus far has been made mainly, independent of *The Prelude,* on the basis of the shorter poems taken chronologically and about whose general chronology and the final form in which the poet left them there can be no doubt. If Professor Harper's theory that *The Prelude* was seriously changed in later years should prove correct, it still remains true that the teachings of the poem as it stands but verifies what may be learned from the shorter poems. The first two books of *The Prelude* were written by 1800 and contain a few passages of still earlier composition. But the remaining twelve books were composed in 1804 and 1805, though also containing some passages of little earlier date. The poem is a spiritual autobiography, recounting the inner life of the author from childhood to maturity. It selects only such incidents as, in the memory of the poet, had a significant bearing upon his inner spiritual development. As such it is both authentic and final, save that, by an inevitable human limitation, it is colored by the philosophy of the poet at the time of composing. That is, the *feelings* the poet had had at any given time are rendered with absolute certainty, but the language and philosophic implications are contemporaneous with the period of composition. Book Thirteen, for instance, which gives an account of how Wordsworth came to select the characters for the poems of the *Lyrical Ballads,* renders with integrity the religious feeling of reverence and awe with which he then approached the divinity in lowly human beings, yet the presentation is touched with his transcendental conceptions of the time he gave the account.

The first two books especially, harmonizing in spirit with the poems of 1799 and 1800, are more strongly naturalistic than the later books. Here the Powers of Nature are all-sufficing to build up the human soul. Diety is conceived as impersonal and pervasive, co-equal with Nature—"the Uncreated," "Thou Soul that are the Eternity of Thought," etc. It is striking that, though occurring frequently throughout the remainder of the poem, the word "God" occurs but once, and that purely incidentally, in the whole of the first two books. But early in Book Three the poet speaks of Deity as "the God who sees into the heart," which suggests the Diety's emergence as a personal Being from the vast order of Nature, and which indicates a new religious attitude. The change is not abrupt, but subtle; yet change it is, and important.

Indeed, the inward meaning of the latter twelve books of *The Prelude* is strikingly similar to that of the poems just considered. Often it is drawn out more specifically in longer and more prosaic passages; but sometimes it is rendered with as much or greater imaginative and spiritual insight than in the shorter poems. As in *Intimations of Immortality* so in *The Prelude* the poet glorifies the inward reality that takes its rise in childhood intuitions and bases his faith in man's greatness and immortality upon it. This is a recurring theme and holds a surprisingly large place in the poem. It was Wordsworth's dearest wish to prove beyond a doubt the continuity of our personal identity through all the vicissitudes of life, the reality of an inviolable inward nature that passeth understanding. By strict logic the following passages belong to the first and second books, but by what they imply they belong where they are. In Book Five the poet says:

> Our simple childhood, sits upon a throne
> That hath more power than all the elements.
> I guess not what this tells of Being past,
> Nor what it augurs of the life to come;—
>
> (lines 508-511)

which is repeated in Book Twelve:

> Oh! mystery of man, from what a depth
> Proceed thy honours. I am lost, but see
> In simple childhood something of the base
> On which thy greatness stands; but this I feel,
> That from thyself it comes, that thou must give,
> Else never canst receive.   (lines 272-7)

Again as in the *Intimations of Immortality* the poet considers the mind as existing in a world of wider compass than that which contains the phenomena of sensation and as of no ascertainable beginning so in *The Prelude* he

believes thought to be of a mysterious origin, other than
that of sensation, and of an imperishable character:

> Hard task, vain hope, to analyze the mind,
> If each most obvious and particular thought,
> Not in a mystical and idle sense,
> But in the words of Reason deeply weighed,
> Hath no beginning.   (Book II, lines 228-232)

In short, this passage, and much else in the remainder
of *The Prelude* and some things in the *Intimations of Immortality,* are in flat contradiction to the fundamental
naturalistic and associational assumption that "all mental
states are derived from sensation."   Thought, not having a beginning, is prior to sensation; mental growth is
rooted, not in sensation, but in self-consciousness. Wordsworth's purpose was to get behind sensation—to find out
what it means, how we may interpret it at all.   We must
postulate an active mind, a self-consciousness, prior to
sensation, in order that it may at all yield any meaning.
Not denying necessarily the psychological method of
association Wordsworth subverts its fundamental philosophical tenet; and this happens midway in the great
years of his work.   If we read him mainly in the light
of *Lines Above Tintern Abbey* he is of course essentially
naturalistic.   Buf if we read him in the light of the great
Political Sonnets and of the *Intimations of Immortality*
and all that goes with it and comes after it he is essentially
transcendental and human; that is, he is more deeply
interested, as he has often told us, in the human mind,
its self-contained and constituent energies, its active,
transcendental powers, than in external Nature and sensation and the language of the sense.   This change in
him accounts in large measure for the differences of
critics in interpreting him.   Those who lay stress on the

earlier poems, as does Leguois, find him mainly a poet
of Nature and a believer in Rousseauistic Naturalism;
those who emphasize the weightier matter of the later
poems find him mainly transcendental, as does Bradley.
A reading of his poems in strict chronological order, with
an open mind as to the important new influences that
entered into Wordsworth's growth, should go far to
harmonize opposing views of critics and should clear up
many of the difficulties of Wordsworth interpretation.

As in the *Ode to Duty* so in *The Prelude* the poet finds
that

> A gracious spirit o'er this earth presides,
> And o'er the heart of man.   (Book V, lines 491-2)

Like *Elegiac Stanzas, The Prelude* recounts the sad
experiences that had humanized the poet's soul and had,
in each case, left him with more strength to combat the
weaknesses of mortal flesh. Examples of this are the
remarkable episode at the close of Book Twelve which
tells of his father's death when the poet was a lad of
thirteen, and the account, in Books Nine, Ten, and
Eleven, of his deepening experiences with the French
Revolution which found him a buoyant youth and left
him "a meditative, oft a suffering, man." (Bk. XIV,
1, 143). Like *The Happy Warrior* this poem accen-
tuates the transcendental power of the human mind
embodied in heroic deeds.

However, *The Prelude* is not merely a poem containing
passages parallel to the shorter poems written at the
same time but makes a distinctive contribution to the
poet's thought. In the early books Wordsworth traces
back into childhood just as far as he can the birth, the
awakening, of his imaginative and moral sense. He
presses hard toward the very origin of "those first-born

affinities that fit our new existence to existing things"
(Bk. I, 1, 555). He finds this awakening very early
indeed in some unusual moments of experience, such as
when by stealth, as a mere child, he rowed a boat of an
evening on the lake, or when at night he watched a storm
from beneath a rock among the mountains. He ascribes
the awakening to some divine ministry of Nature, working by some mysterious active agencies through his sensations. But in the later books, wherever he touches on
the subject, he ascribes the origin of man's greatness not
to a naturalistic but to a transcendental source, as for
instance in the passages just quoted from books Five and
Twelve, especially the lines—

> But this I feel
> That from thyself it comes, that thou must give,
> Else never canst receive;—

which suggests a subjective origin. The immortal soul
has power to thaw "the deepest sleep that time can lay
upon her" (Bk. IV, 1, 167), is not amenable to time, is
transcendental.

Again, in *The Prelude* the poet sets forth certain doctrines about the imagination, the feelings, and the reason.
The three following passages taken in the order in which
they appear in the poem reveal certain interrelations of
the terms:

> But all the meditations of mankind,
> Yea, all the adamantine holds of truth
> By reason built, or passion, which itself
> Is highest reason in a soul sublime. (Book V, lines 38-41)

> Imagination—here the Power so called
> Through sad incompetence of human speech,
> That awful Power rose from the mind's abyss.
> (Book VI, lines 592-4)

This spiritual Love acts not nor can exist
Without Imagination, which, in truth,
Is but another name for absolute power
And clearest insight, amplitude of mind,
And Reason in her most exalted mood.
This faculty hath been the feeding source
Of our long labour.   (Book XIV, lines 188-194)

Love cannot exist without imagination, imagination is reason in her most exalted mood, and passion also is reason in a soul sublime. It may seem absurd to identify these terms in such a way. But Wordsworth is aiming to set forth an entity, a Power, a central energy, the ultimate reality in the human mind, and there is no word that can adequately describe it. He confesses to the sad incompetence of human speech, and the best he can do is to vary the descriptive words. Yet the originality and everlasting freshness and beauty of *The Prelude* is in large measure due to the fact that he breaks through formal language and formal terms and formal psychologies, including the psychology of the Associationists, in his utmost effort to set forth his own intense vision of the inmost nature of our being—its origin, its growth, its continuity of existence, its immortality. He often falters at this almost more than human task. "How awful is the might of human souls," he exclaims in Book Three, and admits that the "high argument" in the main "lies far hidden from the reach of words." He takes courage however when he remembers that the reality he is describing reveals itself in the great moments of life: "There's not a man that lives who hath not known his godlike hours" (Bk. III, 1, 191). The record of these rare but supreme moments, which reassure the poet of man's high destiny, is the heart of *The Prelude*. And the poet has his reward:

> But to my conscious soul I now can say—
> "I recognize thy glory": in such strength
> Of usurpation, when the light of sense
> Goes out, but with a flash that has revealed
> The invisible world;—   (Book VI, lines 598-602)

which is a transcendent experience.

The importance of the principle of transcendence seems to have grown in Wordsworth's mind as he was writing *The Prelude,* it being more marked in the later books. From many instances that abound a few must suffice. In Book Five the poet inquires:

> Oh! why hath not the Mind
> Some element to stamp her image on
> In nature somewhat nearer to her own?
> Why, gifted with such powers to send abroad
> Her spirit, must it lodge in shrines so frail?   (lines 45-49)

There is such a disparity between what constitutes man and what constitutes nature than man, who must needs use a stone or a shell or something that nature supplies when he wishes to make a record of himself, finds that he cannot at all do his gifted powers justice. In Book Eight the poet exalts man as a transcendental Being, who is

> Both in perception and discernment, first
> In every capability of rapture,
> Through the divine effect of power and love;
> As, more than anything we know, instinct
> With godhead, and, by reason and by will,
> Acknowledging dependency sublime.   (lines 489-494)

The godhead in man is even more emphatically asserted in Book Ten but is at the same time conceived to be dependent on the "Power Supreme" whom the poet represents as

Making man what he is, creature divine,
In single or in social eminence,
Above the rest raised infinite ascents
When reason that enables him to be
Is not sequestered.   (lines 424-8)

This transcendental might of the mind, that "dread watch-tower of man's absolute self," is perhaps nowhere in Wordsworth more powerfully set forth than in the last book of *The Prelude*. After a marvellous description of a midnight view from the top of Snowdown, in which he beheld (he says)

The Moon hung naked in a firmament
Of azure without cloud, and at my feet
Rested a silent sea of hoary mist,—

There appeared to him, from out of that vision, "the type of a majestic intellect":

There I beheld the emblem of a mind
That feeds upon infinity, that broods
Over the dark abyss, intent to hear
Its voices issuing forth to silent light
In one continuous stream; a mind sustained
By recognitions of transcendent power,
In sense conducting to ideal form,
In soul of more than mortal privilege.   (lines 70-77)

The power that, amid circumstances awful and sublime, Nature exerts on "the face of outward things" is the express

Resemblance of that glorious faculty
That higher minds bear with them as their own.
. . . In a world of life they live
By sensible impression not enthralled,
But by their quickening impulse made more prompt
To hold fit converse with the spiritual world,
And with the generations of mankind
Spread over time, past, present, and to come,
Age after age, till Time shall be no more.

> Such minds are truly from the Deity,
> For they are Powers; and hence the highest bliss
> That flesh can know is theirs—the consciousness
> Of Whom they are, habitually infused
> Through every image and through every thought,
> And all affections by communion raised
> From earth to heaven, from human to divine;
> Hence endless occupation for the Soul,
> Whether discursive or intuitive;
> Hence cheerfulness for acts of daily life,
> Emotions which best foresight need not fear,
> Most worthy then of trust when most intense.
>
> (lines 89-123)

In Book Twelve he again says that

> The mind is lord and master—outward sense
> The obedient servant of her will.   (lines 222-3)

Such minds must find their permanent home in an order of existence that extends beyond Nature:

> Our destiny, our being's heart and home
> Is with infinitude, and only there;
> With hope it is, hope that can never die,
> Effort, and expectation, and desire,
> And something evermore about to be. (Book VI, lines 603-7)

Thus in *The Prelude* Wordsworth traverses the same ground and with the same underlying purpose as in the shorter poems that synchronize with it. This homogeneity attests once more to the integrity of his mind. Rare are the poets who have revealed their whole minds so fully, who are so frank and yet so dignified and even reserved. Rarer still is the poet who, if he be as profoundly self-revealing as Wordsworth, manifests such little deviation out of his true orbit, such a wide scanning of man and Nature and ultimate truth from a deep-seated center of his own being.

So true is this that many critics have failed to see that

all the while the poet was changing. His growth, however, was continuous and steady. For hardly had he uttered in *Lines Above Tintern Abbey* the markedly naturalistic and necessitarian conception of the mystic unity of all things, in which man and Nature appear but as different manifestations of one impersonal and pervasive Power, when he began to modify the position taken there. The change was slow, subtle, and gradual, but sure. It occurred without a break, and it compassed the gamut from immanence and naturalism in 1798 to immanence and transcendence in 1806.

What was the cause of this gradual change? First, it was due to the natural bent and growth of the poet's mind. That his mind was extraordinarily sensitive to external Nature all agree. But that it was also remarkably sensitive to social, political, and religious influences during this period has not always been so clearly discerned; but such was the case. He aspired to the Wanderer's creed in *The Excursion:*

> Happy is he who lives to understand,
> Not human nature only, but explores
> All natures,—to the end that he may find
> The law that governs each.   (Book IV, lines 332-5)

If he did not realize this ideal fully he at least showed he was eminently capable of growth. He grew in wisdom not merely in regard to individual man but in knowledge of the whole institutional and social fabric of the life of man. This perforce took him out of the perhaps rarer atmosphere but certainly narrower world of the *Lyrical Ballads* of 1798. And in this period he held anything but a dogmatic and final conception of things. An example in point is his changing attitude toward poetic diction as expressed in the advertisement and prefaces to the *Lyrical Ballads* in 1798, 1800 and 1802. In successive publications he was groping toward not only a larger statement of the full significance of the subject but also toward a formula that would square with his artistic growth and practice. He was not deterred by the fact that he thus lay himself open to the charge of inconsistency. Similarly in matters of the spirit he set forth, with what light he possessed at the given time, his full conviction, supported by the whole force of his personality. Thus he spoke authoritatively without being dogmatic, and thus he grew from step to step.

Secondly, Coleridge was a potent influence in hastening that growth. It can be believed, and there is some evidence, that Wordsworth disagreed with Coleridge's theology, as *theology,* and that Coleridge knew that he did. But at the same time he was absorbing the spirit of Coleridge's thought, and appropriating it to his own inner growth. In fact, the transcendental spirit of Coleridge's poems of 1802 and 1807 and *The Friend* in 1809 is strikingly similar to that of Wordsworth's poems after about 1802. Thus Coleridge's progress from Necessity to Transcendentalism parallels, perhaps just a little precedes, Wordsworth's progress from Naturalism to Transcendence, and thus another bond of sympathy was holding the two together in an intimacy remarkable in literary history.

It is therefore no mere accident that Coleridge burst forth into a mighty song of praise of the "Friend of the wise and teacher of the good" after he had read *The Prelude* in manuscript. We know that later Coleridge was disappointed when he read *The Excursion,* but the reading of *The Prelude* almost overwhelmed him. Of course, the beauty and power of the poem go far in

explaining his reaction. But it is very probable that he
himself had not been aware until that moment that
Wordsworth had come so near to his own religious
philosophy, which was a further and a special cause of
his delight and thankfulness. However, Wordsworth
was no whit behind in expressing his indebtedness to
Coleridge. He dedicated the poem to him, which were
a small matter, but in the body of the poem he again
and again addresses him as Friend in the most cordial
and intimate spirit; and in the last book he makes profound acknowledgment of his friend's influence on him:

> With such a theme
> Coleridge! with this argument, of thee
> Shall I be silent? O capacious Soul!
> Placed on this earth to love and understand,
> And from thy presence shed the light of love,
> Shall I be mute, ere thou be spoken of?
> Thy kindred influence to my heart of hearts
> Did also find its way.   (lines 275-282)

To a man as reserved by nature as Wordsworth such a
confession means very much. Those who suppose that
he was so self-centered as not to appreciate others should
read all his expressions of indebtedness scattered through
his works to Spenser, Milton, Burns, his own sister,
Coleridge, and others, and see how hard it would be to
match them from any other great poet. Coleridge, he
further says in this passage, had taught him how
"thoughts and things" may "take on more rational pro-
portions;" how enthusiastic joy and rapture may be
balanced by truth and by trust

> In hopeful reason, leaning on the stay
> Of Providence;—

and how the mind of man may learn to domesticate the
thought of

> The incumbent mystery of sense and soul,
> Of life and death, time and eternity.

Thus the spiritual philosophy of these seers coalesced in the great principle of transcendence. Within the first six years of the new century they had completely broken with the materialistic and associational philosophy of the eighteenth century and had created a body of literature that is, in a very true sense, the guiding spirit of the literature of the century to follow. The spiritual pilgrimage of the two men was from thenceforth to be on the self-same road. How strongly transcendental Wordsworth had become is clearly shown in the very last lines of *The Prelude* (1805), where he looks forward to a not far distant day when he and Coleridge may be "joint labourers in the work" of delivering men from servitude and old idolatry by teaching them the meaning of love and by exalting the powers of the human mind. They together will

> Instruct them how the mind of man becomes
> A thousand times more beautiful than the earth
> On which he dwells, above this frame of things
> (Which, 'mid all revolution in the hopes
> And fears of men, doth still remain unchanged)
> In beauty exalted, as it is itself,
> Of quality and fabric more divine.

IV

The passages quoted from *The Prelude* should be read in their context in order that their importance be not exaggerated. Wordsworth never became an extreme transcendentalist. He was transcendental only in the sense that he gave primacy to the spiritual rather than the material forces of life and that he considered the mind of man as neither wholly derived from nor con-

tained in Nature. That man's being is "above this frame
of things" he presents powerfully in *Loud is the Vale*
(1806), inspired by the news that the dissolution of
Mr. Fox was hourly expected:

> Sad was I, even to pain deprest,
> Importunate and heavy load!
> The Comforter hath found me here,
> Upon this lonely road.

If by the word Comforter, Wordsworth here means, as
is almost certain, the Holy Spirit of the New Testament,
it is a very definite indication of how far, by the year in
which the *Intimations of Immortality* were completed,
he had traveled toward orthodoxy in religion:

> A Power is passing from the earth
> To breathless Nature's dark abyss;
> But when the great and good depart
> What is it more than this—
>
> That Man, who was from God sent forth,
> Doth yet again to God return?—
> Such ebb and flow must ever be,
> Then wherefore should we mourn?

Man thus belongs to an eternal order of existence; and
the contrast between the Nature that was the soul of all
the poet's moral being in *Lines Above Tintern Abbey*
with the "breathless Nature's dark abyss" of this poem
indicates how the poet's attitude toward Man and Nature
has changed within a period of nine years. This does not
mean that Wordsworth ceased to love Nature, for the
one unchangeable fact in his poetry early and late is the
strength of that love. It does mean, however, that since
he gradually ceased to think of Nature as all-sufficing in
the building up of the human soul he will thenceforth use
Nature in his poetry more as decoration and symbol:

Nor will I praise a cloud, however bright,
Disparaging Man's gifts, and proper food.
Grove, isle, with every shape of sky-built dome,
    Though clad in colours beautiful and pure,
Find in the heart of man no natural home;
    The immortal Mind craves objects that endure.
        (Sonnet *Those Words Were Uttered*, etc. 1806)

In *Yes, It was the Mountain Echo* (1806) the poet
treats Nature symbolically. As one can hear two voices
of the cuckoo—the real one and the echo—alike, yet very
different, so, in a parallel way, there are for human beings
"voices of two different natures":

Have not *we* too?—yes, we have
    Answers, and we know not whence;
Echoes from beyond the grave,
    Recognized intelligence!

Such rebounds, our inward ear
    Catches sometimes from afar—
Listen, ponder, hold them dear;
    For of God,—of God they are.

The growth of this tendency toward symbolism may
be traced in the following—*The Simplon Pass* (1799),
The Ascent of Snowdown (1805) as given in Book Four-
teen of *The Prelude,* and *Yes, It was the Mountain Echo*
(1806). In the first the spiritual Power is *in* the object,
so that strictly speaking there is no symbolism. Of
course, the earlier and larger portion of Wordsworth's
Nature poetry is of this kind. In the second symbolism
emerges but is not obtruded. In the last the symbol is
clearly impressed upon the mind.

Various symbolic and inner meanings critics have found
in *The White Doe of Rylstone,* chiefly written in 1807
but not completed and published until 1815. Harper

says: "Other meanings this wonderful poem may have, but surely it teaches that active life is vanity that passeth away." Raleigh thinks the poem is Wordsworth's acceptance of Fate: "The poet neither rebels nor protests against Fate. . . . There is no lack here of the sense of Fate," etc. It may be ventured that the truth Wordsworth wished to convey in this poem is less one-sided than indicated in these quotations. Crabb Robinson says that in 1824 Wordsworth in a controversy "stated that the great difficulty which had always pressed on his mind in religion was the inability to reconcile Divine prescience with accountability in man." Though this poem emphasizes that difficulty it also solves it as far as it can be solved. Recently and on the whole Wordsworth, in exalting the powers of the human mind, had leaned strongly on the side of man's accountability; and though here as in the *Ode to Duty* he does not relinquish man's essential self-possession he pays tribute to the power of the Divine prescience in human life.

From one angle it may be said that the poem is a tragedy resulting from the exercise of human obstinacy. Richard Norton, the Master of Rylstone Hall, is a religious fanatic. Though he knows her heart and her Protestant faith rebel against it, he commands his daughter Emily to embroider Catholic religious emblems upon a banner that he and his sons are to carry in the uprising in the North against Queen Elizabeth. When his oldest son Francis remonstrates against his fanatical course he treats him with scorn and high disdain. When in the field his Chiefs order a retreat without having faced the enemy he impatiently and boldly appears before them, to remonstrate.

Alas! thought he, and have I borne
This Banner raised with joyful pride,
This hope of all posterity,
By those dread symbols sanctified;
Thus to become at once the scorn
Of babbling winds as they go by.

When Francis, who secretly and unarmed has followed his father and brothers, offers advice he is again denounced as a recreant and coward. With his remaining eight sons the father makes a rash night attack upon an enemy castle, unsupported by his superiors or by any of their numbers, and is overwhelmed. At the last when the old man and his sons are sentenced to an ingnominious death, and Francis of his own choice has joined them to suffer with them, the father extorts a promise from Francis to recover the banner and return it to Bolton Priory, the execution of which is the direct cause of the latter's undoing.

What course of action is there for a young man, who in conscience cannot help to carry out a father's plans in time of war? Only such as Francis follows—no active aggression against his father's purposes, but a tendering of whatever human aid he can render to his father and brothers when their lives are in jeopardy. What can a daughter do in time of turmoil when destruction overtakes all the members of her household? Nothing but to suffer and endure. Therein lies the tragedy and also the spiritual victory of the heroine.

From the beginning Francis, clear-eyed, courageous, fearless, foresees in "the headstrong current" of his father's will supported by religious fanaticism, the utter destruction that is to overtake their house. He warns his sister of the impending doom, visualizing the necessity

of inaction and fortitude on her part, with the design to
strengthen her for the shock that is sure to come:

> Weep, if that aid thee; but depend
> Upon no help of outward friend;
> Espouse thy doom at once, and cleave
> To fortitude without reprieve.

A critic already quoted says the poem is Wordsworth's
confession of the uselessness of action, of disillusion "that
lurks at the end of all effort," "a confession of human
failure so sweeping that the Western mind refuses to
join in it." These generalizations seem altogether too
far-reaching for the facts. The poem is Wordsworth's
confession, and no more, that there may arise specific
instances in human life where positive or aggressive
action is of no avail. The story of Emily is very similar
to that of Michael; the latter lost his all when he lost
his son. What reasonable human being would expect any
great action from Michael under the circumstances? His
opportunity for action was strictly limited to the building
of the sheepfold, to which he addressed himself with all
the strength of his vigorous body and broken mind.
Though he failed even here, he somehow calls out our
warmest admiration of the human spirit put to the proof.
In the nature of the case there is no field of action for
Emily. Younger than Michael, she wins a more substantial victory, but purely spiritual and subjective.
"Carrying a serene and perfect sway," she rises *above*
Fate:

> Her soul doth in itself stand fast,
> Sustained by memory of the past
> And strength of Reason; held above
> The infirmities of mortal love;
> Undaunted, lofty, calm, and stable,
> And awfully impenetrable.

The recovery of her self-possession and happiness was greatly aided by the playfellow of her happier days—a white doe, that she met as she returned to the ruins of her former home, and that served as a link between her and "the memory of old loves." The doe is both the embodiment and symbol of the benignant powers of Nature "that calmed her, cheered, and fortified." Emily

> Was happy that she lived to greet
> Her mute companion as it lay
> In love and pity at her feet;
> How happy in its turn to meet
> The recognition! the mild glance
> Beamed from that gracious countenance;
> Communication, like the ray
> Of a new morning, to the nature
> And prospects of the inferior Creature!

Like the hero in *The Happy Warrior* Emily was guided by an "inward light":

> Her sanction inwardly she bore.

In her conduct she reconciled, so far as can be, man's accountability with the Divine prescience. Living out her natural days she at last "was set free and died:"

> Thy soul, exalted Emily,
> Maid of the blasted family
> Rose to the God from whom it came.

The principles of moral idealism are vigorously applied to questions of statesmanship in a group of political sonnets written between 1808 and 1812, referring to various European states and continental heroes. These sonnets make explicit what was implicit in the earlier group of political sonnets (1802, and following). The warrior hero bears an inward light; he lives

To his inner self endeared;
And hence, wherever virtue is revered,
He sits a more exalted Potentate,
Throned in the hearts of men.
        (*Call not the Royal Swede Unfortunate*)

He has almost unlimited power of cheering "desponding men with new-born hope:"

Unbounded is the might
Of martyrdom, and fortitude, and right.
        (*Ah! Where is Palafox, etc.*)

If it be a moral aim for which warriors have fought they cannot lose, even though they be utterly vanquished in the field:

Powers have they left, an impulse, and a claim
Which neither can be overturned nor bought.
Sleep, Warriors, sleep! among your hills repose!
We know that ye, beneath the stern control
Of awful prudence, keep the unvanquished soul.
        (*On the Final Submission of the Tyrolese*)

The soul of a brave people, inspired by a just cause, is superior to the power of armies, "formal, and circumscribed in time and space;" for it is "from *within* proceeds a Nation's health." This inward self-possession of a nation is not due to its "external wealth," nor to the influence of objects of Nature; nor can it be said to be looked for in any particular place on the earth:

And is it among rude untutored Dales,
There, and there only, that the heart is true?
And, rising to repel or to subdue,
Is it by rocks and woods that man prevails?
Ah no! though Nature's dread protection fails,
There is a bulwark in the soul.
        (*And is it among rude untutored Dales*)

But the possession of this bulwark of the soul by a nation postulates a beneficent Divinity that rules over the deeds of men and inspires their heroism:

> O'er the wide earth, on mountain and on plain,
> Dwells in the affections and the soul of man
> A Godhead, like the universal Pan;
> But more exalted, with a brighter train.

And when the odds all seem against a brave man or the cause of an heroic nation, a man must look at the whole connection of events, including the infinite, and take counsel with the Eternal, casting his eye toward immortality:

> We know the arduous strife, the eternal laws
> To which the triumph of all good is given,
> High sacrifice, and labour without pause,
> Even to the death:—else wherefore should the eye
> Of man converse with immortality?
> (*O'er the wide Earth, etc.*)

Man's immortality, the reconcilement of his accountability with the Divine prescience, the secret by which he may overcome pessimism, his relation to his fellowmen and to Nature, and God's relation to Nature, are the high themes of the most ambitious of all of Wordsworth's poems, *The Excursion,* published in 1814.

Some parts of the poem, particularly portions of the first book, date back to the period of the *Lyrical Ballads;* certain other parts were produced in 1802 and 1803; but the great body of the poem was written after 1807. It thus owes its origin and general conception to a time prior to the completion of *The Prelude* and the *Intimations of Immortality.* Yet it faithfully reflects, in the main, the spirit of the poet's thought after 1807. It gives evidence of a certain hardening of the poet's mind. It has lost some of the glow and the spirit of inwardness that characterizes *The Prelude.* It aims to be more objective than *The Prelude,* which is perhaps the cause of its being less spiritually intense and more doctrinnaire.

It is, nevertheless, one of the grandest structures which the genius of Wordsworth has erected.

Coleridge did not consider the poem "equal to the work on the growth of his own spirit"—*The Prelude*. His disappointment, however, was chiefly due to the fact that it did not meet his predetermined expectations, which, even after his having read *The Prelude,* were extremely high. Though full of lofty speculation that satisfied the heart of Coleridge, *The Prelude* also naturally contained much narrative and personal matter; but *The Excursion,* Coleridge hoped, would be purely impassioned speculation. "Of course," he says, "I expected the colours, music, imaginative life, and passion of *poetry;* but the matter and arrangement of *philosophy.*" Had the whole poem been conceived and executed in the strain of

> Authentic tidings of invisible things;
> Of ebb and flow, and ever-during power;
> And central peace, subsisting at the heart
> Of endless agitation;—   (Book IV, lines 1144-7)

one guesses Coleridge would have been satisfied. It was again, as in the case of *The Ancient Mariner,* the younger poet's wishing his own method and purpose on the sturdy mind of his great brother poet, without success.

Though it contains as lofty speculations as can be found in modern literature, it only secondarily has the matter, and does not at all have the arrangement, of philosophy; it is a narrative poem dealing with persons and with concrete facts of life. Any one equipped with the elementary principles of philosophical thinking should have no serious difficulty in reading it. There are four chief personages—the poet, the Wanderer, the Pastor, and the Solitary. A secondary group of personages are those whose lives are narrated by the Pastor and the

Wanderer—usually humble people. Many critics have interpreted the poem as though its only purpose were to make an onslaught on the Solitary's misanthropic ways of thinking and living; but it is actually much more inclusive. Wordsworth's aim seems really more difficult than that which Coleridge had wished for him; for, instead of creating a poem of impassioned abstractions, he purposed to show how the highest transcendental and idealistic truths, upon which he and Coleridge agreed, could be made effective in the life of a misanthrope and how it could actually be embodied in the lives of humblest people. Or, to put it otherwise, his general purpose was to show that in spite of tragedy and suffering, and partly because of it, human life is worth living, and that the universe at heart is good, and not evil; while his specific purpose was to reveal, to put every one in touch with, the inner volitional and emotional springs of life which are the key, not only to successful ethical living, but to a proper and reasonable interpretation of the universe as a whole. As Coleridge later in *The Friend* harmonized the principles of transcendentalism with Christianity so Wordsworth here calls the same high idealistic and religious philosophy in the service of common humanity. That he was only partially successful is due to the amazingly inherent difficulty of the task he set himself. The expenditure of his strong energies of mind in fusing into a holy union the transcendental and the common, the ultimately divine and the simple, accounts for the mighty influence of *The Excursion* on nineteenth century ways of thinking.

In *The Prelude* Wordsworth exalted the mind of man "above this frame of things" and conceived of Divinity as a Power that sees into the heart; but in *The Excursion*

he conceives the Being of God much more distinctly as a
beneficent Person who feels and wills and who is infinitely
exalted above man and all his works, which indicates a
step further toward a conservative view:

> One adequate support
> For the calamities of mortal life
> Exists—one only; an assured belief
> That the procession of our fate, howe'er
> Sad or disturbed, is ordered by a Being
> Of infinite benevolence and power;
> Whose everlasting purposes embrace
> All accidents, converting them to good.
> —The darts of anguish *fix* not where the seat
> Of suffering hath been thoroughly fortified
> By acquiescence in the Will supreme
> For time and for eternity; by faith,
> Faith absolute in God, including hope,
> And the defence that lies in boundless love
> Of his perfections; with habitual dread
> Of aught unworthily conceived, endured
> Impatiently, ill-done, or left undone,
> To the dishonour of his holy name.   (Book IV, lines 10-27)

It is significant that, in Wordsworth's view, the two
outstanding characteristics of God are Will and Love.
Now the counterpart of this Being is resident in man in
terms of a unique union of will and feeling, which has
conscience at the center.   When man realizes as he must,
that his "endowment of immortal power is matched
unequally with custom, time, and domineering faculties
of sense" and that he is a weak child of ill-governed passions and immoderate wishes, the poet asks and answers:

> What then remains? To seek
> Those helps for his occasions ever near
> Who lacks not will to use them; vows, renewed
> On the first motion of a holy thought;
> Vigils of contemplation; praise; and prayer—
> A stream, which, from the fountain of the heart
> Issuing, however feebly, nowhere flows

> Without access of unexpected strength.
> But above all, the victory is most sure
> For him, who, seeking faith by virtue, strives
> To yield entire submission to the law
> Of conscience—conscience reverenced and obeyed,
> As God's most intimate presence in the soul,
> And His most perfect image in the world.
>
> (Book IV, lines 214-227)

Thus conscience, the will, and the feelings, form a single, central, constituent energy of the mind, which, in more general terms, Wordsworth sometimes calls "higher Reason" and sometimes "the imaginative Will." This unique force can never be separated into parts by analytic science. Wordsworth does not deny the validity of the discursive and analytic reason; only, in the light of intuitive Reason or imaginative Will, it is comparatively unimportant and must needs be held in restraint. As in *Intimations of Immortality* here again the imaginative Will, penetrative and indissoluble, postulates man's creative powers, freedom, and immortality.

The will is a disciplining, regulative, and energizing power. It is a mysterious active principle, by which man can make vows, hold vigils, live in the light of high endeavors, lift himself above himself and from "palpable oppressions of despair," and by which, amid all circumstances and changes of life, he can cleave to the law of Duty which links him forever with the Eternal. As in the *Ode to Duty* so here

> Possessions vanish, and opinions change,
> And passions hold a fluctuating seat:
> But by the storms of circumstance unshaken,
> And subject neither to eclipse nor wane,
> Duty exists;—immutably survive,
> For our support, the measures and the forms,
> Which an abstract intelligence supplies;
> Whose kingdom is, where time and space are not.
>
> (Book IV, lines 69-76)

The cardinal feelings are love, reverence, hope, humility, sorrow, and compassion—these humanize man. By self-discipline and "high endeavors" an individual may achieve a lofty eminence among his fellows, but at the same time become dangerously isolated. It is the feelings, particularly those of love and compassion, that give man his inheritance of common humanity. But how may men put themselves at the center of the transcendental law, wherein work together harmoniously the conscience, the feelings of humility and humanity, and the will, now submissive, now energetic, reaching upward to Heaven,

> How acquire
> The inward principle that gives effect
> To outward argument; the passive will
> Meek to admit; the active energy,
> Strong and unbounded to embrace, and firm
> To keep and cherish?   how shall man unite
> With self-forgetting tenderness of heart
> An earth-despising dignity of soul?
> Wise in that union, and without it blind!
>
> (Book V, lines 571-9)

Failure in life, then, attends all who do not possess this inward principle; nor is it easy to acquire, for

> Man is of dust: ethereal hopes are his,
> Which, when they should sustain themselves aloft,
> Want due consistence.   (Book IV, lines 140-3)

Nor is it acquired the same way by any two persons; yet its attainment lies open to all human beings:

> As men from men
> Do, in the constitution of their souls,
> Differ, by mystery not to be explained;
> And as we fall by various ways, and sink
> One deeper than another, self-condemned,
> Through manifold degrees of guilt and shame;
> So manifold and various are the ways
> Of restoration, fashioned to the steps

> Of all infirmity, and tending all
> To the same point, attainable by all—
> Peace in ourselves, and union with our God.
> (Book IV, lines 1107-16)

The many narratives of lives in *The Excursion,* especially in Books Sixth and Seventh, show the success, or half-success, or failure, of various individuals in striving toward the realization of the inward principle. One pair, man and wife, who with much toil had carved from a wilderness in the mountains a home for themselves, showed such high purposes and strength of devotion, and withal such contentment, that "true humility,"

> That best gift of heaven hath fallen on them;
> Abundant recompense for every want.
> (Book V, lines 720-1)

Another showed the quality of perseverance in a remarkable way in his untiring efforts to find precious ore in the mountains; but lacking a balance of qualities he became worthless the moment his perseverance brought him material wealth—an example of half-success.   But

> These elements of virtue, that declare
> The native grandeur of the human soul—
> Are oft-times not unprofitably shown
> In the perverseness of a selfish course.
> (Book VI, lines 665-8)

An illustration of this is a woman whose avaricious thrift and maternal love hopelessly mixed with jealousy caused her to sink into a woful state of moral degeneration.

Again, there are tales of those who suffer beyond their desert in this life.   Like Emily in *The White Doe of Rylstone,* these characters, in varying degrees, rise above their fate, and prove their worth to look forward to a happy immortality.   There are tales also of a blind man, a deaf man, and of other unfortunates.   These narratives

reveal the thoroughly democratic principle that the highest idealistic philosophy may function in the humblest
human beings, and that if man wills to have it so function
there is no room for pessimism in this life even though
outwardly the most disastrous events occur.   The way of
attaining the inward principle of compassion and moral
grandeur is made clear even to a man that has been as
sorely tried by tragic suffering as the Solitary.   These
tales, taken from actual facts, render "heart-felt truth,"

> Tending to patience when affliction strikes;
> To hope and love; to confident repose
> In God; and reverence for the dust of Man.
>
> (Book VII, lines 1055-8)

Nature is frequently used symbolically in *The Excursion:*

> Among these rocks and stones, methinks, I see
> More than the heedless impress that belongs
> To lonely nature's casual work: they bear
> A semblance strange of power intelligent,
> And of design not wholly worn away.
>
> (Book III, lines 80-4)

Thus in the famous passage (Book IV, lines 1132-47)
the ear of Faith listens for "authentic tidings of invisible
things" as a child listens to murmurings of the sea when
he applies his ear to a smooth-lipped shell.   Or again, in
his prayer to Deity the Pastor says:

> We, who—from the breast
> Of the frail earth, permitted to behold
> The faint reflections only of thy face—
> Are yet exalted, and in soul adore!
>
> (Book IX, lines 624-7)

Wordsworth is forced to use symbols in this way because,
in his view, Nature as an entity does not inclusively contain the entity God or the entity Man; yet the objects of

Nature are satisfactory emblems to picture for us his ideas of God and Man.

On the other hand, Nature is far from being a mere symbol, a static emblem, a mere reflector of something other than itself. At her very heart Nature contains an active principle that works similar to the active principle in man, only in a less degree. Though not in herself sufficient to reveal the highest mysteries of God and Man, Nature nevertheless, in her own right, is a vital force, a benign influence, supporting man, a mysterious aid in working out the destinies of the universe; she is a moving force and a moving panorama. What distinguishes Wordsworth as perhaps the greatest of all Nature poets is not so much that he interpreted Nature deeply and philosophically, nor that he has in the aggregate perceived accurately and rendered effectively the greatest number of Nature objects, but that from the beginning he pictured Nature not statically as the older poets were wont to do but rendered her dynamically.   It is not that Nature *is* but that she *acts*. A casual glance, for instance, at Wordsworth's use of verbs in his Nature poetry shows an extraordinarily preponderance of active to passive verbs:

> Where rivulets dance their wayward round,
> And beauty born of murmuring sound
> Shall pass into her face.

"Goings-on" is the key word to interpret Nature.   But what distinguishes Wordsworth's treatment of Nature in *The Excursion* from his earlier poems and makes it unique is that she is at once a symbol of things higher than herself and an active principle at the heart of life. His position is a reconciliation between extreme transcendentalism, like Coleridge's, in which Nature is only a symbol, and pure Naturalism, like that of his own earlier days, in which Nature herself was wholly sufficient.

That Nature contains an inward active principle and is beneficent, that man is a free moral agent and capable of attaining to immortality, that the highest excellencies of character may be achieved by the humblest, that God has created a beneficent universe and presides over all, are eloquently asserted in two long passages in the last book of *The Excursion* and are a sort of summary of Wordsworth's position. *The Excursion,* in brief, is mainly the *Intimations of Immortality* and the *Ode to Duty* written large:

> 'To every Form of being is assigned'
> Thus calmly spake the venerable Sage,
> 'An *active* Principle:—howe'er removed
> From sense and observation, it subsists
> In all things, in all natures; in the stars
> Of azure heaven, the unenduring clouds,
> In flower and tree, in every pebbly stone
> That paves the brooks, the stationary rocks,
> The moving waters, and the invisible air.
> Whate'er exists hath properties that spread
> Beyond itself, communicating good,
> A simple blessing, or with evil mixed;
> Spirit that knows no insulated spot,
> No chasm, no solitude; from link to link
> It circulates, the Soul of all the worlds.
> This is the freedom of the universe;
> Unfolded still the more, more visible,
> The more we know; and yet is reverenced least,
> And least respected in the human Mind,
> Its most apparent home'. (lines 1-20)
> . . . . . The sun is fixed,
> And the infinite magnificence of heaven
> Fixed, within reach of every human eye;
> The sleepless ocean murmurs for all ears;
> The vernal field infuses fresh delight
> Into all hearts. Throughout the world of sense,
> Even as an object is sublime or fair,
> That object is laid open to the view

> Without reserve or veil; and as a power
> Is salutary, or an influence sweet,
> Are each and all enabled to perceive
> That power, that influence, by impartial law.
> Gifts nobler are vouchsafed alike to all;
> Reason, and, with that reason, smiles and tears;
> Imagination, freedom in the will;
> Conscience to guide and check; and death to be
> Foretasted, immortality conceived
> By all,—a blissful immortality,
> To them whose holiness on earth shall make
> The Spirit capable of heaven, assured.
> Strange, then, nor less than monstrous might be deemed
> The failure, if the Almighty, to this point
> Liberal and undistinguishing, should hide
> The excellence of moral qualities
> From common understanding; leaving truth
> And virtue, difficult, abstruse, and dark;
> Hard to be won, and only by a few;
> Strange, should He deal herein with nice respects,
> And frustrate all the rest! Believe it not;
> The primal duties shine aloft—like stars;
> The charities that soothe, and heal, and bless,
> Are scattered at the feet of Man—like flowers.

(lines 209-240)

This philosophy of religious idealism is reconciled with orthodox Christianity in the prayer of the Parson at the close of *The Excursion.* The objects of Nature, beautiful but transitory, are sanctified as symbols of the Eternal Spirit; the Bible is proclaimed as revealing the moral law "working through love"; moral and spiritual progress proceed from belief in "the true and only God, and from the faith derived through Him who bled upon the cross"; the soul, with immortal "energy of love," has the power to triumph over sin and guilt and fleshly limitations.

In the Sonnet *After-Thought* at the close of a series of sonnets on *The Duddon River* (1820) Wordsworth

again asserts the inward, transcendent Faith of the heart.
Man claims a greater immortality than the brook that
flows at his feet; but in comparison to the permanence of
a brook in its form and function man's life seems frail
and brief. Against the conclusion based on knowledge
of appearances and outward facts is the conclusion of an
unerring constituent intuition of the mind:

> While we, the brave, the mighty, and the wise,
> We Men, who in our morn of youth defied
> The elements, must vanish;—be it so!
> Enough, if something from our hands have power
> To live, and act, and serve the future hour;
> And if, as toward the silent tomb we go,
> Through love, through hope, and faith's transcendent dower,
> We feel that we are greater than we know.

V

In *Ecclesiastical Sonnets* (1821), a cycle of one hundred and thirty-two sonnets, Wordsworth dealt with a
Christian religious theme from an historical and institutional point of view. "My purpose," he says, "in writing this Series, was as much as possible to confine my view
to the introduction, progress and operation of the Church
of England, both previous and subsequent to the Ref-
ormation." Being institutional and implying historical
sequences, the subject does not lend itself readily to the
poet who usually composes from reproducing powerful
emotions recollected in tranquility. A glance at some of
the topics, such as conversion, baptism, confirmation, the
sacrament, and at single sonnet titles—*Saxon Conquest,
Crusades, Gunpowder Plot,* etc.—suggests that not often
do deep feeling and imagination and thought conspire together to produce a really creative sonnet impregnated
with religious beauty and emotion. There are many

adaptations, without special originality, of phrases from
the Scriptures, such as,—"the pictured Saviour," "evidence of things not seen," "temples of their hearts,"
"grace descending from above," "Glory to God," etc.
Occasionally, however, when a sonnet topic is somewhat
detached from the sequence and its subject gives the
author a chance to bring his personal self to bear upon it
he produces characteristic work, as in the Sonnet *Mutability*.   Besides, in this series as a whole there is manifest
such a purely objective mastery of technique, such an
objective force of intellect equipped with learning, such a
devoutness of spirit toward traditional religion, such
tranquility of soul, as extorts the reader's intellectual
respect for the work and its author.

The *Ecclesiastical Sonnets* are less important as revealing Wordsworth's religious philosophy, for they do that
only imperfectly, than as revealing a special type of his
religious sympathy.   The principles of Christianity, as
he understood them, had long engaged his profoundest
interest, and were the foundation of some of his greatest
poems; but now he included in the circle of his interest
historic and traditional Christianity.   So far as *Ecclesiastical Sonnets* present fundamental religious principles
they are noticeably like those of *The Excursion,* and suggest no break from the poem to the sonnets.

In fact, *Ecclesiastical Sonnets* and practically all of
Wordsworth's subsequent poetry, which becomes increasingly more religious, is a natural outgrowth of the
principles exemplified in *The Excursion.*   There are many
poems, a few examples of which are *To a Skylark, Composed upon an Evening of Extraordinary Splendour and
Beauty, Presentiments, Devotional Incitements, If This
Great World of Joy and Pain, Humanity, On a High*

Part of the Coast of Cumberland, that would crown a
lesser poet with laurels.   They have an artistic finish,
grace, and devoutness, that often remind one of the
Puritan religious poets of the seventeenth century.

In *Humanity* (1829) Wordsworth again asserts the
interaction, interdependence, and spiritual relations of
Man and Nature and Deity:

> Not from his fellows only man may learn
> Rights to compare and duties to discern!
> All creatures and all objects, in degree,
> Are friends and patrons of humanity.
> There are to whom the garden, grove, and field,
> Perpetual lessons of forbearance yield;
> Who would not lightly violate the grace
> The lowliest flower possesses in its place;
> Nor shorten the sweet life too fugitive,
> Which nothing less than Infinite Power could give.

In *The Primrose of the Rock* (1830) he again emphasizes the universal law that binds the small to the great
in the widest sweep of the universe, with Deity transcend-
ing the law:

> The flowers, still faithful to the stems,
>   Their fellowship renew;
> The stems are faithful to the root,
>   That worketh out of view;
> And to the rock the root adheres
>   In every fibre true.
>
> Close clings to earth the living rock,
>   Though threatening still to fall;
> The earth is constant to her sphere;
>   And God upholds them all.

And in a Sonnet *Desire We Past Illusions,* etc. (1833) he
once more uniquely contrasts the impotence of the discursive reason with the power of the inward imaginative
intuition of the mind—the theme of many of his greater

poems. It represents the final stage of his spiritual development:

> The universe is infinitely wide;
> And conquering Reason, if self-glorified,
> Can nowhere move uncrossed by some new wall
> Or gulf of mystery, which thou alone,
> Imaginative Faith! canst overleap,
> In progress toward the fount of Love,—the throne
> Of Power whose ministers the records keep
> Of periods fixed, and laws established, less
> Flesh to exalt than prove its nothingness.

In the *Lyrical Ballads* of 1798 Wordsworth began with the conception of immanence—a mystic Presence as a divinity in Nature and in the heart of man. This he likewise maintained in later years, only presenting it in more orthodox terms. Throughout also he placed emphasis on the inviolability of personality and the growth of the individual. These are the most important principles in his religious philosophy and indicate the fundamental consistence of his spiritual development. But whereas, in his earlier years, he conceived Deity immanent as an impersonal force, a motion and a spirit that impels all thinking things, and Nature as coequal with Deity, he later gradually came to conceive Deity as a personal entity above Nature, though still working as an active principle through Nature. In a parallel way he by slow degrees began to conceive man as "instinct with godhead" that gives him free-will and places him above Nature both in origin and destiny, though on the one hand he is properly subordinate to Deity "acknowledging dependency sublime" and on the other in close sympathy and communion with the objects of Nature and with his fellowmen. This growth, or change, in him was the cause of the development of his theory of knowledge.

In the early period he accepted the theory of the eighteenth century masters that knowledge is derived from sensation; but he soon began to conceive of thought as having no beginning, as being spiritual in origin and character. Knowledge is both intuitive and discursive. Intuitive knowledge, like the soul, has elsewhere its setting and comes from afar; the mind is essentially transcendent in character. This change in him was also, if not the sole cause, certainly a determining influence on his political and social views. His fundamental conceptions and his particular personal and political experiences undoubtedly acted and reacted on each other. To comprehend the poet aright they must be studied together; together they reveal a unity of development. With the principles of immanence and of individualism running throughout his work and with the principle of transcendence appearing in it fairly early and harmonizing it with liberal Christianity with the spirit of which it was implicitly inspired from the beginning, Wordsworth created a large body of poetry of religious idealism, which, with the teachings of Coleridge, had a mighty influence in determining the current of thought of the nineteenth century.

SHELLEY

SHELLEY

Among the great poets of the early part of the nineteenth century Shelley and Byron were both poets of
religious as well as of political and social revolt. Their
attacks were directed, not in the main against religion and
society as such, but against the established conventions
of religion and society. As regards their feelings—interest in Nature, love of unfettered freedom, etc.—and the
free and personal expression of them they were children
of the nineteenth century, but as regards their thought—
its sources and grounds—they were true products of the
eighteenth century. Byron early and late was a partisan
of the school of Pope, and poems like the *Essay on Man*
contained the type of thinking on the whole best suited
to his mind. Shelley early absorbed the writings of
eighteenth century philosophers—French and English—
and adopted outright as his spiritual leader and guide one
of the latest of them—William Godwin. In this day it
is difficult to conceive how profoundly the youth of the
latter part of the eighteenth and the beginning of the
nineteenth century were influenced by such writers as
Locke and Hume, Voltaire and Pope. As Wordsworth
and Coleridge began their work wholly in the spirit of the
eighteenth century tradition, so did Byron and Shelley.
But whereas Wordsworth and Coleridge effected a constructive reaction against that tradition, Byron and Shelley, either because of their youth or because of lack of
original constructive philosophical thinking, never at-

tained to a clear philosophic conversion from their early masters. To be sure Shelley intermixed a number of Platonic ideas with his own creations; but so did Coleridge in his youth. Yet had Coleridge died at the age of twenty-nine (Shelley died at that age), no one would consider him a Platonist. The claim, made by various Shelley enthusiasts, that Shelley inherited the mantle of Plato is extravagant, to say the least.

It is a striking fact about Shelley that his mind was preoccupied, especially in the formative years of his life, with the subject of religion, and it is significant that the piece of writing which first attracted any considerable attention to him was the essay *The Necessity of Atheism*, published in 1811 when he was eighteen and a student at Oxford. The essay not only is revolutionary in spirit, but also reveals a mind precociously occupied with religious problems. It furnishes the starting point for the study of the growth of the poet's mind.

With condensed expression and close-knit argument the essay attempts briefly to prove nothing less than the nonexistence of Deity. The proof to Shelley seemed easy: there are only three sources of evidence—the senses, reason, and testimony—and these do not suffice to establish belief. The major premise in the essay is really the common eighteenth century dictum that "the senses are the sources of all knowledge to the mind." If we grant this, the argument is logical enough. Shelley, of course, had no doubt of its validity. Yet the truly religious mind, which believes in the primacy of the Spirit over the senses, cannot accept it as valid. It is easier to believe in the existence of Deity than in Shelley's major premise.

In a letter to Elizabeth Hitchener, written in June, 1811, several months after the publication of *The Neces-*

sity of Atheism, Shelley reveals what was probably the
direct source of the major premise in his essay:

> Locke proves that there are no innate ideas, that in consequence,
> there can be no innate speculative or practical principles, thus over-
> turning all appeals of *feeling* in favor of Deity, since that feeling must
> be referable to some origin. There must have been a time when it
> did not exist; in consequence, a time when it began to exist. Since
> all ideas are derived from the senses, this feeling must have originated
> from some sensual excitation, consequently the possessor of it may be
> aware of the time, of the circumstances, attending its commencement.
> Locke proves this by induction too clearly to admit of rational ob-
> jection.[1]

That is to say, the feeling men have for Deity, arising
from a sensual excitation that can be traced to a specific
point of time, proves only a certain psychological process
of the mind and nothing whatever concerning the existence of Deity.

It is also to be noted that twice in the essay Shelley
asserts that "belief is not an act of volition" and that
therefore "no degree of criminality is attachable to disbelief." And in a letter to his father dated February 8,
1811, first published by F. Ingpen in his *Shelley in England* (1917), he attacked Christianity on the same
grounds. Of the coming of Christ as being called good
tidings, he says: "It is hard to believe how those tidings
could be *good* which are to condemn more than half of
the world to the Devil, for, as St. Athanasius says, 'He
who does not believe should go into eternal fire'—as if
belief were voluntary, or an action, not a passion (as it
is) of the mind." Accordingly, to him who perceives
that belief is purely involuntary and who considers there

[1] In another letter to Miss Hitchener, dated June 25, 1811, and in
still another to her, dated Aug. 18, 1811, he repeats these references to
Locke's arguments against innate ideas.

is insufficient testimony to prove the being of Deity, atheism is a necessity.

In the many letters Shelley wrote to Miss Hitchener between June, 1811, and June, 1812, inclusive, there is revealed a growing dislike of Christianity which was to burst forth in full intensity and power a little later in *Queen Mab*. This development of his hatred of Christianity is accompanied, curiously enough, by a growth in his views toward, rather than away from, the tenets of the Christian faith. He is now willing, for instance, to admit the existence of Deity, provided you believe in his kind of Deity:

"I have lately had some conversation with Southey which has elicited my true opinion of God. He says I ought not to call myself an atheist, since in reality I believe that the universe is God. I tell him I believe that God is another signification for the Universe. I then explain:—I think reason and analogy seem to countenance the opinion that life is infinite; that, as the soul which now animates this frame was once the vivifying principle of the infinitely lowest link in the chain of existence, so it is ultimately destined to attain the highest; that everything is animation (as explained in my last letter;) and, in consequence, being infinite, we can never arrive at its termination. How, on this hypothesis, are we to arrive at a First Cause? . . . Southey agrees in my idea of Deity,—the mass of infinite intelligence; I, you, and he, are constituent parts of this immeasurable whole" (Letter to Miss Hitchener, Jan. 2, 1812).

Likewise he asserts his belief in a certain kind of immortality:

As I conceive (and as is certainly capable of demonstration) that nothing can be annihilated, but that everything appertaining to nature, consisting of constituent parts infinitely divisible, is in a continual change, then do I suppose—and I think I have a right to draw this inference—that neither will soul perish; that in a future existence it will lose all consciousness of having formerly lived elsewhere,—will begin life anew, possibly under a shape of which we have no idea (Letter to Miss Hitchener, June 20, 1811).

This view of immortality as animate but impersonal is remarkably similar to that set forth just ten years later in the forty-second and forty-third stanzas of *Adonais*.

But it is the poem *Queen Mab* and the notes appended thereto, printed in 1818, that comprise Shelley's first sustained effort to express the whole of his mind. The poem is notorious as containing an outspoken attack on Christianity. According to the degree of seriousness with which we consider the matter we may either smile or become righteously indignant at his invectives against that religion which he describes as peopling "earth with demons, hell with men, and heaven with slaves."

More important and interesting, however, than the attack itself are the philosophical grounds upon which it is made. At the age of nineteen or twenty Shelley would have scorned the idea of not being able to give a completely rational account of the faith that was in him. "The doctrine of Necessity," he says, "tends to introduce a great change into the established notions of morality, and utterly to destroy religion:"

> Spirit of Nature! all-sufficing Power,
> Necessity! thou mother of the world!
> Unlike the God of human error, thou
> Requirest no prayers or praises.

This is precisely like Coleridge's youthful address to a Necessitarian Deity—

> Of whose omniscient and all-spreading Love
> Aught to implore were impotence of mind—

and is undoubtedly derived from the same general source.

In the more philosophical passages the poet emphasizes the conviction that man and all things, from every atom, "sentient both in unity and part," from "the meanest worm that crawls in dust," to the "interminable wilderness of worlds, at whose immensity even soaring fancy staggers," that all pain and pleasure, all good and evil, "join to do the will of strong Necessity."

There is no question but that at the time of writing the author considered the moral and religious deductions to be made from the poem far more important than its imaginative beauty.   Hence, the "notes."   In a letter to Mr. Hookam, the publisher, in January, 1813, he says: "The notes to 'Q.M.' will be long and philosophical. I shall take the opportunity, which I judge to be a safe one, of propagating my principles, which I decline to do syllogistically in a poem."   In the notes he says:

He who asserts the doctrine of Necessity means that, contemplating the events which compose the moral and material universe, he beholds only an immense and uninterrupted chain of causes and effects, no one of which could occupy any other place than it does occupy, or act in any other place than it does act. . . . Every human being is irresistibly impelled to act precisely as he does act; in the eternity which preceded his birth a chain of causes was generated, which, operating under the name of motives, make it impossible that any thought of his mind, or any action of his life, should be otherwise than it is.

It is well known that Shelley derived many of his doctrines directly from William Godwin's *Political Justice*.[2]   Yet we cannot help being slightly shocked, as

[2] It is clear that Godwin attached very great importance to these views, a point which Shelley could not have overlooked. In the introductory statements in the chapters on *Free Will and Necessity*, Godwin remarks: "It will be found upon maturer reflection that this doctrine of moral necessity includes in it consequences of the highest moment, and leads to a bold and comprehensive view of man and society, which cannot possibly be entertained by him who has embraced the opposite opinion." He also asserts that all his reasoning is based on this doctrine as a major premise.

in this particular instance, to note how the poet echoes the very words of his master. In *Political Justice* we read:

> He who affirms that all actions are necessary, means, that, if we form a just and complete view of all the circumstances in which a living or intelligent being is placed, we shall find that he could not in any moment of his existence have acted otherwise than he has acted. . . . This view of things presents us with an idea of the universe as connected and cemented in all its parts, nothing in the boundless progress of things being capable of happening otherwise than it has actually happened. In the life of every human being there is a chain of causes, generated in that eternity which preceded his birth, and going on in regular procession through the whole period of his existence, in consequence of which it was impossible for him to act in any instance otherwise than he has acted.

A sort of corollary to this doctrine is Shelley's theory that there is no creative mind in the universe. The negation in the poem, "there is no God," Shelley says in the notes, "must be understood solely to affect a creative Deity. The hypothesis of a pervading Spirit coeternal with the universe remains unshaken." This Spirit, which has existed from all eternity and from which flows all life, has no power to make things. That it created the world is a pure superstition, Shelley holds, and the creature of this superstition is the God of the popular religion.[3]

[3] In *The Revolt of Islam* (1817) Shelley says that the idea of the Christian God arose through a wholly subjective experience of pure delusion:

> Some moon-struck sophist stood
> Watching the shade from his own soul upthrown
> Fill Heaven and darken Earth, and in such mood
> The Form he saw and worshipped was his own,
> His likeness in the world's vast mirror shown:
> And 'twere an innocent dream, but that a faith
> Nursed by fear's dew of poison grows thereon.
> —Canto VIII, Stanza VI.

And at this point in the notes there is incorporated the main body of the essay, *The Necessity of Atheism,* with slight modification in expression and occasionally in idea. One significant change occurs in the use of a single word. In the original essay Shelley had said in conclusion that "the mind cannot believe in the existence of a God." In the notes he changed this to—"the mind cannot believe in the existence of a *creative* God." Shelley had now grown to recognize the limitations of his original negation and believed in a living and animating Spirit pervading the frame of things. That is, he was not an atheist, as Southey had told him.

Looking back, then, from *Queen Mab* to *The Necessity of Atheism* one can see that from the beginning the vital thought with Shelley was not Atheism but Necessity. It is necessary that every thought of the mind and every act of life be just what they are, that the mind believe only that which it thinks true, that rewards and punishments based on belief are tyranny, that no personal responsibility really exists, that, in short, Necessity governs all life.

In the imaginative passages of *Queen Mab* this law of Necessity is transformed into a vast and all-pervading Spirit, Soul of the Universe, which in its onward flow of being, from the lowest to the highest links in the chain of existence, is preparing the world for some sudden desirable consummation. Though not perfectly fused with the argumentative elements of the poem, these passages have a poetical atmosphere not to be found in Godwin at all.

In the more polemical parts of the poem and in the notes the poet, as we have seen, on the basis of Necessity, violently attacked Christianity, and also kings and priests and institutions, which he conceived to have been produced by Christianity. The God of the Christian religion commands us to believe certain definite things and threatens our disbelief with everlasting punishment. Christianity assumes "that it is in our power to believe or not to believe; whereas the mind can only believe that which it thinks true." Belief being involuntary, the Christian religion attaches the highest possible degree of merit and demerit to that which is worthy of neither. A philosopher of our own day, the late William James, with his "will to believe," would have been incomprehensible to the philosopher Shelley a hundred years ago.

Godwin said that "man is really a passive and not an active being," and devoted one long chapter in *Political Justice* to prove that the mind is merely a mechanism and that even in volition it is altogether passive. Shelley accepted without qualification the doctrine of his master. It seems in dealing with the principle of Necessity in *Queen Mab,* Shelley was not fully aware that he was handling a two-edged sword. For why should kings and priests and Christians be held responsible for their terrible deeds when, according to the theory of Necessity, they were irresistibly impelled to act precisely as they did act? This, indeed, is the fundamental contradiction in the poem. If Shelley was utterly ineffectual in matters of practical reform it was because he appealed to a principle of belief that has not the remotest connection with the springs of human action.

Shelley's acceptance of the doctrine of Necessity was a temperamental need and not due wholly to chance acquaintance with Godwin's works at a favorable moment in his youth. To conceive of power in terms of personality was instinctively difficult for him; hence the abstractness and utter impersonality of the law of Necessity appealed to him. Then, too, he always longed intensely for a changeless state in a changing world, an immutable and eternal order of things. The conception, therefore, of a pervading spirit coeternal with the universe, never having been created, never to be destroyed, necessary in all its outer activities, with which "is no variableness, neither shadow of turning," seemed the very fulfillment of such intense longings. "The One remains, the many change and pass," he said in a famous figure in *Adonais* written in the mature years of his life. This doctrine also reduces the explanation of the universe to a single principle. To Shelley, who never was able to measure the complex forces that make up human life, the simplicity of this view commended itself.

The doctrine of Necessity had influenced Wordsworth and Coleridge in their youth, the former lightly, the latter seriously; but each turned to opposite views in their mature years. Unlike them, Shelley did not experience any change of heart as regards Necessity. And here one may take issue with various interpreters of Shelley. They say he was materialistic and necessitarian in *Queen Mab,* of course, but as soon as he had outgrown bad boyishness he embraced a philosophy that supersedes and contradicts his juvenile beliefs. True, he swiftly outgrew his early materialism. Indeed, he was not altogether materialistic even when he wrote *Queen Mab,* as the following passage alone proves:

> Throughout this varied and eternal world
> Soul is the only element: the block
> That for uncounted ages has remained
> The moveless pillar of a mountain's weight
> Is active, living spirit.

But on Necessity he never changed his attitude fundamentally. This principle stood to the last in the background of his mind, exercising a shaping and controlling influence over his thought. Naturally, in so poetic and subtilizing a mind as Shelley's, so unpoetic a principle as Necessity underwent many refining modifications. Never again did he render it so crudely and obtrusively as in *Queen Mab,* but wrought it subtly and suggestively into the whole of his composition. Always ignoring some of the grim implications of the law of Necessity, the poet aetherialized it into a vast and indefinite spirit of ideas and being.

The passage just quoted from *Queen Mab* is noteworthy as indicating how early Shelley was inclined to ascribe a greater reality to the immaterial than to the material world; wherein, it has often been pointed out, he is like Plato.[4] But, governed by the law of Necessity, the animating Spirit of this supersensuous world is

[4] In an article, *Platonism in Shelley,* in *Essays and Studies* (Vol. IV, 1913), L. Winstanley presents some striking similarities between passages from Plato and from Shelley. However, many of the Shelley passages, some of which are quoted in the present essay, are in substance less like Plato than Godwin. It is also obvious that Shelley was especially enamoured by the more fantastic parts of Plato, as, for instance, the idea of pre-existence, a preceding Golden Age, alternate periods of order and disorder, etc. Miss Winstanley's oft-repeated statement, in its various forms, "Shelley has embodied all these conceptions in his poetry," seems a little absurd. For Plato, "first among the preparatory preceptors of Christianity," lays special stress on intellectual discipline, travail, and growth necessary to attain the Beautiful and the Good, which is foreign to Shelley. Much of the mist hovering about Shelley's youthful ideas of the Good is dispelled, for example, by a single sentence from Plato's *Republic*: "Whether I am right or not God only knows; but, whether true or false, my opinion is that in the world of knowledge the idea of good appears last of all, and is seen only with an effort."

devoid of will and personality and as such is unethical, wherein Shelley is essentially unlike Plato. Shelley's world is unquestionably full of Platonic forms, but it is also unquestionably impregnated with Godwinian teachings. What seems true is that Shelley attempted to graft Platonic forms on the Godwinian doctrine of Necessity. Godwin was his real master.

In the prose treatise, *A Refutation of Deism,* written in 1814, Shelley's first important production after *Queen Mab,* there is scarcely any modification of the point of view of the poem. In the essay Shelley repeats *verbatim* large portions of the notes to *Queen Mab,* which in turn had been quoted from *The Necessity of Atheism.* These persistent repetitions indicate how deeply ingrained such thoughts were in Shelley.

The essay is developed in the form of an argument between Eusebes, a Christian, and Theosophus, a Deist. The latter attacks Christianity as vehemently as Shelley in *Queen Mab,* and on precisely the same grounds. Especially does he assert that belief, which is a passion, cannot be set up as a criterion of merit and demerit, as is done by Christianity. Eusebes replies, not with a defense of Christianity, but with a vigorous indictment of Deism, in order to force the Deist to accept either Christianity or the alternative, "a cold and dreary atheism."

The Deist bases the argument for his belief in God on the principle of design in Nature. For the sake of the argument the Christian takes the point of view of a professed atheist, and proceeds to destroy the theory of design.

Design presupposes a designer, who may exercise either an arbitrary or a creative will on the Universe, which the atheistical view cannot allow. These negations leave only a law of Necessity to govern all things. At the crux of the argument Eusebes says:

From the fitness of the Universe to its end you infer the necessity of an intelligent Creator. But if the fitness of the Universe, to produce certain effects, be thus conspicuous and evident, how much more exquisite fitness to his end must exist in the Author of this Universe? If we find great difficulty from its admirable arrangement, in conceiving that the Universe has existed from all eternity, and to resolve this difficulty suppose a Creator, how much more clearly must we perceive the necessity of this very Creator's creation whose perfections comprehend an arrangement far more accurate and just. The belief of an infinity of creative and created Gods, each more eminently requiring an intelligent author of his being than the foregoing, is the direct consequence of the premise which you have stated. The assumption that the Universe is a design, leads to a conclusion that there are infinity of creative and created Gods, which is absurd.

After reducing the idea of design to an absurdity, Eusebes concludes that since the Deist considers that the chief characteristic of Deity is intelligence, which has been proved to be a mode of animal being, his God is nothing more than "a vast and wise animal."

The essay closes with a remarkable promise on the part of the Deist:

I am willing to promise that if, after mature deliberation, the argument which you have advanced in favor of Atheism should appear incontrovertible, I will endeavor to adopt so much of the Christian scheme as is consistent with my persuasion of the goodness, unity and majesty of God.

This is remarkable as standing at the close of the last of Shelley's strictly controversial essays. He has, so to speak, come to the end of his argument; Deism has been weighed and found wanting. The arguments of Atheism seem incontrovertible, but the religion of Atheism is too arid, cold, and dreary for acceptance. Some kind of compromise must be made between its irrefutable reasonings and the Christian scheme. This compromise is attempted in the fragmentary *Essay on Christianity,* conjecturally written in 1815.

This essay is noteworthy as being much more sympathetic toward Christianity than anything of Shelley's that precedes it. Here he attempts to show that Jesus' conception of God was very similar to his own: "It is important to observe that the author of the Christian system had a conception widely differing from the gross imaginations of the vulgar relatively to the ruling Power of the universe. He everywhere represents this Power as something mysteriously and illimitably pervading the frame of things." And again: "He [Christ] considered the venerable word [God] to express the overruling Spirit of the collective energy of the moral and material world." Shelley grudgingly admits that Jesus attributed to this Power the faculty of Will, which is not to Shelley's liking. Yet he charitably conjectures that in so speaking of this Power Jesus "intentionally availed himself of a metaphor easily understood." The implication is that Jesus must have viewed God in a strictly necessitarian spirit.

On the other hand, there is expressed in this essay a tendency toward dualism. Even in the passages in *Queen Mab* that deal with reform, where the poet needs must picture a word of struggle between good and evil, there is a tendency to slip away from that necessitarian view of the universe in which everything is connected and cemented in all its parts and nothing capable of happening otherwise than it has happened. Likewise in this essay he conceives that, "according to Jesus Christ and according to the indisputable facts in the case, some evil spirit has dominion in this imperfect world. But there will come a time when the human mind shall be visited exclusively by the influences of the Benignant Power." Jesus, Shelley conceives, was one who was constantly visited by this Power, and who, by purity and goodness, by love and compassion, and by teaching and persuading, opposed the tyrants of this world and thereby forfeited his life. However, this tendency to dualism Shelley subordinates to the conception of that necessitarian power which is "the uniform and unchanging motive of the salutary operations of the material world."

Though in *Queen Mab,* Shelley considered Jesus the author of much evil in the world, he yet there pays tribute to the purity of his life. But now he attests the truth and beauty of his teachings, not only as regards human life, and attempts to harmonize those teachings with his own views. "That those," he says, "who are pure in heart shall see God, and that virtue is its own reward (a Shelleyan doctrine), may be considered equivalent assertions." And the precepts: "Be ye perfect," and "refrain from revenge and retribution," are harmonized with Shelley's views of man's ultimate perfectibility. "We discover," Shelley also asserts, "that He [Christ] is the enemy of oppression and falsehood; that he is the advocate of equal justice; that he is neither disposed to sanction bloodshed nor deceit, under whatsoever pretences their practices may be vindicated. We discover that he was a man of meek and majestic demeanor, calm in danger; of natural and simple thought and habits; beloved to adoration by his adherents; unmoved, solemn and severe."

But in this essay, as well as elsewhere, historic Christianity fares ill at the hands of Shelley, for he considers it to have perverted the teachings of Jesus to superstition and tyranny.   Rightly understood, these teachings, Shelley thinks, are a high expression of the eternal laws of Nature and Necessity:

> The universal Being can only be described and defined by negatives which deny his subjection to the laws of all inferior existences. Where indefiniteness ends, idolatry and anthropomorphism begin. . . . The doctrine of what some fanatics have termed "a peculiar providence"— that is, of some power beyond and superior to that which ordinarily guides the operations of the Universe, interfering to punish the vicious and reward the virtuous—is explicitly denied by Jesus Christ.

—a rather astonishing necessitarian interpretation of the moral teachings of Christ.

The poem *Alastor*, written also in 1815, strikes a similar note.   This poem deals with destiny, but with no special providences.   A passage from the *Essay on Christianity* may serve as a key: "Human life, with all its unreal ills and transitory hopes, is as a dream, which departs before the dawn, leaving no trace of its evanescent hues.   All that it contains of pure or of divine visits the passive mind in some serenest mood."   The two dominant characteristics of the hero are that he is a lone dreamer and that he has the strictly receptive or passive mind, exercising no choice as to his destiny.   He is one who has been deeply impressed by the beauty and magnificence of the external world, has drunk "deep of the fountain of knowledge and is still insatiate," and has seen "the thrilling birth of time."   Says Shelley in the preface: "So long as it is possible for his desires to point towards objects thus infinite and unmeasured, he is joyous, and tranquil, and self-possessed."   But Fate by means of a dream presents to his mind the vision of perfect love in the form of a beautiful maiden.   This vision, though unbidden, is the deciding factor in his life. Having spurned the choicest though imperfect gift which human love offers, he is now and henceforth destined, either with or against his will, to seek for a prototype of his conception of perfection, the infinite in the finite, the eternal in the concrete. In pursuit of this unattainable ideal he roams over the face of the earth. His wanderings through strange lands remind one of the Ancient Mariner's journeyings over strange seas. Both are phantom characters, although the Mariner is much more intensely realized. Both are impelled by powers over which they have no control. But the hero of Shelley's poem, having no belief in special providence or in rewards and punishments, is utterly devoid of moral characteristics. Driven by the force of his own dreams of unattainable perfection, he wanders from place to place. "Blasted by his disappointment, he descends to an untimely grave (preface)."

In the lofty introductory passages of the poem Shelley addresses the "Mother of this unfathomable world," which is no other than the "Spirit of Nature! all-sufficing Power, Necessity," of *Queen Mab*. But here that spirit of Nature, or Soul of the Universe, is more subtly and pervasively rendered. In the favorite figure of the lyre, wholly passive, the poet submits himself to the inspirations and workings of that inscrutable and necessitarian power:

> Serenely now,
> And moveless, as a long forgotten lyre
> Suspended in the solitary dome
> Of some mysterious and deserted fane,
> I wait thy breath, Great Parent.

This principle of Necessity, or Soul of the Universe, is rendered in terms of Beauty in the *Hymn to Intellectual Beauty,* written in 1816. Though Shelley's conception of Beauty in its purely intellectual aspect is certainly influenced by Plato's Beauty as Idea, yet Shelley conceives of Beauty as a Spirit that can hardly be distinguished from the Spirit of Nature of *Queen Mab* and *Alastor* and that works inscrutably on his passive mind:

> Thus let thy power, which like the truth
> Of nature on my passive youth
> Descended, to my onward life supply
> Its calm—to one who worships thee.

The Spirit of Beauty is so supernal and ineffable that no man can see it and live; only its shadow visits this world and also each human heart and countenance, consecrating all it shines upon. And when in a memorable moment in the poet's life the shadow of that Spirit fell upon him he shrieked and clasped his hands in ecastasy, denounced again the poisonous names Christianity had taught him in his youth, and dedicated himself to that Vast Form of Awful Loveliness, which will in time, he thinks, free this world from its dark slavery.

This again indicates that Shelley's approach to Beauty is almost diametrically opposite to Plato's. For Plato urges the advocate of Beauty to begin by making a single form the object of his love, and proceed as on steps from the love of one form to that of two, and from that of two to all forms, point by point through a self-discipline of the mind by its constantly making contrasts in values of the different forms of beauty, until by a long process of chastening it to its proper selections the mind at last arrives "at that which is nothing else than the doctrine of the supreme beauty itself." Shelley on the contrary, without any "former labour" upon which Plato lays so much stress, arrives, by a sort of instantaneous conversion, suddenly into a full sense of the meaning of the absolute Beauty. Plato proceeds from the simple and concrete to the complex and abstract by "contemplating beautiful objects gradually, and in their order;" Shelley flies straight to the empyrean, and, discovering the Abstract Beauty, conceives the Divinity as subtly and as from afar operating for the good of this dense world by supplanting its ugliness, deformity, disproportion, and darkness, with a new super-Harmony of light and love and life, a prophecy of a far-off millenium. Though Shelley was not a modern Plato he was uniquely himself.

Some critics have found similarities between this poem and Wordsworth's *Intimations of Immortality*. But Wordsworth really worshipped at a different shrine. He raised his song of thanks and praise for those first-born affections in us, for the fact that the child is father of the man, for "the primal sympathy, which having been, must ever be,"—in brief, for the human heart by which we live, its tenderness, its joys and fears. He emphasized the individual worth of the soul on the basis of certain central and indestructible qualities which reside in it, and which are the real roots of man's spiritual freedom. In Shelley's *Hymn*, on the other hand, personality has but a phantasmal existence." [5]

Likewise in the poem *Mont Blanc*, also written in 1816, Shelley muses on his "own separate phantasy," his passive mind, as he calls it, through which flows "the

[5] Compare the following from *A Refutation of Deism*: "Mind cannot create, it can only perceive. Mind is the recipient of impressions made on the organs of sense, and without the action of external objects we should not only be deprived of the existence of mind, but totally incapable of the knowledge of anything. It is evident therefore that mind deserves to be considered as the effect, rather than the cause, of motion." If the individual mind is indeed no more than that, then we truly are but "phantoms" in our personal existence.

everlasting universe of things," and with what different results from those obtained by Wordsworth! In *Mont Blanc* we are told that personality itself is but a phantom and that all things that move and breathe with toil and sound live and die, and pass away, and that the adverting mind is taught that

> Power dwells apart in its tranquillity
> Remote, serene, and inaccessible,

governing, however, in its secret strength by a Law of Necessity, thought, and life, and being. Thus Necessity is here rendered in terms of Power.

It has already been noted that in *Queen Mab* and in the *Essay on Christianity* there was a modification of this view toward dualism. Since both the poem and the essay deal with reform and reformers, it is natural that such a tendency should appear. Likewise in *The Revolt of Islam,* written in 1817, which is even more than *Queen Mab* a reform poem, though not so crude a one, the dualistic view is quite naturally emphasized:

> Know then that from the depth of ages old
> Two Powers o'er mortal things dominion hold,
> Ruling the world with a divided lot,—
> Immortal, all-pervading, manifold,
> Twin Genii, equal Gods—when life and thought
> Sprang forth, then burst the womb of inessential Nought.
> —Canto I, Stanza XXV.

These powers are the Spirit of Evil and the Spirit of Good. The former is represented by the priests and the tyrants in the poem; the latter by the characters Laon and Cythna. But these two characters are merely passive, obedient only to the Spirit of Good. They love and suffer and forgive and endure, and seal their lives in martyrdom for the cause of good. The struggle is really not so much a struggle between Laon and the tyrants as between the Spirits of Good and of Evil, of which their human representatives are the mere instruments. Yet this dualism is only apparent, not real; for there is a power behind Good and Evil that is far greater than they. As Cythna says in a notable passage:

> One comes behind
> Who aye the future to the past will bind—
> Necessity, whose sightless strength forever
> Evil with evil, good with good, must wind
> In bands of union which no power may sever:
> They must bring forth their kind, and be divided never!
> Canto IX, Stanza XXVII.

This idea is perhaps repeated in Shelley at critical places more often than any other, and if there is any single conception that may be spoken of as truly fundamental or central in Shelley's faith, it is here expressed. The fine phrase "sightless strength" is especially to be noted.

In the preface Shelley says that the poem is a succession of pictures illustrating "the awakening of an immense nation from their slavery and degradation to a true sense of moral dignity and freedom; the bloodless dethronement of their oppressors, and the unveiling of the religious frauds by which they have been deluded into submission." However, the attack on religious frauds is by no means as intense as in *Queen Mab*, and it is the last one on any extensive scale in Shelley's writings. He had still five years to live and his greatest works to produce, but he had already arrived at a settled conviction as to the moral greatness of the Founder of Christianity, even though he occasionally and to the last had his fling at Christian followers. In *The Triumph of Life* written just at the close of his career he speaks of

> Gregory and John, and men divine,
> Who rose like shadows between man and God;
> Till that eclipse, still hanging over heaven,
> Was worshipped by the world 'oer which they strode,
> For the true sun it quenched.

That is, the Christian world worshipped the followers of Jesus as Deities. Likewise in a note to the last Chorus in *Hellas* he says "the sublime human character of Jesus Christ was deformed by an imputed identification with a power, who tempted, betrayed, and punished the innocent beings who were called into existence by his sole will," etc. Or again, in *Prometheus Unbound* he speaks of the perversion of the spirit of Christ's teachings, which, with the other instances, indicate how heavily to the last the horrors of Christian superstition, as Shelley saw it, weighed on his mind:

> One came forth of gentle worth
> Smiling on the sanguine earth;
> His words outlived him, like swift poison
> Withering up truth, peace, and pity.
> Look! where round the wide horizon
> Many million-peopled city
> Vomits smoke in the bright air.
> Mark the outcry of despair!
> 'Tis his mild and gentle ghost
> Wailing for the faith he kindled.
>
> —Act I, lines 546-555.

This contention that the human race has so long been utterly incapable of comprehending the essential teachings of Jesus implies a certain profound pessimism, on Shelley's part, concerning the present race of man. Yet Shelley was easily capable of conceiving as roseate all things at a far distance. This explains why he so frequently betook himself to a Golden Age of the past and still more frequently to a Golden Age of the future. It also perhaps explains why after *The Revolt of Islam* he considered it futile to oppose what he conceived to be the corruptions of present Christianity by means of the doctrine of Necessity, and did not urge it further.

II

The idea of Necessity, nevertheless, continued to dominate all of Shelley's later meditative poetry. We have seen that he interpreted Necessity in terms of Power in one poem and in terms of Beauty in another, and that he identified it with the Soul of the Universe. The most striking characteristic of Shelley's thinking, as thinking, is that it is extraordinarily indefinite and abstract, so that his terms may oftentimes be interchanged without doing violence to his thought. "One mind, one power, one all-pervasive spirit, that is after all the cardinal principle of Shelley's philosophy and faith," says A. T. Strong in *Studies in Shelley* (1923).[6] Love, Wisdom, The Spirit of Beauty, God, have all in Shelley so wide a cosmic signification that in the last analysis they mean much the same thing. The word Power, for instance, may almost anywhere be substituted for the word Necessity without any appreciable difference of meaning. The chief ad-

[6] Had Mr. Strong stuck to this text he would have avoided the pitfalls of over-ingenuity in which his essay on Shelley's faith abounds. In the same breath he speaks of the speculations of Shelley with the speculations not only of Plato, but also of Aristotle, Spinoza, and Kant. Presumably these are the philosophers chiefly worthy to be compared with Shelley. Indeed he holds that Shelley surpassed Spinoza in keenness and penetration, and although he admits that Shelley knew nothing whatever of Kant, he yet feels in his soul that Shelley came very close to grasping Kant's "Categorical Imperative." It is really refreshing to go back to Leslie Stephen and Matthew Arnold on Shelley after reading the dithyrambic expositions of Shelley's faith by Miss Winstanley and Mr. Strong.

vantage Necessity has over various other terms is that it has a more definite connotation, giving the reader a clue to follow the poet in his subtle speculations, and it connects Shelley with a school of thinkers from whose dominance he never clearly emancipated himself.

The chief difference between Godwin's conception of Necessity and Shelley's mature conception of it is that Godwin, insensible of the existence of mystical or spiritual reality, thinks of the law of Necessity as binding and cementing together, in a logical and prosaic manner, all parts of the visible world and human life, whereas Shelley holds that the law obtains equally in the spiritual as in the material world.   The two most fundamental characteristics of the "one mind, one power, one all-pervasive spirit" of Shelley, are, first, that it is self-executing, not in a mechanical, but in a spiritually operative sense, whereby it necessitates all life, and secondly, that it is impersonal.   Like Wordsworth in his early Naturalism, Shelley preferred to use more general terms like the Soul of the Universe for the word God, since the latter was always in danger of suggesting something personal, or individual, or, as Shelley would say, anthropomorphic. All Being, including the mind of man, was to him impersonal.   So he generally spoke of the mind as a 'phantom,' and his chief characters in his poems—Laon, Cythna, Asia, Prometheus, etc.—are not at all flesh and blood individuals, such as Wordsworth or Browning would create, but are either instruments of some cosmic power or symbols of it.   In most general terms the conception that an impersonal, spiritual Power pervades all objects of the universe and necessitates their being and action may be called Pantheistic, though this element in

Shelley, like Wordsworth's early Naturalism, is relieved by a high spirituality.

Because of the spiritual and supersensible elements in Shelley, he has often been called an idealist. However, his idealism, if we call his philosophy so, is but an attenuated and necessitarian sort of idealism. He has sometimes been said to be transcendental; but his work is surely of a different kind than that which has been made familiar to us by Coleridge. One of the cardinal points in Coleridge's transcendentalism is that it starts with the conception that there is a free, creative and self-determining power within the individual mind:

> From the soul itself must issue forth a light, etc.—

This is foreign to the native tendency and also to the developed philosophy of Shelley. Coleridge's many expressions of profound indebtedness to Kant and Shelley's one reference to Kant,[7] which is sharply satirical, in his poetry indicates the gulf that lay between the mind of Shelley and the mind of a true transcendentalist. Shelley was rather the advocate of the cosmic, spiritual, impersonality of all things.

The same dualism and the same overarching Necessity, with its impersonal pantheistic implications, noted in *The Revolt of Islam*, controls the action and the thought in *Prometheus Unbound*, the most ambitious of Shelley's poems, begun in 1818 and completed in 1819. Interpreted from one angle, Prometheus personifies the Mind of Man, or Reason, and represents the Spirit of Good. From another angle he represents Revolutionary Liberty, which is also the Spirit of Good. Jupiter, the anthropomorphic God, created by Prometheus (the Mind

7 Shelley owned a complete edition of Kant's works.

of Man) through error, personifies authority and institutions and their tyranny, and represents the Evil Spirit and all things contemptible. Though Prometheus and Jupiter are the chief antagonists and the reader is led to expect a conflict between them, no such conflict is presented in the poem. Nor is Jupiter directly dethroned by Prometheus; the latter only loves and suffers and endures, and thereby purifies his own nature. He is the supreme example of the passive mind, awaiting calmly his hour, not for action, but for his release. It is significant that though Prometheus must be purified in mind neither his character nor his conduct determines the time of his release. He does not know when it shall be; he knows only it will come. It is predetermined, necessitated. Demigorgon, who is Eternity, and Fate, Time, Occasion, Chance, and Change, vast, vague, and imageless expressions for Necessity, fix the moment of the downfall of Jupiter and the redemption of Prometheus; and it comes instantaneously. When this happens the action of the poem is completed.

The slight motivation of the narrative is due partly to the fact that the poem is primarily lyrical. As a lyric its plan of construction is extremely simple. The poem naturally falls into two distinct parts, with two emotional centers (The Division occurs between Scenes 1 and 2 of Act III). The first part represents the Mind of Man (Prometheus) as bound and enslaved; the second as absolutely free. There are scarcely any intermediary stages. The poem does not deal with the life of the present or with human characters as such. The first part deals with the past, and the second presumably with the distant future—a millenium—in the treatment of which the poet achieved an extraordinarily intense and sustained

lyricism. But the vast interspace between Prometheus
bound and Prometheus free is given over to the abstractions Time and Demigorgon,—which is the main cause of
the rather impalpable motivation and the passive character of the poem.

But it may be urged that in the poem the principle of
Love at least is an active agency, independent of the law
of Necessiy, which rescues life from that fatalism toward
which all of Shelley's writings tend.[8] In one line in a
famous passage the independence of Love is asserted:

> For what would it avail to bid thee gaze
> On the revolving world? What to bid speak
> Fate, Time, Occasion, Chance, and Change? To these
> All things are subject but eternal Love.
>   —Act II, Scene 4.

However, in the notes to *Queen Mab* where love is
represented as most lawless, indisciplinable, "compatible
neither with obedience, jealousy, nor fear," it is declared
in the same breath to be an involuntary affection, "inevitably consequent on the perception of loveliness," the
lover being a slave to its mandates. And though in the
preface to *The Revolt of Islam* Shelley states that "love
is celebrated everywhere as the sole law that should govern the moral world," it seems that in the poem itself he
makes it a servant of Equality:

[8] That Shelley was aware of this tendency is shown in a note from
the essay *On the Punishment of Death*, where he makes an unsuccessful
attempt to distinguish between Necessity and Fatalism: "The savage
and the illiterate are but faintly aware of the distinction between the
future and the past; they make actions belonging to periods so distinct,
the subjects of similar feelings; they live only in the present, or in the
past as it is present. It is in this that the philosopher excels one of the
many; it is this which distinguishes the doctrine of philosophical necessity from fatalism." But this makes no real or fundamental distinction.
It simply exalts Necessity into a dignified Fatalism.

> Eldest of things, divine Equality:
> Wisdom and love are but the slaves of thee!

And Equality is but another name for that inscrutable, illimitable and destiny-shaping power, the mother of all things:

> O Spirit vast and deep as Night and Heaven!
> Mother and soul of all to which is given
> The light of life, the loveliness of being . . .
>   . . . Now millions start
> To feel thy lightnings through them burning;
> Nature, or God, or Love, or Pleasure,
> Or Sympathy, the sad tears turning
> To mutual smiles, a drainless treasure,
> Descends amidst us.

Thus Love, like the words Necessity and Power already noted, is a word almost interchangeable with Wisdom, or Nature, or God, and though it has a human side, it is chiefly a cosmic force as impersonal and impalpable as Time, or Nature, or any other of Shelley's abstractions, which exist and work in a necessitarian spirit almost exclusively independent of the human consciousness.

Likewise Asia, who represents Love in *Prometheus Unbound,* is the instrument of a similar impersonal and cosmic power that, in its destined moment, illumines

> Earth and heaven
> And the deep ocean and the sunless caves
> And all that dwell within them.

Naturally Asia, as a character, is as actionless and unindividualized as either Prometheus or Jupiter. She passively awaits the predetermined hour of her reunion with Prometheus.

The philosophy of *Prometheus Unbound* is thus essentially the same as that of *The Revolt of Islam,* except that the application of the principle of reform is much more general and correspondingly more indefinite. The symbolism of Prometheus as the Mind of Man and as Liberty and of Jupiter as the Institutions of Man and as Tyranny leads to a highly allegorized legend, leads away from every day human nature into the impalpable and the abstract. The interpretation of allegory, it may be contended, should confine itself to the broad outlines of the story. Shelley's native tendency to refine and subtilize upon his own general conceptions has led many a critic to attempt minute and detailed interpretation of his legend. They surely deceive themselves if they suppose by such method to find 'deep truth'—they rather lose themselves in a labyrinth of tangled conceptions. It is far better to hold to the broad generalizations of the allegory. The indefinite and somewhat vague characters are the instruments respectively of Good and Evil, while Necessity's 'sighless strength' is the determining factor in the conflict between them, giving Mankind ultimately the victory, yet working almost exclusively "beyond and above consciousness."

In the *Defense of Poetry,* written in 1821, Shelley says that poetry "acts in a divine and unapprehended manner, beyond and above consciousness." His philosophy of poetry thus harmonizes with his philosophy of life—in fact, is drawn out of it. Consider further the following sentences from the essay: "A man cannot say, 'I will compose poetry.' The greatest poet cannot say it; for the mind in creation is as a fading coal, which some invisible influence, like an inconstant wind, awakens to transitory brightness; this power arises from within, like the color of a flower which fades and changes as it is developed, and the conscious portions of our natures are unprophetic either of its approach or its departure."

. . . "It is as it were the interpenetration of a diviner nature through our own; but its footsteps are like those of a wind over the sea, which the morning calm erases, and whose traces remain only, as on the wrinkled sand which paves it." . . . "It is not subject to the control of the active powers of the mind, and its birth and recurrence have no necessary connection with the consciousness or will."

Of course these sentences should be read in their context so as not to take on an exaggerated importance. But allowing for their disseverance here they are characteristic of Shelley's approach to his subject and indicate his fundamental point of view. How diametrically opposite in meaning is that last sentence, and for that matter the spirit of all of them, to the view of the transcendentalist Coleridge when he speaks of the imagination as "first put into action by the will and understanding, and retained under their irremissive, though gentle and unnoticed, control." Shelley's passages are as dissimilar to Coleridge's mature critical writings as they are similar to the early writings of Coleridge when he was a Necessitarian and spoke of all life as 'organic harps diversely framed' over which sweeps, 'plastic and vast, one intellectual breeze.' The following passage, reported to Medwin by Shelley, even more sharply contrasts Coleridge and Shelley as critics of poetry, accentuating Shelley's conception of the passively receipient character of the poet's mind. In speaking of the poet Shelley says: "Imagination steals over him— he knows not whence. Images float before him—he knows not their home. Struggling and contending powers are engendered within him, which no outward impulse, no inward passion awakened. He utters sentiments he never

meditated. He creates persons whose original he had
never seen. But he cannot command the power that
called them out of nothing. He must wait till the God
or dæmon genius breathes it into him."

Thus the pure, the great, and the mighty poets are
most helpless as individuals; that is, to the degree that
they become perfect instruments for the cosmic, the
inevitable, the impersonal, 'the eternal, the infinite, and
the one,' to have free course through their minds do they
produce great poetry. This is the most characteristic
contribution of *The Defense of Poetry* to criticism, and
its philosophy is essentially in harmony with that of his
poetry; nowhere in modern criticism is there such an
insistence on the idea that the poet, when he writes
supremely, is the passive instrument of cosmic processes,
of the Absolute.

The shaping hand of an impersonal Power is clearly
discernible in the last portion of *Adonais,* written in
1821. Here it is transformed into a Light, a Beauty,
a Benediction, a sustaining Love 'through the web of
being blindly wove'; it is Nature; it is Eternity; it is
the "one Spirit's plastic stress" that

> Sweeps through the dull dense world, compelling there
> All new successions to the forms they wear.

This is the recurrent and central position with Shelley.
The endless forms and concrete objects of this dull world
are 'compelled' to take on whatever life and activity they
possess by the power of the One Spirit. But the forms
and objects themselves are fugitive and transitory; the
fleshly part of man's being is refractory to the perfect
working of the Spirit through him. Death must inter-
vene, so that the soul may be made one with the Universal
Spirit. Thus the poet says in a famous passage:

> The One remains, the many change and pass;
> Heaven's light forever shines, Earth's shadows fly;
> Life, like a dome of many-colored glass,
> Stains the white radiance of Eternity,
> Until death tramples it to fragments—

This One, this compelling and self-executing Power, however impersonal and however vaguely described, makes our present finite life seem, by contrast, a mere dream, a phantasmagoria. To die and to be immortal is to be made one with this inscrutable, impalpable, and impersonal Force. This remerging in the general Soul, with the loss of personal identity, it will be remembered, Tennyson called "a faith as vague as all unsweet." Tennyson believed passionately in the integrity of our personal individuality and in a personal immortality, which makes him a different kind of idealist than Shelley:

> Eternal form shall still divide
> The eternal soul from all beside;
> And I shall know him when we meet.
> (*In Memoriam,* XLVII)

In *Hellas,* written in 1821, the cosmic Power is rendered chiefly in terms of mind, or Thought, which is typified by the ideal Greece, or Hellas. Says Ahasuerus, the Jew, to Mahmud, the Sultan:

> Talk no more
> Of thee and me, the future and the past;
> But look on that which cannot change—the One,
> The unborn and the undying. . . . This Whole
> Of suns, and worlds, and men, and beasts, and flowers,
> With all the silent or tempestuous workings
> By which they have been, are, or cease to be,
> Is but a vision;—all that it inherits
> Are motes of a sick eye, bubbles and dreams;
> Thought is its cradle and its grave, not less
> The future and the past are idle shadows
> Of thought's eternal flight—

The individual is nothing, the One is all. Men are mere
visions, "idle shadows of thought's eternal flight." Not
the concrete thoughts of individuals, but Thought in the
abstract is the reality. It has nought to do "with time,
or place, or circumstance," but like an eyeless Destiny it
controls all finite things.

Necessity is described in the poem as "the world's eyeless charioteer, Destiny." Even Mahmud recognizes
that nothing can happen until its destined hour. When
Hassan speaks to him of the time Ahasuerus is to appear
to Mahmud, the latter declares that the Jew will come

> When the omnipotent hour to which are yoked
> He, I, and all things shall compel—enough.

And the spirit of this is caught up and given universal
application in the great Chorus that immediately follows.
Not only men but generations and ages and worlds are
subject to an inexorable Destiny. Here as in other places
Shelley suggests with extraordinary vividness the vastness of the cosmos and the littleness of individual being:

> Worlds on worlds àre rolling ever
> From creation to decay,
> Like the bubbles on a river
> Sparkling, bursting, borne away.

But abstract Thought abides. Shelley was not profoundly interested in the Greece of the present; but he
worshiped the Golden Age of Greece of the past, and
persuaded himself there would be a Golden Age of
Greece in the future. Thought, or Greece, a synonym
of Thought, abides forever:

> But Greece and her foundations are
> Built below the tide of war,
> Based on the crystalline sea
> Of thought and its eternity.

The fragment *The Triumph of Life* (1822), the last of Shelley's compositions, is interesting as showing that to the very end he tended more and more toward pure abstractions. The poem is based upon a dream that visited the poet's passive mind—"a vision on my brain was rolled." In his dream he perceived a chariot in which sat a Shape, while around the chariot and following it were many human shapes. This pageantry represents Life. The charioteer was a Janus-visaged Shadow, and "all the four faces of that charioteer had their eyes banded." This Shadow, then, is "the eyeless charioteer, Destiny," the sightless Necessity of the other poems. The purport of the poem is to render Necessity in terms of Life,—an appropriate fragmentary conclusion to the brief life and the works of Shelley.

There is thus from *Queen Mab* to *The Triumph of Life* a series of lengthy poems that are full of speculative and abstract reasoning, which indicates that Shelley's philosophical thinking was an integral part of his poetry. The thought is sufficiently self-consistent, but it is from beginning to end tenuous and indefinite in character. What gives it vitality and saves it to poetry is the fact that in all its best parts it is sustained by an intense lyric quality. However, the last poems are more abstract than the earlier ones; besides Shelley often thought of himself as a philosopher, and it may be conjectured that had he lived longer his tendency to the abstract would have gained the victory over his lyrical gift, as it actually did over Coleridge after the age of thirty. Ill health and a tendency to abstract reasoning were common to both, though Coleridge's lyrical qualities were probably less considerable than Shelley's.

III

It should also be remembered that throughout his literary career Shelley believed in the perfectibility of man, based on the more fundamental belief in the essential unreality of evil. Godwin had said that "under the system of Necessity the idea of guilt, crime, desert, and accountableness have no place." Likewise in *The Revolt of Islam* Shelley speaks of the mere "temporary triumph of oppression" and "the transitory nature of ignorance and error." And Mrs. Shelley, writing of her husband's philosophy, says: "The prominent feature of Shelley's theory of the destiny of the human species was that evil is not inherent in the system of creation, but an accident that might be expelled."

Thus it requires but a small amount of self-exertion to get rid of an accident or a mere error and to attain to perfectibility. There is no purifying, developing, and enriching of the personality in the process. In fact, it can hardly be spoken of as a process, but rather as a mere instantaneous change. So that when in *The Revolt of Islam* Cythna asserts to the sailors that they might "arise and will" to change the world, she means that somehow there has been a slight aberration on the part of mankind from the law of Necessity and Nature and that the error might be instantaneously corrected. A strong desire seems to be sufficient to rend the flimsy partition between the ignorance and error of the present and the golden age of wisdom and freedom of the future, which desire is destined some time to arise and be realized on the instant. In speaking of Shelley's frequent use of a veil as a symbol in his poetry Mr. Strong in *Studies in Shelley* says: "The very fact that he portrays life in the

image of the Veil shows that he regards the fabric sever-
ing good from evil, error from truth, as of the thinnest,
and as destructible in the very moment in which the heart
of man should be converted to desire for the change."
This doctrine of desire and of immediate satisfaction on
the appearance of desire no doubt has its virtues, but
assuredly it does not possess the virtue of self-discipline.
Thus the millenium for which Shelley ardently hoped is
to come not by large numbers of individuals exercising
contrition for their own individual shortcomings and
wickednesses, such as Christianity suggests, and gradually
bettering their characters and thereby adding to the slow
advancement of the race toward a more perfect society,
but it is to come by mankind brushing aside the thinnest
of veils that hides from it the true and the good, with the
implication that this can be done instantly whenever the
desire arises. In brief, Shelley had no conception of the
will as operative in making one's life 'daily self-surpassed'
and thereby achieve character by slow growth; nor did
he possess any adequate philosophic theory of Free-will.

"The vulgar," said Godwin, "will universally be found
to be advocates of free-will. . . . This having been the
conception of the masses of mankind in all ages, and the
idea of contingency and accident having perpetually
obtruded themselves, the established language of morality has been universally tinctured with this error."
Shelley took pains not to be classed among the vulgar by
his master. Yet the fact is that his language, as well as
the language of Godwin himself, and indeed the language
of any human being, so far as he is human, is tinctured
with this so-called error. "It is a received opinion in
metaphysics," says Bagehot, "that the idea of personality
is identical with the idea of will." And for any one who

has much to say to his fellow-men, it is manifestly impossible to prevent the idea of will from coloring his language. A number of examples can be found in Shelley's writing.[9] No doubt as the poet approached maturity he began to recognize the actual feelings of actual persons around him and to perceive that their actions seemed in nowise to have been determined by a chain of causes generated in the eternity of time before their birth.

For all that, however, the poet was to the end remarkably true to the law of Necessity and its pantheistic impersonal implications. In the fragmentary essay *On Life*, assigned by Rossetti to 1815, but conjecturally assigned by Dowden to 1819, Shelley says: "The words I, You, They, are not signs of any actual difference subsisting

[9] Three of the most striking examples are as follows:
From *Julian and Maddalo* (1818):

> We are assured
> Much may be conquered, much may be endured
> Of what degrades and crushes us. We know
> That we have power over ourselves to do
> And suffer—what, we know not till we try,
> But something nobler than to live and die.

From *A Philosophical Review of Reform* (1818): "We derive tranquility and courage and grandeur of soul from contemplating an object which is because we will it, and may be, because we hope and desire it, and must be if succeeding generations of the enlightened sincerely and earnestly desire it."

From *Prometheus Unbound* (1818): Prometheus to Jupiter:

> O'er all things but thyself I gave thee power,
> And my own will.

These passages seem numerous around the year 1818. It may be that at this time Shelley was groping toward a real sense of will and personality. But the philosophy of his youth was too strong for him to succeed. The exceptions here simply prove the rule.

between the assemblage of thoughts thus indicated, but are merely marks employed to note the different modifications of the one mind." These words, he also says, "are grammatical devices invented simply for arrangement, and totally devoid of the intense and exclusive sense usually attached to them." Totally devoid of individuality and will!

Thus from Shelley's general world view there arise two significant negations—the negation of will or personality and the negation of evil. The holding of these views interfered seriously with the poet's constructive thinking. The tenuity complained of by many readers of Shelley's poetry, "the incurable want, in general, of a sound subject matter," as Matthew Arnold phrased it, is not due primarily to the fact that Shelley considered the supersenuous world more real than the senuous world, as so many Shelley advocates declare, but rather to the fact of his denial of the reality of evil and the reality of will and personality.

His attitude toward evil tends to turn some of his serious work into mockery. A poet who goes forth to do battle with evil must at least consider the foe a reality, a force to be grappled with, an adversary worthy his best steel. But in Shelley's dualistic poems we are often reminded that the Good is opposed by a mere phantom, and that we have been invited to witness a combat with shadows, however fierce the onslaught upon them.

The other negation is more vital; it robs Shelley's poetry greatly of the power of personality and of moral profundity; it hinders it from treating human beings as human beings, and lies at the root of the poet's own saying: "As to real flesh and blood, you know I do not

deal in those articles; you might as well go to a ginshop
for a leg of mutton as to expect anything human or
earthly from me." And this fact, in turn, makes it
necessary for him constantly to resort in his poetry to the
personification of abstract objects and to the use of various forms of symbolism. Exceptions like *Julian and
Maddalo* indicate what the poet might have accomplished
had he possessed a vital interest in the separate individuality of human characters.

This negation of will and personality also precludes
any serious volitional appeal in Shelley's poetry.

> I could lie down like a tired child,
> And weep away the life of care—
>
> Oh, lift me from the grass!
> I die! I faint! I fail!

is the prevailing tone of his finest lyrics. It is not merely
that the poet feels no sense of deep personal unworthiness
or of profound sinfulness within him, but chiefly that his
own separate phantasy seems to have such a slight hold
on things. The wild lyricism and the extraordinary
poignancy of his verse have their source in the poet's sense
of his own helpless, fleeting, shadow-like being, and in his
sense that the will of man is impotent and has nowhere
to turn for strength, for assurance, and for a satisfying
and an abiding peace. His spirit rises swiftly to some
lofty pinnacle of aspiration and hope, and as swiftly
descends to the depths of despair. It is striking, for
instance, that the great Chorus at the close of Hellas,
where the poet feels the thrill of near approach to the
Golden Age,—

> The world's great age begins anew,
> The golden years return—

should end with almost a tragic note:

> Oh, cease! must hate and death return?
> Cease! must men kill and die?
> Cease! drain not to its dregs the urn
> Of bitter prophecy.
> The world is weary of the past,
> Oh, might it die or rest at last!

From these negations the poet had only two ways of escape. The first was to a dream world of clouds and sunsets, to

> The loftiest star of unascended heaven,
> Pinnacled dim in the intense inane,

or to a sinless Eden,

> Around mountains and islands inviolably
> Prankt on the sapphire sea,—

Fortunately, however, Shelley was natively gifted with keen powers of perception. "He could interpret," says Mrs. Shelley, "without a fault each appearance in the sky; and the varied phenomena of heaven and earth filled him with deep emotion. He made his study and reading-room of the shadowed copse, the stream, the lake, and the waterfall." In his early poetry, as for instance, ✓ *Alastor,* he lavishly decorates his verse with many lovely images of Nature. But even here "the meeting boughs and implicated leaves" that wove a twilight over his path were but an aid to his pursuit of "love, or dream, or God, or mightier Death." And in all his later poetry there is the dominant tendency to personify objects of Nature or to use images as symbolic in the service of indefinite or abstract conceptions. Hence the attenuated and somewhat thin 'idealism' so characteristic of Shelley's poetry.

The *Ode to the West Wind* (1819) is not only pro-

foundly characteristic of this attitude of mind but illustrates all the essential characteristics of Shelley's genius.
A superb lyric rhapsody, it still has clinging to it something of Shelley's spirit of reform. Though beginning
with a rather naturalistic description of the west wind,
the poet, as he proceeds, is borne up, as it were, on the
wings of his own singing, and by the spell of his own
inward ecstacies the wind is transformed into some vast
and mighty Power, or at least the symbol of such, to
which he bows in devout worship. Had he remained
wild and free as in his youth, he cries,

> I would ne'er have striven

> As thus with thee in prayer in my sore need.
> Oh lift me as a wave, a leaf, a cloud!
> I fall upon the thorns of life! I bleed!

> A heavy weight of hours has chained and bowed
> One, too, like thee: tameless, and swift, and proud.

The unbroken and full-throated flow of the verse, the
even gradation from pure objectivity in the beginning
to almost complete subjectivity at the end, the movement
from the faint 'I hear' at the first to the vehement,
climactic 'Be thou! spirit fierce, My spirit! Be thou
me, impetuous one!' at the close, are all nothing short
of marvelous. The poet creates a deep sense of the helplessness of a fettered soul wildly longing to be free. The
release comes when the shadowy personal identity is
made one with the tumult of the mighty harmonies of the
West Wind, and thereby becomes a fit instrument to
arouse the unawakened earth and to regenerate mankind.
Precisely the same mental process is developed and
precisely the same results are obtained in *To the Skylark* (1820), which also illustrates all the essential
elements at Shelley's genius. Under the pressure of the

poet's ecstasy the bird becomes an unbodied joy, a tumult of mighty harmonies, filling the spaces of the universe. This rapture and dazzling splendor produces in the mind of the poet langour and dissatisfaction, from which he escapes by losing himself in that splendor of harmonious madness, and fancying the wisdom thus learned to be revealed to mankind:

> The world should listen then, as I am listening now.

Thus if we recognize the limitations put upon him by his own negations, we may assert that Shelley made the utmost of his ideal world, investing it with an inscrutable Power, imageless and unspeakable, yet necessary and self-executing and compelling in all its aspects, a Power that forever dwells apart, toward which the poet's being forever pants and aspires. In this view man is conceived but as a waterspout in the eternal storms of Being.

Nor is this conception without permanent value; there are always minds who love to contemplate the eternal and immeasurable flux of things, to think of past and present as idle shadows of thought's eternal flight, to detach the self thus and see how frail and trivial is man in his little span of years, how insignificant and impotent his little systems, how great and incomprehensible the cosmos! Such find a certain amplitude and vastness in Shelley's cosmos, and a kinship with his bold and speculative mind,

> Swiftly leading to those awful limits which mark
> the bounds of time, and of the space when time
> shall be no more.
>
> (Fragment: To Harriet)

The other way of escape was toward the simple, passive, non-resitant life, so like certain aspects of Christianity. "I agree," says Shelley, "with the Quakers so

far as they disclaim violence, and trust their course wholly
and solely to its own truth." So he sang of those passive
qualities which have an abiding interest and an unfailing
esthetic charm—love which is truth, gentleness which is
brave, endurance which wins by silent resistance, fortitude which does not anger at provocation, forgiveness
which takes no account of revenge, sorrow and melancholy which luxuriate in their own helplessness, and yearn-
ings for the infinite which cannot be satisfied:

> To thirst and find no fill—to wail and wander
> With short uneasy steps—to pause and ponder—
> To feel the blood run through the veins and tingle
> Where busy thought and blind sensation mingle;
> To nurse the image of unfelt caresses
> Till dim imagination just possesses
> The half created shadow.
>
> (Fragment: Unsatisfied Desire)

"I shall say what I think," says Browning. "Had
Shelley lived he would finally have ranged himself with
the Christians." But what Shelley might have become is
not so important as what he actually was. Whether, he,
or any other man, was a Christian depends almost wholly
on our definition of Christianity. Perhaps no one would
be so bold as to declare what the teachings of Jesus were
in their entirety. At least it is not a fit subject on which
to dogmatize. On the other hand, an original poet
asserts with assurance only what he sees and feels to be
true in his own inner experience. Such experience being
inevitably circumscribed in a finite creature, it seems that
a poet can at best express only a limited number of great
convictions, which may or may not be fundamentally
similar to the essential teachings of Jesus. It is in this
sense only that Browning himself may be considered a
Christian; for there are important aspects of Christianity

which he barely touched, because they were not vital to his experience. Now Shelley undoubtedly expressed some convictions that are fundamentally similar to the teachings of Jesus, but because they are not so numerous nor so broad-based nor so heartily sympathetic with Christianity as those of Browning, men have usually accorded to Browning the name of Christian, but have persistently withheld it from Shelley. This is undoubtedly a fair distinction, when it is understood as indicating a difference in degree and not in kind. This distinction is further strengthened when it is remembered that Shelley constantly refused to distinguish the good from the evil in historic Christianity and as a consequence failed to credit the good in it.

Nevertheless, in his later years Shelley not only more than once spoke and wrote of the sublime personality of Jesus, but in *Hellas'* (1821) he wrote some lines concerning God which might even have been acceptible to orthodox Christians of Shelley's day:

> In the great morning of the world
> The spirit of God with might unfurled
> The flag of Freedom over Chaos.

And in a passage (quoted approvingly by Browning) in *The Boat of the Serchio* (1821) Shelley seems to have identified his own view of Necessity with strict predestination:

> All rose to do the task He set to each,
> Who shaped us to his ends and not our own.

The question may here be raised, how can Shelley's ideas about the unreality of evil and the negation of personality, his belief in Necessity and his attitude toward Christianity, have any bearing on our estimate of his poetry, as poetry? For the reason that Shelley is primarily a rhapsodist and that his poetry at its best is very ethereal and has pronounced charm of style the question has more than once been answered in the negative. But the answer here is that his views have a great deal to do with the final estimate of his work as a poet. The conception of impersonality and the principle of Necessity and its negations were not merely a matter of speculative opinion with him, but were the breath of his habitual thinking; they were deep-seated convictions; they entered into the very warp and woof of his thought; they mark out definitely the limits of his own world, giving it color and atmosphere. His mind would soar upward and sentiment wed itself to thought; so that in Shelley's world, as in any artist's world, the intellectual and moral elements are of essential importance. His studiousness led him deeply into eighteenth century philosophers, and others. In his mature years he was no mere imitator, nor was he especially a breaker of new ground, such as was Coleridge. But from his studies he fashioned certain instruments of thought, which he felt intensely, which he in a sense lived, and which he applied to the current feeling and thought of his own day—the feeling especially for Nature and the general feeling of unrest and of the need of the reorganization of society. In the main he gave a highly modern, emotional, and romantic expression to the deterministic current of eighteenth century thought.

BYRON

BYRON

Throughout his literary career Byron manifested so strange an admixture of courage and self-pity, sincerity and posing, faith in man and cynicism, radicalism and respect for tradition, serious thought and flippant comment, such a rapid shifting not only from one mood to another but from one idea to another, that it is extremely difficult to find a center from which to interpret his poetry. Nevertheless there is a serious strain of constructive thinking in him. If we leave out of account the more frivolous and the merely amusing of his verse, and also consider only incidentally his satiric writings, remembering that he was perhaps mainly a satirist, we can find certain basic principles of thought in his work, a view of the cosmos, a characteristic reaction to Nature and to human life; and can also discern a certain development of his views. Admittedly an incomplete interpretation of the poet, this approach to him has the advantage of setting forth whatever constructive philosophy there is in his world.

Like Shelley Byron was intensely modern in his emotions but backward looking in his thought. Again like Shelley he was a poet of revolt, an innovator, but his innovations were born of personal moods or of the temper of the times. He was too impatient of careful and constructive thinking to develop an original attitude of philosophical consistency, and when he did think he slipped back into fairly well defined formulae of eighteenth century ideas. His indebtedness to the eighteenth century ran deeper than merely the ardent advocacy and imitation of the poetry of Pope; whenever he adverted to first principles it gave him the foundation of his thought. We may not say with Goethe that when Byron reflects he is a child, but rather that when he reflects he is the child of the eighteenth century.

In general Byron's early work, as for instance, the first two Cantos of *Childe Harold,* is highly emotional and romantic—strong in the love of Nature and of unrestrained freedom, while his later work becomes gradually more intellectual; each contact with the rationalistic and skeptic spirit of the eighteenth century, reacting favorably on certain rebellious elements in his own nature, disillusioned him as to the worth of his emotions and in the end transformed him into the author of the satire of *Don Juan.* "My passions were developed very early," he says in *Detached Thoughts.* "Perhaps this was one of the reasons which caused the anticipated melancholy of my thoughts,—having anticipated life." There was also a sharp conflict between his thought as personal energy and desire and his thought as an inherited philosophy, which tended to the same end—the mock spirit of *Don Juan.*

I

As every one knows the first two Cantos of *Childe Harold,* published in 1812, when Byron was twenty-four, took the world by storm. The passionate energy in them, the spirit of adventure, the graphic and picturesque descriptions of places of historic interest, the rapid, kalidoscopic, movement from scene to scene, dazzled the reading public. The Cantos do not contain any philoso-

phic profoundities; yet here for the first time Byron suggests the beginnings of a philosophy of life. He preaches
individualism undisciplined and freedom unrestrained.
He sets up an antimony between Man and Nature,
embracing as an individual the solitude and loveliness
of Nature and scorning companionship with man:

To sit on rocks, to muse o'er flood and fell,
To slowly trace the forest's shady scene,
Where things that own not man's dominion dwell,
And mortal foot hath ne'er or rarely been;
To climb the ›trackless mountain all unseen,
With the wild flock that never needs a fold;
Alone o'er steeps and foaming falls to lean;
This is not solitude; 'tis but to hold
Converse with Nature's charms, and view her stores unroll'd.

But midst the crowd, the hum, the shock of men,
To hear, to see, to feel, and to possess,
And roam along, the world's tired denizen,
With none who bless us, none whom we can bless;
Minions of splendour shrinking from distress!
None that, with kindred consciousness endued,
If we were not, would seem to smile the less,
Of all that flatter'd, follow'd, sought, and sued;
This is to be alone; this, this is solitude.

                                        Canto II, 25, 26.

There is also in these Cantos an implicit spirit of
satire which becomes explicit in his later writings. He
implies a cynical attitude toward womankind:

But pomp and power alone are woman's care,
And where these are light Eros finds a feere;
Maidens, like moths, are ever caught by glare.

                                        Canto, I, 9.

He makes sneering remarks concerning Sabbath religious
worship in London, where the "spruce citizen, wash'd
artisan, and smug apprentice gulp their weekly air" as
they make their way to church:

Ask ye, Bœotian shades, the reason why?
'Tis to the worship of the solemn Horn,
Grasp'd in the holy hand of Mystery,
In whose dread name both men and maids are sworn,
And consecrate the oath with draught, and dance till morn.

                                        Canto, I, 70.

As he reviews the past of Spain and Greece he is deeply
impressed by a profound sense of the futility of life, the
fatuity of personal existence, by a sort of Calvinistic
sense of Fate:

                        Shall man repine
That his frail bonds to fleeting life are broke?
Cease, fool! the fate of gods may well be thine!
Wouldst thou survive the marble or the oak,
When nations, tongues, and worlds must sink beneath the stroke?

                                        Canto II, 53.

Or again, in speaking of the Acropolis at Athens he says:

Look on this spot—a nation's sepulchre!
Abode of gods, whose shrines no longer burn.
Even gods must yield—religions take their turn;
'Twas Jove's—'tis Mahomet's—and other creeds
Will rise with other years, till man shall learn
Vainly his incense soars, his victim bleeds,—
Poor child of Doubt and Death, whose hope is built on reeds.

                                        Canto II, 3.

The cynicism in these Cantos may be a mere pose of the
youthful Byron, but the sense of man's mortality, of
doubt and chance and mutability in man's being, which
underlies the poem, reveals a note of deep reality in
Bryon's thought.   Both the negative and the cosmo-
politan attitude toward all religions as here revealed is
also a characteristic note.

Soon after the publication of the first two Cantos of
Childe Harold Byron protested against identifying the
hero with himself.   Though no doubt it is wrong to make

such identification outwardly and literally, the serious
and deeper experiences as represented in the poem are
Byron's own. The hero's love of loneliness, his worship
of the great things in history, his special devotion to the
country of Greece, his sense of the futility of life, and
the negation of religion, can be with confidence ascribed
to the author himself.

The feeling of man's futile existence, of his smallness
as set against his pretensions, Byron not only attests in
this poem but in various passages in his letters written
soon after the poem. In writing to Mr. Gifford, for
instance, June 16, 1813, Byron says: "It was the com-
parative insignificance of ourselves and *our world,* when
placed in competition with the mighty whole, of which it
is an atom, that first led me to imagine that our pretensions to eternity might be over-rated." This cosmo-
politan attitude, as it were, toward the universe as a
whole he again speaks of in a letter to Miss Milbanke,
March 3, 1814: "Why I came here, I know not. Where
I shall go, it is useless to inquire. In the midst of myriads
of the living and the dead worlds—stars—systems—
infinity—why should I be anxious about an atom?"

Byron's anxiety about the atom, however, was always
sufficiently great. Indeed the intensity and energy with
which his personality undisguised asserts itself in his
poetry is one of the marked characteristics of his genius.
Under but the slightest disguise the heroes of Byron's
oriental tales, as Selim in *The Bride of Abydos* (1813),
Conrad in *The Corsair* (1813), and Lara in *Lara*
(1814), the poet asserts his own egoistic energy and
undisciplined personality, in a blaze of oriental color and
with melodramatic effect. But it required the sting of a
sharp reversal of personal fortune completely to reveal

the poet to the world. When in 1815 he married Miss Mibanke and a year afterwards they parted and the society of London that had lionized the poet suddenly turned against him as though he were a criminal, Byron became so enraged that he hurled himself without any disguise whatever and with all the personal energy at his command, which was nothing short of volcanic, upon, or against, the world. In the Third Canto of *Childe Harold,* written in the summer of 1816 after his separation, he cries:

> I have not loved the world, nor the world me;
> I have not flatter'd its rank breath, nor bow'd
> To its idolatries a patient knee,—
> Nor coin'd my cheek to smiles,—nor cried aloud
> In worship of an echo; in the crowd
> They could not deem me one of such; I stood
> Among them, but not of them; in a shroud
> Of thoughts which were not their thoughts, and still could,
> Had I not filed my mind, which thus itself subdued.
>
> I have not loved the world, nor the world me,—
> But let us part fair foes; I do believe,
> Though I have found them not, that there may be
> Words which are things,—hopes which will not deceive,
> And virtues which are merciful, nor weave
> Snares for the failing; I would also deem
> O'er others' griefs that some sincerely grieve;
> That two, or one, are almost what they seem,
> That goodness is no name, and happiness no dream.
>
> Stanzas 113, 114.

But the experience of anger and suffering through which Byron passed was the immediate cause of a rapid unfolding of his poetical powers, as revealed in this Third Canto of *Childe Harold* (1816). A fuller and more sustained flow of verse, greater richness and variety of imagery, a deeper current and wider sweep of thought, characterize this Canto as compared to the earlier ones.

Proud and haughty in spirit the poet poured out his wrath against the mass of humanity, against the crowd. He clung to the faith in the very few—the heoric and the mighty of the earth—and by implication placed himself in their society. Such, as himself, are original, unconventional, are scornful of the ideas and customs of the masses, and will be free. Byron puissantly asserted the might of the mind, like a transcendentalist. But whereas Coleridge and Wordsworth in their mature years expressed their faith in the free, active and creative power of the mind, based on a reasoned philosophy, and accompanied by the principle of self-discipline, Byron asserts the freedom and power of the mind, blindly as it were, unreasoned and undisciplined.

On the other hand, there is for Byron the cosmos— "The myriads of the living and the dead worlds—stars— systems—infinity—" which, when set over against the individual mind makes that mind, however great and powerful, a mere atom and its efforts ultimately futile. The exhilarating contest between the might of a great personality and the cosmic processes of impersonal Nature is exhibited in Byron's poetry on a grand scale:

> Above me are the Alps,
> The palaces of Nature, whose vast walls
> Have pinnacled in clouds their snowy scalps,
> And throned Eternity in icy halls
> In cold sublimity, where forms and falls
> The avalanche—the thunderbolt of snow!
> All that expand the spirit, yet appals,
> Gather around these summits, as to show
> How Earth may pierce to Heaven, yet leave vain man below.
>
> Canto III, 62.

The upper regions, so to speak, of the cosmos are wild, chaotic, dazzling; inspiring yet appaling to the human mind. And though at the last the mind of man is swallowed up in the abyss and is ultimately as helpless as the smallest atom, man's ability to measure his strength for a time with the huge and mighty forms of Nature gives the poet "a fierce and far delight,"—such as nothing else can. The wild, stormy, gigantic, untamable, elemental energies of Nature Byron exults in and describes incomparably; they have a kinship with his own inward, unsubdued, and uncontrolable energies of mind.

The Third Canto is Byron's great Nature poem. Its exalted tone and atmosphere owe something to the indirect influence of Shelley. The influence of Wordsworth's early Naturalism, however, is more obvious. In certain passages, quite un-Byronic, Wordsworth's ideas emerge:

> Are not the mountains, waves, and skies, a part
> Of me and of my soul, as I of them?
> Is not the love of these deep in my heart
> With a pure passion?
>
> Stanza 75.

Wordsworth's description in *Lines Above Tintern Abbey* of his youthful experience with Nature—

> The sounding cataract
> Haunted me like a passion; the tall rock,
> The mountain, and the deep and gloomy wood,
> Their colors and their forms, were then to me
> An appetite; a feeling and a love—

is distinctly echoed by Byron in—

> I live not in myself, but I become
> Portion of that around me; and to me
> High mountains are a feeling, but the hum
> Of human cities torture—
>
> Stanza 72.

However, Wordsworth would not have subscribed to the last clause just quoted; for it was characteristic of Wordsworth that he contemplated Nature, not as something to flee to, but as a Power to humanize and socialize man, a shaping influence "on that best portion of a good man's life, his little, nameless, unremembered, acts of kindness and of love." In the concluding passage of *Lines Above Tintern Abbey* he speaks of the steep woods and lofty cliffs as dear, both for themselves and for his sister's sake—for the human association with them. But Byron was anti-social in his relations to Nature. The mountains and wild ocean shores were places of refuge from the society of man. Byron loved the ocean because it was untamable; he loved a mountain storm because it was 'wrathful'—these were soothing to his own rebellious, anti-social nature.

Again, in his early Naturalism, Wordsworth conceived of Nature as functioning so vitally in human character and of character as reacting so vitally to Nature that the entities Man and Nature are inseparable. In characteristic poems, such as, for instance, the Fourth *Lucy* poem one cannot tell where Nature ends and character begins or where character ends and Nature begins. The product is creatively a single unit. Byron, on the other hand, who has no such conception of the vital interaction between Man and Nature, uses the more conventional method of parallelism: he describes a scene in Nature at length, and then runs parallel to it a human or personal experience. In a magnificent passage in the Third Canto—Stanzas 92 to 96 inclusive—he describes a storm at midnight in the Alps. Then in stanzas 96 and 97 he makes the transition from description to the personal feeling:

> Sky, mountains, river, winds, lake, lightnings! ye,
> With night, and clouds, and thunder, and a soul
> To make these felt and feeling, well may be
> Things that have made me watchful; the far roll
> Of your departing voices, is the knoll

> Of what in me is sleepless,— if I rest.
> But where of ye, oh tempests, is the goal?
> Are ye like those within the human breast,
> Or do ye find at length, like eagles, some high nest?
>
> Could I embody and unbosom now
> That which is most within me,—could I wreak
> My thoughts upon expression, and thus throw
> Soul, heart, mind, passions, feelings, strong or weak,
> All that I would have sought, and all I seek,
> Bear, know, feel and yet breathe—into *one* word,
> And that one word were Lightning, I would speak;
> But as it is, I live and die unheard,
> With a most voiceless thought, sheathing it as a sword.

A powerfully expressed cry of desire for self-expression!

From this emotional despair and from the defiance of the world in this Canto it is but a step to the moral despair and defiance of the powers in heaven and earth in *Manfred, a Dramatic Poem,* written in 1816-17. In this dramatic piece Byron reverses the ordinary motive of tragedy. It is usual in a tragedy that the hero struggle against opposing forces unto death, that death is avoided until the last. Though Hamlet, for instance, meditates suicide he nevertheless fights manfully for self-preservation. Manfred, however, has from the beginning an intense and fixed longing for forgetfulness—self-oblivion—death; he is possessed "with the fierce thirst of death—and still unslaked!" (Act II, 1, 48):

> There is a power upon me which withholds,
> And makes it my fatality to live,—
>
> Act I, 2, 23-24.

This fatality not only determines that he must live but also determines a certain fixed hour for his death. In the first act Manfred calls up the spirits and powers of the air and demands that they give him self-oblivion, which they cannot do. In the second act he attempts to commit suicide by casting himself from the crags in the Alps, but is prevented by a Chamois Hunter. In the third act the Abbot attempts to rescue him from evil ways and from communion with evil spirits who have come to claim possession of him; but he is immune from the power of both—the demons vanish before his moment of death arrives, and the Abbot stands by helplessly.

Besides, Manfred had been fated to an illicit love of the mysterious Astarte. Like him in lineaments—"her eyes, her hair, her features, all,"—she was perhaps his sister or some one near in kin. Her unlawful love of him perhaps caused her premature death. The relationship and the experience, whatever it was, is only vaguely and distractedly hinted at in the poem, is a thing that remains unspeakable, and is of course the cause of Manfred's despair and agony and longing for death.

The fatality that determines that Manfred shall live and that fixes his hour of death likewise gives him the power, and also the license, to defy all things in life. Like the speaker in *Childe Harold* Manfred has ostracized himself from mankind and defies all their conventions. He loves not the world nor the world him:

> From my youth upwards
> My spirit walk'd not with the souls of men,
> Nor look'd upon the earth with human eyes;
> The thirst of their ambition was not mine,
> The aim of their existence was not mine;
> My joys, my griefs, my passions, and my powers,
> Made me a stranger; though I wore the form,
> I had no sympathy with breathing flesh.
>
> Act II, 2, 50-57.

Not only are the spirits of the earth, air, stars, etc., who represent the forces of Nature, inferior to the power of Manfred, but even the Destinies who claim—

> Our hands contain the hearts of men,
> Our footsteps are their graves;
> We only give to take again
> The spirits of our slaves!—
>
> Act II, 3, 54-57

are defied by his superior power. He boldly presents himself before their king, the great Arimanes, ruler of darkness and all evil, and, refusing to bow down in worship before him, demands that he raise the spirit of the dead Astarte. And though he recoils for a moment when her phantom, refusing to grant him forgiveness, disappears, he immediately recovers, and one of the spirits says of him:

> He mastereth himself, and makes
> His torture tributary to his will.
>
> Act II, 4, 159-160.

In like manner he defies, though in a more tolerant spirit, the power of the Church as represented by the Abbot. Nothing can break his will, strong and persistent and indomitable. The efforts of the demons to possess him only makes his will grow stronger; the penances and spirit of submission suggested by the Abbot merely intensify its power; torture and despair increase its fierceness. Addressing himself to the spirit that comes to take possession of his soul he cries:

> Must crimes be punish'd by other crimes,
> And greater criminals?—Back to thy hell!
> Thou hast no power upon me, *that* I feel;
> Thou never shalt possess me, *that* I know:
> What I have done is done; I bear within
> A torture which could nothing gain from thine:
> The mind which is immortal makes itself
> Requital for its good or evil thoughts,—
> Is its own origin of ill and end
> And its own place and time: its innate sense
> When stripp'd of this mortality, derives

No colour from the fleeting things without;
But is absorb'd in sufferance or in joy,
Born from the knowledge of its own desert.
                                    Act III, 4, 123-130.

This is perhaps the nearest approach in Byron to Coleridge's and Wordsworth's conception of the transcendental might of the mind; but its spirit is headlong, un-
compromising, self-assertive, defiant. It is most likely
that Byron was indebted directly to Coleridge for the idea
that the mind "is its own origin of ill and end and its
own place and time," deriving "no colour from the fleeting things without." This conception is not usual with
Byron and is indeed in contradiction to the general trend
of his thought, which is deterministic and necessitarian.
To be sure Byron natively was assertive, aggressive, and
independent. But his thought, as philosophic thought,
was Calvinistic determinism, which implies a profound
fatality. Calvin and Jonathan Edwards were content
to live in a world that was predestined and predetermined,
and submitted themselves to it in all patience of heart
and mind. Byron, living in a Revolutionary and individualistic age, cried out for a self-destined and a self-
determined world. But how could he have one world
when impelled to believe only in its opposite? For
Byron there was no real solution of this contradiction,
no adjustment or harmonization of conviction and
conduct!

Fatality overarches the spirit of defiance and self-
assertion in *Manfred:* "Fatal and fated in thy sufferings,"
says the Witch of the Alps to Manfred. "Hitherto all
hateful things conspire to bind me in existence," says
Manfred himself. He was bound and fated to love
criminally, to live and despair and to defy, even unto

death.   Shelley's Prometheus was likewise fated; but Prometheus passively and pacifically awaited his hour of release that was to inaugurate a golden age, while Manfred despairingly, fiercely and defiantly awaited his hour of destruction and death!   Each clearly symbolizes their respective authors' conception of human destiny.

But it is to be noted that Manfred does not defy God in his heaven, and therefore he is not blasphemous.   He dares the worst that can come to him from evil spirits, from humans, and from Nature.   It is well that there is an eternal law, even though a fatality, to which he submits; it is well that he recognizes, though only at the last and dimly, an immortality of the mind.   These elements lend a kind of grimness and also a grandeur to the tragedy.   This grandeur is immensely heightened by the fact that the setting of the story is the most rocky and cavernous and wildly beautiful parts of the Alps mountains, of which, for background and science effects, the poet takes full advantage.

In Byron's career this poem represents the height of despair and defiance.   In his Swiss Journal and Letters of the year preceding he says: "The recollection of bitterness, and more especially of recent and more home desolation, which must accompany me through life, have preyed upon me here; and neither the music of the shepherd, the crashing of the avalanche, nor the torrent, the mountain, the glacier, the forest, nor the cloud, have for one moment lightened the weight upon my heart, nor enabled me to lose my own wretched identity in the majesty, and the power, and the glory, around, above and beneath me."   It seems that the anguish and torture and despair, and the defiance of all things human and earthly, worked itself out in the speeches and action of

Manfred, who is a kind of glorified Byron. After this the poet is more calm.

The spirit of calmness pervades a brief but very fine poem entitled *Prometheus,* written in the summer of 1816. Unlike Shelley, who makes his Prometheus representative of humanity and thinks of him as a symbol, Byron treats Prometheus as a separate and real personality. He expresses profound admiration for his self-restraint and his silent endurance and suggests that when man acts as nobly as Prometheus he reveals himself half-divine. Also in 1816 Byron wrote *The Prisoner of Chillon,* which sympathizes deeply with the prisoner, who must endure patiently and as best he can the long tortures of silent suffering. In this summer he also wrote two poems to his sister—*Stanzas to Augusta* and *Epistle to Augusta*—in the latter of which he is willing to admit, somewhat pathetically, that the misfortunes that have overtaken him are due to his own error of judgment:

> The fault was mine; nor do I seek to screen
> My errors with defensive paradox;
> I have been cunning in mine overthrow,
> The careful pilot of my proper woe.—

which is the first step toward achieving patient endurance. But there is likewise a Fragment, produced in the same summer, which in the following passage expresses a more common theme of Byron:

> Oh Earth!
> Where are the past?—and wherefore had they birth?
> The dead are thy inheritors—and we
> But bubbles on the surface; and the key
> Of thy profoundity is in the grave.

And similarily is the terrible vision *Darkness,* also written in 1816, which shows extraordinary fertility in portraying a state of man's and the earth's ultimate destruction. The

power of defiance and endurance and the fearful hope-
lessness and empty void that hangs about man's ultimate
destiny are alternately sung by Byron in this period of
pain and suffering and the dark gropings of his mind.

It was fortunate that his friend Hobhouse at this
juncture encouraged him in the study of traditional and
historic Italy and aided him in gathering material there-
from for a poem.   This turned out to be the Fourth
Canto of *Childe Harold* (1817).   Byron became obviously deeply immersed in the spirit of historic Italy, and
thus found a partial escape from the despair that had
possessed him.   He now recognized, as he did in the
Epistle to Augusta, that

> The thorns which I have reap'd are of the tree
> I planted;—they have torne me—and I bleed:
> I should have known what fruit would spring from such a seed.
>
> Stanza 10.

A deeper calm and serenity and a richer objectivity is
present in this Canto as a whole than is usual with Byron.
The past glories of Venice and Rome, which had fasci-
nated him in his boyhood, now laid a deeper spell upon
his imagination by intensive and intimate study.   The
mighty men of Italy's past—a long roll—were heroes
that Byron could sincerely worship.   Italy, "Mother of
Arts," "Parent of our Religion" (st. 47), a land

> Which *was* the mightiest in its old command,
> And *is* the loveliest, and must ever be
> The master-mould of Nature's heavenly hand,—
>
> Stanza 25.

stirred him to affectionate interpretation and unstinting
praise.   The fallen state of Venice and the general abject
condition of present Italy, in contrast to the glories of
her past, aroused him to noble utterance in the cause of
freedom as against tyranny.

Although the poem is obviously more objective than others of his, yet Byron does not at any place or for any length of time get far away from his personal experience. Indeed, this Canto shows a growth in his skill to interweave the objective with the personal. The wrecks of ancient grandeur about him everywhere again and again suggest that he himself is standing "a ruin amidst ruins." In addressing himself to Time and in speaking of the Coliseum he remarks:

> Amidst this wreck, where thou hast made a shrine
> And temple more divinely desolate,
> Among thy mightier offerings here are mine,
> Ruins of years—though few, yet full of fate:—
> If thou hast ever seen me too elate,
> Hear me not; but if calmly I have borne
> Good, and reserved my pride against the hate
> Which shall not whelm me, let me not have worn
> This iron in my soul in vain—shall *they* not mourn?
>
> Stanza 131.

As though compensating for the self-restraint practiced through most of the Canto he near the end breaks out in a vindictive attack upon his enemies and in a most violent expression of his personal grief:

> Have I not had to wrestle with my lot?
> Have I not suffer'd things to be forgiven?
> Have I not had my brain sear'd, my heart riven,
> Hopes sapp'd, name blighted, Life's life lied away?
> And only not to desperation driven,
> Because not altogether of such clay
> As rots into the souls of those whom I survey.
>
> Stanza 135.

And though he wrote strongly for the freedom of Italy and the freedom and independence of all the world he yet asserted more profoundly than ever before the emptiness in the last analysis of all human endeavor:

> There is the moral of all human tales;
> 'Tis but the same rehearsal of the past,
> First Freedom and then Glory—when that fails,
> Wealth, vice, corruption,—barbarism at last.
> And History, with all her volumes vast,
> Hath but *one* page,—'tis better written here
> Where gorgeous Tyranny hath thus amass'd
> All treasures, all delights, that eye or ear,
> Heart, soul could seek, tongue ask.—
>
> Stanza 108.

This is the recurring note and the deeper strain in Byron. And if what he says be true it may well be asked whether the freedom he struggles for is worth the having. Such pessimistic fatalism and the idea of freedom are, to say the least, strange bedfellows. But for Byron life was immediate sensation, absorption, intense thought, activity, a striving, a continuous contest! It was zestful and tremendously exciting; the struggle for freedom must be made even though all its ultimate contingencies be enveloped in an utter fatality, even though freedom itself be a form of fatality. As has been said, Byron suggests no grounds for the resolving the antinomy of moral freedom and philosophic fatalism. The essence of Coleridge's exposition of this matter eluded Byron and elicited only the cynical remark that Coleridge has taken to

> Explaining metaphysics to the nation—
> I wish he would explain his explanation.
>
> Dedication to *Don Juan.*

Yet there is in this Canto, as in *Manfred,* an emphasis on a kind of immortality of the mind. In the early part of the Canto Byron speaks of the beings of the mind, that is, creations like the character Pierre or the character Othello in poetry, as immortal, multiplying in us a brighter ray and more beloved existence and with fresher growth replenishing the void (Stanza 5). In the latter

stanzas he asserts a sort of indestructible energy as a part
of the mind itself:

> But there is that within me which shall tire
> Torture and Time, and breathe when I expire.
>
> Stanza 137.

In stanza 155 this strain approaches again more closely
Coleridge's transcendental conception of the mind, with
the emphasis upon its subjective, inward reality of greatness. The poet is speaking of the Dome of St. Peter's:

> Enter: its grandeur overwhelms thee not;
> And why? it is not lessen'd; but thy mind,
> Expanded by the genius of the spot,
> Has grown colossal, and can only find
> A fit abode wherein appear enshrined
> Thy hopes of immortality; and thou
> Shalt one day, if found worthy, so defined,
> See thy God face to face as thou dost now
> His Holy of Holies, nor be blasted by his brow.

This is a high note for Byron, but he strikes it only
occasionally. Had he had a steady faith of this sort his
poetry would be other than it is. Of course, a mere
belief or non-belief in a future life may not have much
bearing on the quality of a poet's work, but a conviction
of the innate worth and greatness of our human nature,
which is truly the only worthy basis to postulate man's
immortality, is a fundamental characteristic of the faith
of the creative and constructive thinking poets of the
world. Byron possessed only glimmerings of such a
faith; he had a far greater working faith in the essential
worthlessness of our human nature, and he remained for
the most part a poet of satiric intent, of disillusionment,
and of the destructive elements of life. His fertility in
the use of imagery suggesting decay and destruction is
simply amazing. In the Third Canto of *Childe Harold,*
for example, he compares a broken heart to a mirror:

> Even as a broken mirror, which the glass
> In every fragment multiplies; and makes
> A thousand images of one that was,
> The same, and still the more, the more it breaks;
> And thus the heart will do which not forsakes,
> Living in shatter'd guise, and still, and cold,
> And bloodless, with its sleepless sorrow aches,
> Yet withers on till all without is old,
> Showing no visible sign, for such things are untold.
>
> Stanza 33.

Or again in the Fourth Canto, where he expresses his faith in the doctrine of original sin—

> Our life is a false nature, 'tis not in
> The harmony of things,—this hard decree,
> This uneradicable taint of sin,
> This boundless upas, this all-blasting tree
> Whose root is earth, whose leaves and branches be
> The skies which rain their plagues on men like dew—
> Disease, death, bondage—all the woes we see—
> And worse, the woes we see not—which throb through
> The immedicable soul, with heart-aches ever new.—
>
> Stanza 126.

he not only illustrates his fertility in the use of imagery of destructive things but also shows what a case hardened Calvinist he was in his philosophic outlook. Unquestionably this fixed attitude of mind had a powerfully negating influence upon his constructive thinking and feeling. Unless he could break away from this point of view he was bound to grow into the negative and ironic position of the author of *Don Juan*. As a matter of fact in *Don Juan* the destructive strain, accompanied by a light touch and a mocking spirit, shows itself as nearly inexhaustible as we may suppose any human being capable of producing!

II

But Byron's interest in the spiritual interpretation of life did not cease. His early Calvinistic training and his early love of the Bible, especially the Old Testament, had entered ineradicably into his being. In a letter to Gifford he speaks of the "Calvinistic School, where I was cudgled to Church the first ten years of my life," and of the fact that he cannot get rid of its effects on him. And in 1821 he writes to Murray to send him a Bible. "Don't forget this, for I am a great reader and admirer of those books, and had read them through before I was eight years old,—that is to say, the *Old* Testament, for the New struck me as a task, but the other a pleasure."

His earlier reactions to the 'hated' Calvinism taught him in his boyhood was to deny all worth to religion and particularily to Christianity. "I will have nothing to do with your immortality," he writes to Hodson in 1811. "We are miserable enough in this life, without the absurdity of speculating upon another." As compared to other religionists Christians he considers hypocrites: "I will bring you ten Mussulmans shall shame you in all good-will towards men, prayer to God, and duty to their neighbours." In another letter (1811) to Hodson he says: "One remark, and I have done; the basis of your religion is *injustice*," etc. In another letter to this friend (1811): "There is something Pagan in me that I cannot shake off. In short, I deny nothing, but doubt everything." These skeptical opinions of his youth he gradually modified, and the earlier teachings took possession of him. For ten years later (1821) he wrote: "Of the Immortality of the Soul, it appears to me that there can be little doubt, if we attend for a moment to the action of the Mind. . . . It acts also so very independent of body. . . . That the *Mind is eternal,* seems as probable as that the body is not." (*Detached Thoughts,* 1821-22). Or again, in a letter to Tom Moore, March 4, 1822: "I am no enemy to religion, but the contrary. As a proof, I am educating my natural daughter a strict Catholic in a convent of Romagna; for I think people can never have *enough* of religion, if they are to have any. I incline, myself, very much to the Catholic doctrines."

This interest in spiritual values, no doubt, lead him to write *Cain: A Mystery* (1821), which caused such a storm of wrath on the part of the public against the author for his supposed impiety and blasphemy as is to-day almost unbelievable. Byron defended the poem to his friend, Tom Moore: "With respect to 'Religion,' can I never convince you that I have no such opinions as the characters in that drama, which seems to have frightened everybody? Yet *they* are nothing to the expressions in Goethe's *Faust* (which are ten times hardier), and not a whit more bold than those of Milton's Satan." Four days later he again writes to Moore: "This war of 'Church and State' has astonished me more than it disturbs; for I really thought *Cain* a speculative and hardy, but still harmless, production." Still again to John Murray: "If Lucifer and Cain speak as the first Murderer and the first Rebel may be supposed to speak, surely all the rest of the personages talk also according to their characters—and the stronger passions have ever been permitted to drama." Of course Byron's defense in the

main was right and the judgment of his public was wrong.
However, Byron's public was perhaps right in one particular. It may be surmised that it accepted Lucifer as
speaking in his proper person but objected to the
author's obvious and open sympathy for the murderer
Cain, whose ideas are in harmony with Lucifer's—therein
lay the scandal, and in a sense still lies. Certainly the
personages talk according to their characters; but Byron
shapes his characters according to his own choice. Adam
and Eve and Abel he makes commonplace, formal, conventional and stupid. Cain he makes original, daring,
aspiring, human, and even loveable. This contrast
results in an emphasis which perhaps Byron did not
intend but which in a measure accounts for the wrathful
protests against the author.

What Byron really intended was to create in Cain
such a character as would cause his every act to clash
with those in his immediate environment, as would make
all his acts, including the final act of murder, seem inevitable, or fatal. Have given the character of Cain and
his conventional relatives as Byron created them, the
outcome must be what it is, and not otherwise. The
doctrine of necessity, or fatalism, Stopford Brooke contends in his essay on *Cain* in *Naturalism in English
Poetry,* Byron believed in and also hated. There can
be no question about his belief; and what is more important he believed in the doctrine feelingly as well as
intellectually. Cain cannot help it that he was born with
a thirst for knowledge, with a questioning mind which
doubts dogma and demands proof, with a moral feeling
of injustice due to his parents' sin visited upon himself
and his children. In his first soliloquy he says:

> They have but
> One answer to all questions, " 'Twas *his* will,
> And *he* is good." How know I that? Because
> He is all-powerful, must all-good, too, follow?
> I judge but by the fruits—and they are bitter—
> Which I must feed on for a fault not mine.

Cain loves his wife Adah and his children most tenderly, and out of this affection there is born his imaginative sensitiveness to the evil sown in the world by his parents and its influence of agony "through thrice a thousand generations." He is not only angry at his parents because they accept the All-powerful as the All-good unquestioningly but that

> They pluck'd the tree of science,
> And sin—and, not content with their own sorrow,
> Begot *me—thee*—and all the few that are,
> And all the unnumber'd and innumerable
> Multitudes, millions, myriads, which may be,
> To inherit agonies accumulated
> By ages!—and *I* must be sire of such things!

This again is the doctrine of original sin in which Stopford Brooke also holds Byron believed and which he hated. Had Byron been familiar with Coleridge's conception of original sin as "sin originant, underived from without," that is, originating in the will of the individual rather than from some one else, it would have dispelled many mists for him; but he thought of it in the rigid eighteenth century manner as an adamantine chain connecting ourselves in a fatalistic way with the first sinner. It is doubtful whether Bryon ever seriously considered an alternate view, so deeply was his intellectual inheritance ingrained in him. He frequently considered himself, as he says in a letter, "as destined never to be happy, although in some instances fortunate." With the sense

of this destiny hanging over him we may be lenient with
his unusual sympathy with Cain, whom he considered
destined to commit murder.

In the play the conditions of life weigh upon Cain so
heavily that, like Manfred, he wishes to die, but cannot;
he is fated to live on:

>   I live,
> But live to die; and, living, see no thing
> To make death hateful, save an innate clinging,
> A loathsome, and yet all invincible
> Instinct of life, which I abhor, as I
> Despise myself, yet cannot overcome—
> And so live. Would I had never lived!

Lucifer, the evil one, and a sorrowful but scoffing per-
sonage, engages Cain's interest and promises to satisfy
his longings for knowledge, on the condition that Cain
bow down and worship him. Cain disdainfully refuses;
like Manfred, he is not overwhelmed by supernatural
beings and takes a proud and haughty attitude toward
them. Lucifer tacitly rescinds the condition by assuming
that since Cain has not bowed to the Almighty he perforce has bowed to Lucifer. Cain even accounts himself
superior to Lucifer in the fact that he can love, but submits his mind to the superior knowledge which Lucifer
is to impart to him.

Here, one thinks, Byron had an opportunity to produce
profound tragedy—experience and knowledge to be
gained at certain fundamental spiritual risks! Byron
however seems to content himself by impressing us with
the vastness of Space, by juggling a little with Time, and
by presenting rather ineffectively a vague picture of past,
present, and future worlds. Lucifer carries Cain off into
internimable space where he beholds lights and glorious
worlds, "distant, dazzling, and innumerable," which

> Sweep on in your unbounded revelry
> Through an aerial universe of endless
> Expansion—at which my soul aches to think—
> Intoxicated with eternity!
>   . . . Let me die, as atoms die
> (If that they die), or know ye in your might
> And knowledge!

When Lucifer has returned Cain to his own earth he feels that years had rolled over his absence, while Adah informs him that but two hours had elapsed since he left her. Lucifer had hinted the mystery:

> With us acts are exempt from time, and we
> Can crowd eternity into an hour
> Or stretch an hour into eternity.

The dramatic purpose of this journey of Cain and Lucifer seems to be to make Cain, when he returns to earth, feel his littleness, be utterly discontent with his lot, almost hectic with longings to break with his environment, more deeply confirmed in his own half-formed disloyalty to his parents and in his hatred of Jehovah, ready to do some wild deed of rebellion. When Abel inquires, meekly enough, what he had seen, he answers almost savagely, with flushed cheeks and with eyes flashing with unnatural light:

>   The dead,
> The immortal, the unbounded, the omnipotent,
> The overpowering mysteries of space—
> The innumerable worlds that were and are—
> A whirlwind of such overwhelming things,
> Suns, moons, and earths, upon their loud-voiced spheres
> Singing in thunder round me, as have made me
> Unfit for mortal converse: leave me, Abel.

He is as one possessed. It is to be noted that aside from the little jealous feeling Lucifer had adroitly insinuated into Cain's mind, Cain had not up to this point held any grudge against his brother; his whole mind had been directed toward the fierce injustice of his parents' sin and the Almighty's rule, as he saw it.   Infected with the pessimistic but mocking spirit of Lucifer, flushed with a sense of new power and new knowledge, inspired by the immensities of eternal existence, he cannot adjust his mind to that of his commonplace, simple, and formalistic brother.

But Abel at this moment is especially, almost stupidly, persistent.   Cain's constant refusal to worship the Almighty or to sacrifice to Him was reaching a crisis; humbly but stubbornly Abel insists on Cain's making his offering, which he finally does in a sullen spirit; then when his offering of fruit is rejected he breaks out in a wild fury, not against Abel, but against Jehovah for "his high pleasure in the fumes of scorching flesh and smoking blood" of Abel's sacrifice.   He conceives Jehovah as bloodthirsty, and to avenge himself on Him he attempts to hurl Abel's altar to the ground, which Abel, who loves Jehovah more than life, defends.   Cain, snatching a brand from the altar, strikes him on the temples.   In a moment Cain is hanging over the dying body of Abel, crying out in anguish of spirit:

> Abel! I pray thee, mock me not!   I smote
> Too fiercely, but not fatally.   Ah, why
> Wouldst thou oppose me?   This is mockery;
> And only done to daunt me:—'twas a blow—
> And but a blow.   Stir—stir—nay, only stir!
> Why so—that's well! thou breath'st! breathe upon me!
> Oh, God! oh, God!

Fated from his birth to be the emblem of all future murderers of the world, he has now, in an impulsive moment, fulfilled his destiny.   His fatal and fated deed brings death into the world, agony of silent suffering to Zillah, a fiery curse from his mother Eve upon the murderer, and a sense of the devastation of the original wrong-doing in Adam, thus multiplying evil in the world—sin upon sin in endless succession to all future ages—just what Cain so passionately wished might *not* come through him! Thus fatalistically works out forever more the law of original sin.

If Byron's unusual sympathy with Cain in the first part of the story need any justification, it is to be found in the manner of treating the effects of the crime on Cain. The poet does not extenuate it. Unlike Manfred, who is filled with despair and defiance by a crime, Cain is stunned into a new sense of humanity by it:

> What shall I say to him?—My brother!—No:
> He will not answer to that name; for brethren
> Smite not each other. Yet—yet—speak to me.
> Oh! for a word more of that gentle voice,
> That I may bear to hear my own again!

All the past, with its soaring aspirations and its knowledge of infinitude, seems but a nightmare in the presence of this new reality:

> I am awake at last—a dreary dream
> Had madden'd me.

He is willing to undergo any punishment that may be meted out to him, for he cannot bring himself to forgive himself the awfulness of his crime. Addressing the spirit of Abel he says:

> I think thou wilt forgive him, whom his God
> Can ne'er forgive, nor his own soul.

Even of the mark the Angel of the Lord sets on Cain's forehead to exempt him from such a deed as he has done he remarks:

> It burns
> My brow, but nought to that which is within me.

And his love for Adah, which has never wavered, he is willing to renounce. "Leave me," he says to her, believing it will be so. But the love of Adah is single and is not shaken. She abhors the crime, but leaves its punishment as a matter between Cain and his Maker. Out of the general darkness there shines the love of Cain and Adah unsullied, and they together, with their children, depart for the wilderness, not hopelessly. But to the last Cain asserts the fatality by which his career has been determined:

> After the fall too soon was I begotten;
> Ere yet my mother's mind subsided from
> The serpent, and my sire still mourn'd for Eden.
> That which I am, I am; I did not seek
> For life, nor did I make myself.

Heaven and Earth (1821), another 'Mystery,' follows *Cain,* dealing with the love of the daughters of the world for the Sons of God, just before the Flood. The poem is not to be compared, as a performance, with *Manfred* or with *Cain,* although the setting is extraordinarily dramatic and effective. It does not seem to have a very distinctive theme. Noah appears to be a sort of eighteenth century Calvinist. When Shem advises him not to go nearer the cave's mouth to avoid danger Noah replies:

> Do not fear for me:
> All evil things are powerless on the man
> Selected by Jehovah.—Let us on.

Japhet, who, loving Anah, a descendant of Cain, and wishing to save her, refuses to go with Noah and expresses doubt of God's justice in destroying such creatures as Anah. Noah sternly rebukes his son, and is about to renounce him forever, when the Angel of the

Lord admonishes Noah to be a father still, and suggests that Japhet, in spite of himself, will be saved from destruction, which proves true in the sequel. Anah and Ablibamah, descendants of Cain, who are in love with two Sons of the Most High and for the like of whom the Flood was especially ordained, are carried out of the reach of the Flood's destruction by their angelic Lovers. Helpless women and innocent children, both individually and in choruses, appear before Noah, crying with anguish to be saved from the Deluge, but are ruthlessly swallowed up by the waves. The most impressive part of the poem is the description of the onrushing flood, presented with graphic power and in a sublime spirit. The theme, if any, seems to be to show how the Flood, ordained and executed by Jehovah, arbitrarily and without principle destroyed and saved human life—a characteristic subject for Byron's genius. The rule of arbitrariness and of fatality to all living things takes the place of the law of reason.

III

It is noticeable in Byron's art that whenever he treats of a subject not directly related to his personal experience he is comparatively unsuccessful, as in the historic plays he assayed in his later years, such as *Marino Faliero* (1820) and *The Two Foscari* (1821), and others, which proves that opportunity for him to achieve distinction did not lie in handling impersonal themes. It is also a marked perversity of his genius that whenever he reaches a spiritually lofty level as in the last part of *Cain* and in certain parts of *Childe Harold* he immediately recedes to an opposite or at least a decidedly lower level. The explanation, broadly speaking, lies in two facts, first, that as between the existence of good and evil in this world, Byron felt that the evil is almost overwhelmingly greater, that life is mainly destructive rather than constructive, that happiness is scarcely ever achieved, heroism, is after all, exceptional, freedom is in the last analysis a vain hope. And so whatever good and true and beautiful thing he may present, the destructive, doubting, scoffing spirit is not far off and soon makes itself felt. Sordid details are disproportionately abundant in comparison to attractive details. In *Heaven and Earth* the poet makes the Spirit of the Cave prophecy the state of mankind after the Flood:

> This remnant, floating o'er the undulation
> Of the subsiding deluge, from its slime,
> When the hot sun hath baked the reeking soil
> Into a world, shall give again to time
> New beings—years, diseases, sorrow, crime—
> With all companionship of hate and toil,—

and much more in the same vein. To be sure Japhet makes a beautiful prophecy of the harmony and happiness that will come to the world at the advent of the Redeemer. But Byron's feelings are plainly with the Spirit of the Cave. Secondly, his most striking literary quality was variety, or mobility, the power of swiftly shifting from point to point, from idea to idea, from one feeling to another, from high to low and low to high, with speciousness, producing a dazzling effect, but an effect revealing upon analysis a lack of calm penetration, of conscious and sustained nobility of thought, of profound intellectual consistency.

Byron's grand forte was medley, but extraordinary medley. It was given to him to write in the mature years of his life *Don Juan,* by far the longest of his

poems, a serio-comic narrative poem, full of broad good
humor and also fierce satire and a mocking spirit, full of
long speculations with a purposeful tendency to anti-
climax, of downright vulgarities and of pure emotion,
of the claptrap of cheap fiction and of subdued tragic
beauty—all blended together by a conversational and
realistic tone and by the swift, shuttle-like, kaleidoscopic
movement of the author's mind, triumphing over all
obstacles and revealing all his gifts and powers of expression.   The outstanding note, however, is satire and the
mock spirit, the logical outcome of Byron's intellectual
growth.   The poem contains no new philosophy but
traverses many of the familiar paths of his earlier poems,
with a turn that laughs them out of court, such as, for
example, the following echo of some of the grand heroics
of *Childe Harold:*

> He thought about himself, and the whole earth,
>   Of man the wonderful, and of the stars,
> And how the deuce they ever could have birth;
>   And then he thought of earthquakes, and of wars,
> How many miles the moon might have in girth,
>   Of air-balloons, and of the many bars
> To perfect knowledge of the boundless skies;—
> And then he thought of Donna Julia's eyes.
>
> Canto I, 92.

Life for Byron was a struggle, a contest, but in all its
ultimate contingencies, a fatality.   His natural affections,
as we have seen, matured early, and, violently uprooted
by the stormy events of his life, ran their course rapidly.
As he says in the Fourth Canto of *Childe Harold:*

> Alas! our young affections run to waste,
> Or water but the desert; whence arise
> But weeds of dark luxuriance, tares of haste,
> Rank at the core, though tempting to the eyes,
> Flowers whose wild odours breathe but agonies,

And trees whose gums are poison;—such the plants
Which spring beneath her steps as Passion flies
O'er the world's wilderness, and vainly pants
For some celestial fruit forbidden to our wants.

Stanza 120.

But his thought, as thought, ran a similar course,
although not so swiftly. In the Third Canto of *Childe
Harold* he declares that

I have thought
Too long and darkly, till my brain became,
In its own eddy boiling and o'erwrought,
A whirling gulf of phantasy and flame.—

Stanza 7.

which, on the face of it, indicates a kind of intellectual
malady. There can be no question that Byron thought
keenly and brilliantly on political, social, and every day
personal matters. But when his thinking adverted to his
deeper self or to first principles a heavy hand was laid
upon him by an inherited philosophy whose postulates he
could not refute. Intellectually the dead past and the
living present were at enmity in him; his thought was at
war with itself, tending to self-destruction. If he hated
the doctrines that were cudgled into him in his youth, as
Stopford Brooke maintains, it was because he saw no way
of escape from them. Here the wisdom of Coleridge
and Wordsworth, who successfully effected a constructive
reaction against those same inherited beliefs, was vastly
greater than that of Byron. The most self-assertive poet
of his age, Byron yet in the mature years of his life
declared: "I have always believed that all things depend
upon Fortune, and nothing upon ourselves" (*Detached
Thoughts,* 1821-22). But there must be a limit to self-
assertion that labors under the fearful handicap of
helplessness; and there are signs of its flagging in

Byron's work. The conflict between his native individualism and his deep sense of fatality underlying all things could have but one issue at the last—cynicism and satire. First emotion, then self-assertion and defiance, and at last satiric mockery—this is the general course of his development. In Shelley a similar conflict ended in a kind of present melancholy with hopeful dreams of the future. Byron laid great stress on personal, experiential, and phenomenal existence; Shelley considered these things as phantasms. The great law of fatality drove Byron into a world of satire and ironical laughter; Shelley it drove into sadness and dreams of far off millenniums. Neither, in their short lives, found a satisfactory solution of the sorrows of mortal existence.